BETWEEN AUTHOR
AND READER

D1569643

PSYCHOANALYSIS AND CULTURE
Arnold M. Cooper, M.D., and Steven Marcus, Editors

BETWEEN AUTHOR AND READER

A Psychoanalytic Approach to Writing and Reading

STANLEY J. COEN

COLUMBIA UNIVERSITY PRESS

New York

Columbia University Press
New York Chichester, West Sussex

Copyright © 1994 Columbia University Press
All rights reserved

Library of Congress Cataloging-in-Publication Data

Coen, Stanley J.
  Between author and reader: a psychoanalytic approach to writing and reading
/ Stanley J. Coen.
    p.   cm.—(Psychoanalysis and culture)
  Includes bibliographical references (p.) and index.
  ISBN 0–231–07356–9   ISBN 0–231–07357–7 (pbk.)
  1. Psychoanalysis and literature.   2. Reader response criticism.
3. Psychology in literature.   I. Title   II. Series.
  PN56.P92C64   1994   801'.92—dc20   93–24579
                                                    CIP

Casebound editions of Columbia University Press books
are printed on permanent and durable acid-free paper.

This book incorporates, in thoroughly revised form, material previously published elsewhere. Grateful acknowledgment is made to the following for permission to adapt and revise what they have published of mine: the Journal of the American Psychoanalytic Association for "How to Read Freud: A Critique of Recent Freud Scholarship," 36 (1988): 483–515, and a book review of Psychoanalysis and Discourse by P. J. Mahony, 40 (1992): 925–928; The Analytic Press for "The Author and His Audience: Jean Genet's Early Work" from The Psychoanalytic Study of Society 10 (1984): 301–320, W. Muensterberger, L. B. Boyer, and S. A. Grolnick, eds.; Leo Goldberger, editor in chief of Psychoanalysis and Contemporary Thought and Psychoanalysis and Contemporary Science, Inc., for "Introduction to Essays on the Relationship of Author and Reader: Transference Implications for Psychoanalytic Literary Criticism" from Psychoanalysis and Contemporary Thought 5 (1982): 3–13; The Johns Hopkins University Press for "Louis-Ferdinand Céline's Castle to Castle: The Author-Reader Relationship in Its Narrative Style" from American Imago 39, no. 4 (1982): 343–368, and "Freud and Fliess: A Supportive Literary Relationship" from American Imago 42, no. 4 (1985): 385–412; the Psychoanalytic Quarterly for book reviews of On Defining Freud's Discourse by P. J. Mahony, 60 (1991); 681–683, and His Brother's Keeper: A Psychobiography of Samuel Taylor Coleridge by S. Weissman, 60 (1991): 513–515; Joseph Reppen, Ph.D., editor, for book reviews from Review of Psychoanalytic Books of The Literary Use of the Psychoanalytic Process by M. A. Skura, 2 (1983/84): 169–172, and Powers of Horror: An Essay on Abjection by J. Kristeva, 3 (1984): 250–252.

    The author also thanks the following for permission to quote from texts whose copyright they hold: Grove Weidenfeld for Our Lady of the Flowers by Jean Genet, 1943, translated by B. Frechtman, Grove Press, Inc., 1964, and for Justine; or, Good Conduct Well Chastened by D. A. F. Sade, 1791, in The Marquis de Sade: The Complete Justine, Philosophy in the Bedroom, and Other Writings, compiled and translated by R. Seever and A. Wainhouse, Grove Press, Inc., 1965; Peter Owen Ltd., Publishers, for The Marquis de Sade: Selected Letters, selected by G. Lély, translated by W. J. Strachan, and edited by M. Crosland, October House, 1966; Georges Borchardt, Inc., for Castle to Castle by Louis-Ferdinand Céline, 1957, translated by R. Mannheim, Penguin Books, Ltd., 1976.

Printed in the United States of America
c 10 9 8 7 6 5 4 3 2 1
p 10 9 8 7 6 5 4 3 2 1

*For those who have taught me the joys and struggles in
reading and writing by their love of the written word,
through their help, and by their own example*

CONTENTS

PREFACE

This book combines my interests in psychoanalysis, literature, and literary criticism. It especially addresses the issue of what author and reader want from each other and how each negotiates his or her needs in their literary encounters. Its focus is on problems of methodology in psychoanalytic literary criticism, on the uses of psychoanalysis in literary criticism, and on models of the psychology of writing and reading. Central to this book is the conviction that psychoanalytic literary criticism does not draw primarily on abstract psychoanalytic theory but on the skillful, complex exploration of one's reading experience, which is enriched by the reader's access to his or her own feelings and needs. In this sense, a psychoanalytic literary criticism combines the disparate talents of the literary critic and the practicing psychoanalyst. My book advocates the reader's access to as much of his or her inner experience during reading as possible. This approach parallels what is required of the practicing psychoanalyst: that he or she be able to feel and need passionately together with his or her patient and then subject these feelings and needs to self-scrutiny for the sake of understanding that patient. My model of the psychoanalytic literary critic is the literary critic, trained in the *method* of practicing psychoanalysis, who can read carefully, closely, critically, drawing on her or his own thoughts, feelings, fantasies, and imaginings.

As you will discover, my psychoanalytic interests in perversion and in pathological dependency (Coen 1992) have influenced my choice of the writers I have studied and the models I have constructed here. I do not aim to provide a definitive statement about the psychology of writing and reading. On the contrary, I encourage the opening of questions about what authors and readers want from one another. My models of author/reader interaction are focused around the authors I have studied. Although these models are highly selective, they do offer a broad approach to a psychology of writing and reading. I present fantasied models of the dependent author's need for the reader's acceptance that will enable the author to manage the intolerable dark side of his psyche. Eschewing biographical reconstruction of the author's conflicts, my book emphasizes imaginary models of the author/reader interaction that attempt to enhance and enrich the reader's experience of the text. I also assess a variety of contemporary approaches to psychoanalytic literary criticism. The reader should bear in mind that when I examine male authors addressing an imagined male audience, my use of gender will reflect this situation.

My teaching of psychopathology at the Columbia University Psychoanalytic Center for many years has influenced these explorations. So has my participation in a study group on psychoanalysis and literature at Columbia, originally founded by Lionel Trilling, and in the Interdisciplinary Colloquium on Psychoanalysis and Literary Criticism, which I have chaired at the American Psychoanalytic Association since 1984. I have especially admired those colleagues who have been able to combine the talents, skills, and callings of the psychoanalyst and literary critic: Patrick Mahony, Paul Schwaber, Jay Martin, Janet Hadda, William Richardson, Alan Bass, Gail Reed, and Cynthia MacDonald. I am indebted to a number of other colleagues who have encouraged my interest in psychoanalytic literary criticism: Francis Baudry, Jose Barchilon, Professor Robert Belknap, Arnold Cooper, John Gedo, James Gorney, the late Seymour Grolnick, James Hamilton, the late Robert Liebert, Roy Schafer, and Professor Murray Schwartz. I thank the distinguished critics who have participated with our Interdisciplinary Colloquium at the American Psychoanalytic Association for what they have taught me: Professors Stanley Fish, Patrick Mahony,

Shoshana Felman, Cynthia Chase, Samuel Weber, Barbara Johnson, Wayne Booth, Peter Brooks, and Joan Scott.

The opportunity to present earlier versions of some of these ideas to the Association for Psychoanalytic Medicine and the American Psychoanalytic Association was very helpful.

I also thank my wife, Dr. Ruth Imber, for her love and help with this project, as with so much else. I thank my children for their love and forbearance so that I could complete this book. My patients have helped me grasp many of the ideas presented here, especially when I had to struggle with their difficulties and my own within the treatment. Jennifer Crewe, Arnold Cooper, and Professor Steven Marcus helped me to bring this book to publication. I am grateful to my manuscript editor, Susan Heath, for helping to clarify my writing. Anne McCoy and Eve Bayrock expedited the editing and production of my book.

BETWEEN AUTHOR
AND READER

INTRODUCTION: WHAT DOES PSYCHOANALYSIS HAVE TO DO WITH WRITING AND READING?

Within both psychoanalysis and literary criticism there has been a shift of focus away from efforts to determine meanings within the psyche or text toward the complexities of relationships. Intrapsychic conflict is now understood by psychoanalysts to include conflict about needs, feelings, and attitudes between self and others. An object relations perspective comes together with a drive model when the latter is understood to derive from the affective history of one's relations with others. Psychoanalytic treatment similarly is no longer regarded primarily as the analyst's attempt to interpret defenses against unconscious conflict so as to retrieve repressed childhood memories with their associated painful feelings. Rather, psychoanalytic treatment is now regarded as a dynamic interaction between analyst and patient, each becoming involved, to different degrees, in an affective force field that is to be understood and interpreted.

The psychoanalyst no longer sits outside the treatment process, always able to observe and interpret it dispassionately. It is no longer expected that the well-analyzed psychoanalyst becomes immune to neurotic reactions to his or her patient. On the contrary, the analyst is now expected to use his affective reactions, neurotic and otherwise, in order to understand what is transpiring, outside his conscious awareness, between himself and his analysand. Countertransference, rather than being primarily a sign of the analyst's deficiency, has become a vehicle through which the analyst has the potential to use himself constructively for the patient's benefit.

It is now understood that certain defenses operate not only within one person's mind but also between two people. This concept applies especially to dependent patients who seek others to help them contain or avoid what is troubling within them. Thus, such people may protect themselves by attributing an ugly aspect of the self or of an internal parental object to the analyst (by projection, projective identification, externalization, and transference). Here intrapsychic and interpersonal become inseparable. The patient actually attempts to induce certain affects in and elicit certain roles from the analyst. The analyst must allow himself to resonate with such feelings and roles in order to understand what is being enacted between patient and analyst.

The psychoanalyst no longer assumes a privileged position as outside conflict (the patient's and his own). He is now expected to struggle with his patient's conflicts and his own, to immerse himself affectively within both of these, while still being able to maintain his perspective primarily on what the patient, not the analyst, needs. This is obviously difficult to do. It means that the analyst must be drawn into the patient's needs and feelings and his own—especially as they are played out between himself and his patient—without either avoiding or enacting these needs and feelings. The analyst must feel love and hate strongly with his patient and still be able to manage those feelings within himself. What the analyst cannot bear to feel within himself he cannot help his patients to tolerate, manage, and integrate.

Most contemporary psychoanalysts believe that the unfolding transference neurosis is a *construction* that derives, in part, from the interaction at multiple and varying levels of (un)consciousness between two people, analysand and analyst. This human interaction between the analytic couple resonates with and is intended to amplify, recover, and replay the history of the patient's childhood conflicts and fantasied relationships. Inevitably, the analyst will also be drawn into neurotic interactions with the patient, which derive from the needs primarily of the patient but also, to a degree, from those of the analyst. The analyst is expected to be sufficiently capable of self-observation so that she can use her own feelings, wishes, defensive reactions, and so forth, to monitor the patient's contributions to the analyst's reactions.

Analytic interpretation, in these terms, is regarded as a subjective, dynamic reading by the analyst (influenced by the patient) of this complex interaction in the consulting room. However, the focus and goal of such psychoanalytic interpretation is always intended to help the patient to tolerate observing his or her own conflicts more fully so that he or she now has the possibility of resolving them in a more satisfactory way. The aim of psychoanalytic interpretation is always to advance the psychoanalytic process, not merely to offer understanding. Psychoanalytic interpretation to a patient thus differs from literary interpretation of a text to a reader. The former aims to to heighten feelings, self-observation, and motivation for change. The latter may aim to influence, persuade, and convince the other to accept one's perspective, but does not include in its agenda the notion that neurotic conflict is to be addressed and modified.

By examining intensely interactive writings of certain dependent authors, this book will consider similarities and differences between literary, therapeutic, and love relationships. We will especially need to explore what author and reader want from each other and what this has to do with other nonliterary relationships. Ways to process and understand what happens between reader and author need to be found in order to grasp more clearly the reader's position and role in relation to the author and her text. Like the psychoanalyst, the reader is now understood to have a more complex and difficult job.

Similarly, the literary critic has lost her privileged place outside the text. Most contemporary schools of criticism problematize the position of critic/reader and eschew the effort to extract single meanings embedded within the text. "Even in science," Heisenberg writes, "the object of research is no longer nature itself, but man's investigation of nature" (1958: 24). (See Bleich's [1978] essay "The Subjective Paradigm" for an excellent summary of the applicability of contemporary philosophy of science and hermeneutics to literary criticism.) Reader-response criticism has applied dynamic psychological process to reading and interpreting. This approach intentionally shares many similarities with the analyst/analysand interaction.

The task of this book will be to explore such initial efforts to develop a psychology of writing and reading. Psychoanalysts have needed much encouragement to make full use of their own "analyzing instrument" (Isakower 1963). Rarely does a psychoanalyst reveal much detail about the workings of her mind while she is analyzing. It is refreshing and unusual when a well-known psychoanalyst discloses publicly that he learns certain negative aspects of an analysand when he imagines why his fantasied affair with the analysand would be unsatisfactory. Surprisingly, we know even less about the mind of the critic at work, about the intermediate steps by which the critic derives her readings. In this book I emphasize that a psychoanalytic literary criticism should begin with such data—details, literary and psychological, of the critic's reading experience—and I explore what has been written about such confluence between psychology and criticism. My model of the psychoanalytic literary critic will be the literary critic who has been trained in the *method* (not only in the theory) of practicing psychoanalysis. When a skilled critic, who is also a sensitive psychoanalyst (say, Patrick Mahony), combines both the techniques of criticism and those of psychoanalysis, the results can be highly rewarding. Listen to how Mahony works (1989: 94):

> My own approach presumes that Freud's texts, like crystals, have fault lines, and I wonder where they are and how wittingly as well as unwittingly they are covered up. I muse about whether Freud's self-irony fully accounts for the gaps or contradictions in his report. Given the foiling nature of the unconscious, these questions are where I begin, not end, my enquiry. In addition, by splitting my ego into participant and observer roles, I aim to respond antiphonally to the dual activity that characterized Freud's own compositional creativity.

In his writing about Freud's texts, Mahony emulates with his reader—and with Freud-as-writer—Freud's interactive engagement with his reader and his work (see chapters 6 and 7 of this book). This leads to a creative enactment in reading Mahony reading Freud. Mahony shows us (and encourages us to join in) the ways in which he allows himself to resonate creatively as reader/rereader/interpreter of Freud as creative writer/mentor/psychoanalytic explorer. Writing and reading become exciting, creative acts, when one allows oneself to discover where one is going, while immersed in writing or reading. Writing and reading become creative literary and psychoanalytic experiences of working out and working through. Both author and reader struggle to work through conflicts in the acts of writing and reading, seeking creative expression and integration. To read an author's text, using this model, we have to attend to the author's creative and conflictual needs, both within her text and toward her readers. And we have to attend to our own attempts as readers to seek creative solutions to our conflicts—conflicts within ourselves and toward the author.

I shall present samples from my own work and from others in order to describe and conceptualize the process of the mind of the psychoanalytic reader/critic at work. In doing so, I shall grapple with complexities of the psychological interaction between and among author, text, and reader. The authors discussed in this book include Genet, Céline, Sade, and Freud. I selected each work because it revealed an intense, self-conscious involvement with the reader. In retrospect, it is now clear that these were dependent authors who sought intense imaginary contact with their readers. Study of such work facilitates investigation of the psychological field in which the reader becomes involved with author, text, narrator, and characters. This book outlines one model of the author/reader relationship: the formulations offered here apply especially to dependent authors and may or may not apply to other authors and readers. Nevertheless, I believe there is *some* universal applicability to the themes discussed here. My model of the author/reader relationship is intended to stimulate critics to explore different models of this relationship with other authors. My book is one approach to a psychology of writing and reading; it will need to be emended as others provide detailed descriptions of what transpires between themselves and other authors.

Certain themes are central to this book. Other authors and other works can certainly be expected to lead in other directions. Here, however, problems of need, dependency, and the dangers of rage and destructiveness take priority in the relationship between author and reader. The writings I examine seem preoccupied with the need for their audience's enthusiastic response, admiration, and acceptance of what these authors find most intolerable and reprehensible within themselves. Although there is a universal need for acceptance and absolution of what is intolerable within, the writings I explore in this book bring such dependent need into the foreground of the reading experience. Such writing seeks the temporary illusion that one's badness has been mastered by magical transformation into something good and poetic. Indeed, creativity tends to be idealized by many, in psychoanalysis and in literature, as capable of such noble transformations. My book considers that writing and reading, at least in relation to the works I investigate here, may have to attend to issues of need and destructiveness, and I present models for the management of the need and destructiveness within the writing and reading I examine.

The reader should know how I came to these investigations and some of my motivation and aims. Indeed I would emphasize that authors of psychoanalytic literary criticism and of psychoanalytic writings should have access to and disclose some of their needs and aims in pursuing a given work so that the reader can locate himself in relation to the author and his work. Scott (1988, 1991, 1992) has written persuasively that authors (of historiography) tend to obscure their own position in relation to their writing task. Attempts to influence and persuade others then remain naively undisclosed, as if only the present author was able to demonstrate, without bias, what others had heretofore missed. Authors' wishes to powerfully overcome their readers, subjecting them to their own views, have also been described by Foucault (1971), Certeau (1983), Fish (1980; 1982, unpublished), and Mahony (1982, 1984a, 1986 [about Freud]). I thoroughly disagree with the position that authors of criticism should strive to present an objective position—as if that were even possible (e.g., see Scott [1991] on R. G. Collingwood). Recent guidelines for assessing papers on applied psychoanalysis (to which I have contributed) for the *Journal of the American Psychoanalytic Association* ask that authors identify some of their aims and intentions in their work when describing the methodologies they employ at the interface of psychoanalysis and another discipline (Simon 1992, unpublished).

Power and politics certainly can come together when authors seek to influence readers. I was shocked (and should not have been) by an experience I had with my earlier (1992) book on psychoanalysis. On the same day, I received letters from two distinguished psychoanalysts who had read the book in order to provide blurbs for the jacket. Although both praised the book, each declined to endorse it. The first contended that endorsement would be tantamount to a political statement accepting my work within the most traditional psychoanalytic technique, even though it was applied to more troubled patients with whom such standard technique must at times be modified. The second colleague especially praised what he found original and innovative in the approach to psychoanalytic work, but he nevertheless objected that my theoretical position remained within the mainstream of traditional psychoanalysis. He could not endorse it because his endorsement would indicate that the work was radically rejecting of traditional psychoanalysis, which, he argued, it was not. Did the other colleagues who did indeed endorse the book do so free of such political motivation or perhaps because they wished, in part, to advance views we shared about the boundaries, possibilities, and limitations of psychoanalytic work with certain more difficult patients?

Three strands have come together in my writing the present work. My psychoanalytic teaching of perversion led me to read Genet's fiction in the search for new ways of understanding impersonation and wishes to play at changing gender. I was fascinated to learn (from James Gorney) that my fledgling attempts to use my own personal reading experiences to understand Genet's writings were akin to contemporary reader-response criticism. I then set about educating myself more thoroughly in current literary criticism. This became a wonderful opportunity to read more literature and criticism, alone and with colleagues in New York City and during meetings of the American Psychoanalytic Association. It is now clearer to me how much my psychoanalytic interest in pathological dependency (Coen 1992) has also influenced my choice of the writers I have studied and the formulations I have offered. I came to understand perversion as one variety of pathological dependency, in which one person makes sexual use of others in order to manage certain conflicts. This theme of perverse misuse of others has intrigued me both in my patients and in the writers I have chosen to study. In a sense, this book explores literary dimensions of dependency as dependency affects writing and reading. My focus in this book is therefore highly selective, congruent with these areas of my special interest in psychopathology: perverse, dependent, exploitive, hateful and destructive, and creative literary attempts to contain, manage, and transform this dark underside of the human psyche into something beautiful and universal.

Although I believe that the issues I emphasize in this book do apply generally in the psychology of writing and reading, they may be much less important with other authors. That is to be expected. I do not claim to offer a comprehensive integration of the psychology of writing and reading. On the contrary, the purpose of this book is to open psychological exploration of writing and reading further through its idiosyncratic, personal, selective emphasis. I offer a model for understanding what certain authors (perverse, angry, dependent) want from their writing and from their readers. I want to stimulate and encourage others, psychoanalysts and literary critics, to explore further what writer and reader want from each other and how they attempt to manage such wishes in their literary encounters.

The reader should not interpret my ideas in this book too concretely. The models of author/reader interaction constructed here are intended to be imaginative fictions, certainly not attempts to recapture what the author really intended. In fact, I am generally critical of psychobiographical attempts to explain (away) fiction. The models of author/reader engagement presented here are to be assessed by their usefulness in enhancing understandings of a work and, more generally, of the psychology of writing and reading. Thus do not worry too much whether an author really set out to master certain conflicts through his writing. That will probably be impossible for us to decide from his books unless we actually have that author on our psychoanalytic couch. Instead, concentrate on whether the work is enriched and invigorated by the readings offered here, and consider whether these readings add to your understanding of what author and reader want from each other.

Skillful readers of patients and of texts—psychoanalysts and literary critics alike—are attentive, responsive, and creative in raising questions about what cannot be so easily explained. They seek to open new possibilities of meaning, leading in unexpected directions, rather than to close off such excited discovery with definitive answers. Perhaps the best answer to the question of what psychoanalysis has to do with writing and reading is that it can heighten the reader's awareness of her complex responsiveness. As I shall indicate, the best psychoanalytic literary criticism has been done by those capable of combining their talents as psychoanalysts and as literary critics. This does not mean that they have used *theoretical* knowledge of psychoanalysis to explain fiction. Usually that leads to unsatisfactory readings of fiction, just as it leads to lifeless, unpersuasive readings of patients. Rather such psychoanalysts and critics have been able to allow themselves to draw on emotional responses, to a patient or to a text, which they have then been able to examine more dispassionately in order to understand the other better. There is always the risk, as literary critics turn to psychoanalysis or as psychoanalysts turn to literary criticism, of appropriating theory rather than method. I am indebted to my colleagues who combine the skills of the psychoanalyst and the literary critic for this model of *practical criticism*, in which psychoanalyst and critic come together.

The ideas offered in this book on the psychology of writing and reading are always to be read with the above caveat—that psychoanalytic theory is never to be pasted onto texts. I hope readers will be able to integrate this approach into their own techniques of reading texts in order to use themselves in richer and more complex ways to become better psychoanalytic critics.

Chapter 1

AN OVERVIEW OF
PSYCHOLOGICAL APPROACHES
TO WRITING AND READING

This chapter offers a critique of psychological approaches to writing and reading by psychoanalysts and literary critics. Psychoanalysts have written surprisingly little about the psychology of writing and reading. Thus, for example, the interrelations between and among author, text, and audience have received relatively little psychoanalytic attention. Literary critical models of reading have tended not to be psychological, emphasizing instead theories of the process by which meanings are created in reading a work. Exceptions will be noted, and implicit meanings of psychological interaction between and among author, text, and audience will be elaborated from the literature I review. This chapter seeks to develop such psychological models of literary interaction. My own models, drawing on the authors studied here in chapters 2–5, are discussed in chapter 8 of this book.

Psychoanalytic Beginnings

The early psychoanalysts were eager to demonstrate through the study of art that their ideas about psychopathology applied, at least to some degree, to the general population of nonpatients (Kris 1952). Psychoanalytic aesthetics thus began with a political strategy! Much of early psychoanalytic writing seems to have been aimed at influencing and persuading others of the importance and validity of Freud's discoveries (cf. Mahony 1984a, 1986). Freud (1914) reported that he felt troubled by the "powerful effect" that certain works of art exerted on him. If he could understand rather than just experience such aesthetic moments, he could feel safer to enjoy the work of art.

Freud claimed (1914) that his interest in applied psychoanalysis derived from such needs to explain his aesthetic experiences to himself. He believed that it was the artist's *intention* that the viewer or reader be powerfully gripped during the aesthetic experience by something akin to what had led the artist to create. In this early model, when the work is interpreted the artist's "intention" is discovered. At the same time, Freud acknowledged how difficult it is to use interpretation to reach the artist's conscious or unconscious intentions.

It should be no surprise that Freud's followers would observe that Freud's own feelings had influenced his aesthetic interpretations (e.g., Jones [see Strachey 1953:230; Jones 1955:366–67] on Freud's interpretation of Michelangelo's "Moses"). Bleich (1977) uses this same example to argue that the interpretation explains the intention of the *interpreter* rather than that of the artist. Better that the critic be aware of her own subjective contributions to her interpretation, Bleich explains, than that she imagine she can actually recover the artist's intention.

Certain of the artist's needs of her audience have been described, such as self-enhancement to counter feelings of guilt and mortification; communication, sharing, and tension regulation; and avoidance of separateness with the possibility of new synthesis (Sachs 1942; Kris 1952; Greenacre 1957; Kavka 1975; Niederland 1976; Noy 1979; Myers 1979; Rose 1980). More recent psychoanalytic literature has emphasized the multiple functions art serves for creative integration and adaptation of inner and outer reality (e.g., Waelder 1965; Rose 1978, 1980; Roland 1978; Rothenberg 1978; Noy 1979). But the author/reader relationship has been relatively undeveloped in psychoanalytic writing.

Author, Text, and Audience

Psychoanalytic Approaches

Kris (1952) points out that the creative artist must have some "idea of a public," real or imaginary. The audience's approval alleviates the artist's guilt and enhances his self-esteem, balancing narcissistic tensions that may have been disturbed by the creative process. Kris, more knowledgeable about aesthetics than Freud, emphasized that the audience recreates the work through its ambiguity rather than discovers the artist's intention. The artist may have a fantasy relationship with the audience to whom he proffers his artistic creation as a kind of love gift (Greenacre 1957:490) or with whom he shares personal experiences and meanings (Noy 1979). Fantasies of the audience—and, in fact, the entire creative experience—may assist a temporary regression that then leads to forward movement (Rose 1972, 1973, 1980).

Artists may imagine that their work, now regarded as beautiful and perfect, will serve to repair their damaged self-image or stand in for a missing other (Niederland 1976). In this model, artists identify with their creations so as to enhance themselves or to fill in what they feel is missing within themselves. This idea applies especially to the artist who has a sense of defect and seeks to emphasize a capacity for magical transformation or recreation as defense against helplessness, mortification, or loss.

I was originally influenced in these investigations (see chapter 2 in this book, on Genet) by Khan (1965) and Bach and Schwartz (1972), who suggest the existence of a writing perversion that certain gifted authors can substitute for perverse sexual behavior. The *implicit* hypothesis maintained that the relationship between a perverse writer and his audience may approximate a perverse sexual experience. Khan noted that confession is a function of perverse behavior. He referred to the "extravagant sincerity" of writers such as Oscar Wilde, André Gide, Henry Miller, and Jean Genet. Khan suggested that such confession, whether through sexual contact or writing, approximated dreaming or hallucinating more than organized ego activity.

Bach and Schwartz (1972) speculate that one goal of the Marquis de Sade's writing *The 120 Days of Sodom* in prison was its effect on imaginary readers. Following Heinz Kohut, they interpret this as Sade's wish to so devastate his readers with "horror, disgust, and outrage" that they would have to affirm his grandiose self as it appears in the exercise of his sadistic power. Imaginary readers are "both his mirroring audience and his victims" (p. 470). They suggest that the "brilliance, intensity, and sensation" of Sade's fantasies were the means by which he evoked such vivid reactions in his characters and in his readers. Bach and Schwartz's major emphasis, however, is on Sade's delusional attempt *within the text* to validate grandiose self-images and idealized object-images as defenses against psychotic fragmentation. Nevertheless, these psychoanalysts at least imply that certain authors' fantasies of their relationship with their readers may serve to manage their intense needs of other people who are felt to be necessary for one's survival.

Psychoanalysts have described different narcissistic motivations for creativity, unrelated to an audience but with emphasis on the functions of the text as object. The artist may regard his artistic creations somewhat as an adult version of the infantile transitional object (P. Weissman 1971). In that case, his creations tend to remain in the background of the artist's psyche, only temporarily infringing on the artist's relations with living people, and are relinquished with varying degrees of difficulty. On the other hand, some artists might use the created object, prominently and permanently, more as a fetish to bolster the self. Following a psychotic period, Edvard Munch has been described (Rose 1978) as withdrawing from people into an intense involvement with his pictures, which he is said to have regarded as love objects. Munch beat a painting with a whip, as if to improve its character. Oscar Wilde's creative process has been described (Kavka 1975) as an attempt at self-cure of the author's damaged self-esteem through the reestablishment of self-cohesion. In this schema, Wilde's creations are thought to serve as others who would enhance the self (self-objects) so as to repair his self-esteem.

Literary Critical Approaches

Contemporary literary criticism has been shifting its focus from the interpretation of meanings embedded within a text to the processes of writing and reading. This is true of the French structuralists and post-structuralists (e.g., Barthes, Derrida), of certain psychoanalytically influenced critics (e.g., Holland, Schwartz, Bleich), and of other proponents of reader-response criticism (e.g., Rosenblatt, Fish, Iser, Gadamer, Poulet). Philosophical approaches to the phenomenology of reading have moved criticism away from attempts to determine objec-

tive meanings hidden within a text, meanings the reader needs to extri-
cate. The subjective experience of the reader; interaction between reader, text, and, at times, the author; and the values and premises with
which the reader approaches interpretation of the text have been
emphasized. As within psychoanalysis proper, so too within literary criticism, revisionists have focused on problems of indeterminacy, uncertainty, perspective, hermeneutics, and subjective and communal
assumptions and agreements. Literary critics have come to focus more
on how a reader reads a text and on what happens to her as she does so,
equating this with the "meaning" of the text.

The psychoanalyst's position in the consulting room, and her attitudes toward what her patients tell her, have often been ignored when
she has tried to decipher hidden meanings contained within the written text. In the consulting room, no psychoanalyst would attempt to
understand the content of a patient's communications without simultaneously considering why the communication is being made , how it
is being reported, who the patient imagines the analyst represents at the
moment, what responses the patient hopes for from the analyst, and so
forth. Thus content is always considered by a psychoanalyst in relation
to transference, defense, wish, and the functions of the communication.
Sometimes the actual content of the communication seems to have predominant importance; sometimes what stands out most is the effect the
patient seeks to have on the analyst—that is, what the patient needs
right then from the analyst and is attempting to elicit via his verbal
communication. Treating the written word as objectively capable of
unique interpretation, without attention to the complex field of interaction between and among author, text, and audience, leads to
methodological reductionism in both psychoanalysis and in literary
criticism.

We now expect that the analyst will frequently, if not continuously,
lose her (privileged) place as outside of conflict (the patient's and her
own). Self-analytic scrutiny of the analyst's affective displacements from
a position of reasonably neutral empathic understanding allows for a
richer and deeper grasp of the patient's conflicts by the analyst's resonating with some aspects of them within herself. At varying times, the
analyst may find herself emotionally in the position of the patient, a
portion of the patient (e.g., the patient's conscience), or of a parent.
Construction of meanings within the analytic situation can become
problematic in this antipositivist collaborative model. How are meanings to be negotiated when the participants thoroughly disagree and

neither can hear the other? It is to be hoped that the analyst's self-analytic processing of what she experiences within the analytic situation
allows the analyst to preserve her function of aiding the patient to
understand herself. It should also be clear by now that the literary critic has also become implicated in similar struggles. Literary criticism,
psychoanalysis, and contemporary epistemology have contributed to
problematizing the position of the critic.

The New Criticism, most influential in the 1940s, held that the
author's intentions could not be recovered. In contrast to this position
Dilthey (1833–1911) claims that a text is to be understood by attempting to reexperience the author's thoughts (see R. S. Steele 1979). This
nineteenth-century hermeneutics has been subsequently criticized, perhaps most cogently by Gadamer (1975). Gadamer regards interpretation as an event in which the interpreter gives his own subjective meaning to the content of the text, recreating and making it the interpreter's
own. The aesthetic experience is related to play in that the subject loses
herself, becoming absorbed in the experience while simultaneously giving it her own meanings. Gadamer emphasizes the impossibility of
attempting to reconstruct the author's own "mental experiences" (p.
335).

Reading is an event during which meanings are created and the reader achieves a communion with the text but not with the author. "What
is fixed in writing," Gadamer argues (p. 357), "has detached itself from
the contingency of its origin and its author and made itself free for new
relationships." Reminding his readers that Aristotle included the attitude of the spectator in his concept of the aesthetic experience (*Poetics*), Gadamer stresses the role of an audience for completing the experience of a work of art. "Artistic presentation, by its nature, exists for
someone, even if there is no one there who listens or watches only" (p.
99, emphasis added).

According to Gadamer, the artist must limit the "free invention" (p.
118) of his mind and text because he seeks to communicate with other
people; he must choose his material in order to have an effect on those
other people. The text's "written marks" (p. 349) are brought to life
by the meanings attributed to them by the reader. Thus, Gadamer's
perspective is that the partners in the literary experience are the text,
not the author, and the interpreter. Nevertheless, Gadamer under-
stands the reading of a text as akin to conversation in that a common
expression is shared between reader and author. This last point provides enough ambiguity to encourage the possibility of the reader's

communion with the author and not merely with his fixed, inanimate text.

Despite warning of the pitfalls, Bleich (1975) also finds it tempting to use the reader's responses as if they reflect something of the author's mind and intentions in creating his work. Bleich regards Edel's biography of Henry James as an example of "responsible discussion of the author's 'intention', as well as his overall relationship with a particular work" (p. 753). Schwartz (1975, 1978) clearly shifts the focus from reader and text to a triangular relationship between critic, text, and author. Although Schwartz is psychoanalytically sophisticated, he seems to preserve an emphasis that is primarily literary in his writings. Nevertheless, by his shift to a dynamic perspective on the relations between critic, text, and author, Schwartz helps to establish a psychoanalytic literary criticism. He uses Erikson's (1954) reinterpretation of Freud's dream of "Irma" as illustrative of the interpreter "actively mixing himself with his subject" (p. 763) rather than with his or her text. For Schwartz, this leads to the "externalization of a relationship between Erikson and Freud, self, and other" (p. 763).

Schwartz's (1975) idea of literary "potential space," similar to Gorney's (1980), emphasizes "the interpenetration of what is given (e.g., the material properties of objects or the historical meanings of words) with what is imagined (e.g., the personal value of objects or the private associations of language)" (p.764). "Literature is written language located in potential space," Schwartz contends (p. 765), "the language *we* locate there."

In practice, however, psychoanalytic approaches to literary criticism have not maintained a perspective on the triangular interaction between and among author, text, and reader. Subjectively interactional psychoanalytic literary criticism (as represented by Holland [1975a, 1975b, 1976, 1978]; Schwartz [1975, 1978, 1982]; English 692 [1978]; and Bleich [1967, 1975, 1976, 1977]), focuses predominantly on the position of the critic or reader, leaving the triangle of author, text, and reader skewed. This subjective psychoanalytic literary criticism relies too exclusively on the content of the reader's responses for its understanding and identification of unifying themes within the text.

How the reader relates to the text and to the author of the text has not been sufficiently considered. I refer to the quality of one's relationships to others, human as well as literary figures and texts. Readers have complex configurations of feelings and ideas in relation to texts and to their fantasies of the author in the background. How do readers' responses, that is, feelings and ideas, relate to an author's needs and purposes, conscious and unconscious, in writing the text? How can readers' responses be used to study an author's psychology, including his creation of the text? Kris (1952:255) warns that "effect is a function of [the artist's] intent but not of intent only; it must be separately considered." The complex interaction between author, text, and reader requires further clarification in order to understand the psychological meanings (i.e., needs) of the author and of the creation of his artistic product. Literary texts should not be *reduced* to psychopathology or even to psychological meanings alone. Rather, the focus needs to be on how to use readers' responses to a given text in order to generate more compelling, richer readings. Such readings would draw upon universal psychological themes experienced within the relationship between the three contributors to the literary experience (author, text, and audience).

The author's attitudes toward and relation to her text and audience have been insufficiently considered. Even where theoretical consideration has been given to the uses an author makes of her text and her readers, in *practical criticism* this has tended to be neglected in favor of explication of embedded meanings within the form and content of the text. The multiple functions that the audience—as well as the text—as object, provides for the author require further consideration. The same applies to the reader's needs of the author and the text. What are the methodological problems in using readers' responses to study an author's needs in creating her work? What are the similarities and differences in the literary relationship between author, text, and audience and in other relationships with more directly available and responsive living people? This latter question will provide an organizing perspective toward the authors studied in this book (see chapters 2–5, and 8) as imaginary literary relationships are compared with relations with live human beings.

Where is the author of a text to be located? Is she to be found as an overriding, synthesizing, creative presence within her work or is she to be sought as existing separately outside of the work she has authored? Poulet (1970) argues that the author with whom we need to be concerned does not exist apart from her work. The author has, however, imbued this work with her own subjective presence that we, the readers, can realize if we so allow ourselves. For Poulet, nevertheless, the reader is much less concerned with the author than with the coming to life of the work within the experience of reading. Holland (1970) aptly notes that this position neglects the very active and creative role of the reader.

Booth's (1979) concept of the "implied author" refers to the creating person who is implied by the choices made in crafting the work precisely as it has been crafted. Booth's concept of the "implied author" is predominantly a literary rather than a psychological construct. Booth has in mind freeing the picture that can be constructed of the author of a given work by the specific choices made at each step of the literary rendering and from identity with the "flesh-and-blood author." Booth stresses that the reader's picture of the "implied author" must be compatible with established biographical facts about the author, a view that Cooper (1982) questions.

Bleich (1978) makes clear that readers need to invent their own fantasied construct of the author while reading. Fish (1970) also works with a concept, less clearly delineated, of an "author" implied by the strategies with which the reader contends. For Fish as for Poulet (1970), these literary strategies emphasize the reading experience rather than psychological understanding of the encounter between author and reader.

Green (1978) suggests that psychoanalytic critics confine our literary efforts to the goal of helping the reader understand the effects a text has on her rather than attempting to find and psychoanalyze the author. For the classroom teaching of literature, helping students understand how they have been affected by a text is a legitimate goal (Richards 1929; Rosenblatt 1938; Holland 1973, 1975a, 1978; Bleich 1978; Fish 1980). However, problems arise in the theory and practice of literary criticism concerning the use to be made of such subjective responses to the text. Encouraging students to observe and report their personal associations to literary works may help their psychological and literary maturation. Literature professors and students may engage in ersatz psychotherapy, which may be helpful or harmful to either party. The problem is how to relate such subjective responses to understanding the text.

Some would argue that all subjective reactions have equal value, but that some are more persuasive and fit the prevailing needs of an interpretive community more successfully (Bleich 1967, 1975, 1976, 1977, 1978; Fish 1980). Others would preserve the objective status of the text while emphasizing its interaction with the reader's subjective responses (Rosenblatt 1938; Holland 1970, 1973, 1975a, b, 1976, 1978). Some (e.g., Fish) claim that texts are produced during reading by the application of given interpretive modes, that texts do not exist prior to interpretation. Others differentiate the text from the work, one of which, depending on the critic, is constituted from the other when interpreted (Rosenblatt 1938; Barthes 1973, 1979; even Kris 1952). The current debate within psychoanalysis between proponents of hermeneutic and natural science perspectives toward interpretation in the psychoanalytic situation reflects, in part, the persistent unwillingness of many psychoanalysts to accept this shift toward a subjectively interactional interpretive paradigm. That psychoanalysts and literary critics have been so interested in hermeneutics recently (see Steele 1979) testifies to a heightened awareness of and interest in the processes of understanding and interpretation. These are human activities that serve human, personal, and communal needs. Contemporary experimental fiction that is seemingly "unreadable," ambiguous, contradictory, that overemphasizes its own formal structure, that stresses the narrator's dialogue with the reader (Céline's *Castle to Castle* or Calvino's *If on a winter's night a traveler* are only two of many examples) makes the reader self-consciously aware of her own participation in "reading" the novel. The problem becomes how to use the reader's heightened awareness of her own subjective responses.

Could it be that a skilled critic is a skilled critic, without a psychoanalytic perspective adding much to such talent? For example, Felman's (1977) superb explication of Henry James's *Turn of the Screw* beautifully and persuasively describes the structure of the text and the structure of the reader's (her own) experience of it during reading. She uses this experience in a polemic to argue her own position that ambiguity, contradiction, uncertainty, and conflict are the very stuff of life, that they cannot be reduced without doing violence not just to texts but to life itself. To my mind, nothing is gained by then attempting to connect these exceedingly complex structures—of text and reader experience of text—with the nature of the "unconscious"—unless the connection is metaphorical. But since the images are already so well rendered by the text, there is no reason to do even this. The images themselves perform a function analogous to that of our constructs of the unconscious: they account for an aspect of life. Summoning up the authority of Lacan's name or his construct of the unconscious does not advance Felman's already persuasive argument. A literary not a psychoanalytic perspective has clarified the text and the "structure of the reading experience."

Fish (1970) aptly warns, as does Kris (1952), that critics need to resist the psychological pressure toward simplification and closure, that literature is ambiguous and complex, not possessed of single, specifiable meanings that can be used to paraphrase a work. Holland (1975) points out that all constructions of meaning serve psychological purposes. Attempts to unify, to seek converging themes, serve to reduce anxiety about divergence, complexity, unfamiliarity, helplessness, and so on. Although Holland admirably confesses his own personal need to handle anxiety by organizing complex issues in terms of a unifying theme, this has been his approach to practical criticism. Schwartz and Willbern (1982) criticize Holland's work on reader-text interaction for preserving the emphasis on the identification of a single, central explanatory principle at the heart of the writing-reading experience. Like Felman, Holland is a fine critic but whether his criticism is enriched by the "psychoanalytic" meaning he offers is open to question. Although Schwartz and Holland both point to how critics or readers use themselves subjectively while reading, neither has offered specific examples of how they have used their own subjective reading experiences in formulating and writing criticism.

Schwartz (1975, 1978, 1982) delineates what critics do and why they do it. He explores how reading is subjective. In this book I will emphasize that a psychoanalytic literary criticism needs such detailed data of the critic's reading experience, both literary and psychological. I will consider the similarities and differences between the critic's position and the psychoanalyst's, as each is influenced by and participates in an intense affective process that he or she attempts to understand and interpret.

According to Schwartz (1978), the literary relationship occurs between people; the reader seeks an experience, not with a text but with his own (fictional) "embodiment" of the author. Schwartz (1978, p. 150) maintains that "the author I seek is actually always a fiction I recreate through his fictions." The "other" with whom the critic shares the literary experience includes the author as well as the critic's own audience of readers and critics. Bleich (1978:161) suggests that the more unfamiliar a reader is with an author or "his language system," the greater will be his need to "invent an author as part of the normal activity of response and interpretation." The reader's focus on a construct of the author may serve a variety of psychological functions.

Initial Convergence of Literary Critical and
Psychoanalytic Approaches

Winnicott's (1967) concept of "potential space" has influenced two psychoanalytic commentators on the relationship between author and reader. Green (1978) describes writing as "communication with the absent" (p. 282); the absence as well as the illusory representation of the reader are both intensely felt and "fashioned" by the writer. The reader's experience of the writer mirrors the writer's experience of the reader. The author's and reader's doubles, "ghosts which never reveal themselves—communicate through the writing" in "this no-man's land . . . this site of a transnarcissistic communication" (Green 1978:283). Green hints that one motivation of Proust's (or at least of the literary Marcel's) writing was a search for contact with a mother who desired literary more than live objects.

Gorney (1980) describes a dialectic of coauthorship, an imaginary relationship between reader and writer when a reader interprets a text. "It is within the field of illusion provided by the text," Gorney writes "that a discourse between author and reader is established, interpretation occurs and meaning is freshly created" (p. 14). Gorney (1979:4) argues that language and literary creation, with the role of illusion, aim at a "wished-for recognition of a real or fantasied other" or at least the illusory re-creation of an absent other. Following Lacan (1977), he believes that the primal requirement of language is to manage "the absence of the mother by evoking her presence through the symbolic power of the word" (1979:2).

To my mind, the usefulness of these initial approaches to a psychology of reading and writing are marred by reducing the psychological relationship between author and reader *only* to the most primitive needs. That is, language is to evoke the presence of the other, or the illusory potential space is to reestablish early relations with transitional objects. Care must be taken not to equate adult creativity with early infantile development (see Rose 1978; Brody 1980; Skura 1981). The development of the creative imagination cannot be reduced to simple infantile needs.

Psychoanalytic authors have tended to refer concretely to the "transitional" quality of the creative imagination as if there were some kind of direct link to earliest development. They seem to have been seeking a metaphor for creative attempts to bridge and integrate inside and outside (cf. Rose 1978). Certain wishes—such as those for narcissistic affirmation, alleviation of guilts and fears, for immortality, and protection against loneliness and depression—are universal and certainly may influence (consciously and unconsciously) every author's dialectic with her audience. These authors' objects—substitute inanimate literary objects as well as the imaginary (and real) people who read their writings—may be regarded in diverse ways and may function to gratify various needs.

Holland (1975) attempts to establish the rudiments of a developmental line for reading and being a reader. Holland suggests that the reader regards the text as well as its author as a "gratifying other," experienced in relation to earliest maternal nurturance. For the toddler being read to is a "mixed human and literary experience" (p. 126). Holland quotes Fraiberg (1968) as saying that at a certain point in childhood, pleasure in reading and in language becomes somewhat independent from the people who had taught these skills to the child. "The book itself has taken over as a partner and is invested with some of the qualities of a human relationship," Fraiberg states. Reading and books serve as extensions of one's primary relationships. Holland's aphorism, "other is other, be it book or mother" (p. 127) aptly expresses how a reader approaches a text.

To examine narrative style psychologically, as I attempt to do in this book, requires clarification of the multiple functions—aesthetic, literary, as well as psychological—served by narrative style. Much of the intensely interactive quality of the writing I examine is mediated through its narrative style and the role of the narrator. This book will highlight contrasts between literary communication and the text as an aesthetic object. Hence, literature should not be viewed exclusively as written communication but is perhaps best conceived more broadly as the human construction of aesthetic objects that are rendered through language (see Booth 1979, especially his [chapter 2] discussion of Ronald Crane; see also Rose 1980). This tension between communication and aesthetic object will be especially emphasized in my discussion of certain letter writing (see chapter 4 in this book on Freud's correspondence and chapter 5 on Sade's).

Toward a Psychoanalytic Literary Criticism

Fish (1980) offers an approach to the *methodology* of subjective criticism of the formal properties of the text. (He points to what one struggles with while reading: "Patterns of expectation and disappointment, reversals of direction, traps, invitations to premature conclusions, textual gaps, delayed revelations, temptations," all of which can be related to "intentions" or strategies of the author (pp. 344–45). The text, Fish suggests, should be questioned as to its effects on the reader: "What is the reader doing? What is being done to him? For what purpose?" (p. 345). As one attempts to answer such questions, the reader-response critic delineates "the structure of the reading experience."

This provides a close reading of the text, Fish argues, without the assumption that what is recovered are innate features of the text. It provides, that is, a careful description of the text that is consistent with a given set of interpretive assumptions and strategies for approaching it. Fish has turned the affective fallacy around to argue that what the poem *does* is precisely what it means. Wimsatt and Beardsley (1954) had warned ("the affective fallacy") that the psychological effects of a poem should not be confused with what the poem itself is. Fish's approach is not, however, a psychoanalytic approach.

Skura (1981) (see chapter 6 in this book) also presents fine examples and arguments for detailed examination of the complexities of reading a difficult text, paying attention to the very struggle to deal with and integrate the text. The meaning of the text, Fish and Skura argue, cannot be unrelated to the problems that are posed for the reader in reading it. Skura's central contention for both psychoanalysis and literary criticism is that what is most important is continual examination of process—psychoanalytic process or reading process—as the overall framework within which the constituents (content, function, mode of representation, rhetorical function) are to be considered. Skura argues that radical questioning of our assumptions in reading and the ability to shift levels and modes of reading, to tolerate ambiguity, contradiction, uncertainty, and complexity lead to more interesting readings of texts.

Felman (1987) makes similar, wise observations (see chapter 7 in this book) about the complexities of reading. I do not agree with Skura's application of terms from the psychoanalytic process to the reading process. For example, Skura refers to the reader's struggle with the complexities of a text as "working through"; I do not think the analogy is helpful. I certainly do agree with her that what psychoanalysis contributes most is not specific psychosexual fantasy content but a complex approach to understanding people and their conflicts. But reading literature is not analogous to the psychoanalytic process.

Skura's transference model of exchanges between author and reader through the text is well presented in terms of the variety of relationships the text "presumes" with the reader.

Reed (1982, 1985) suggests exploring contradictions in texts and in readers' and critics' responses to them (see chapter 6 in this book). She (1982) uses the concept of parallelism to explore the contradictions in critics' understandings of a text (by Diderot). Examining readers' and critics' responses to texts certainly may help to identify important problems in reading texts and may help to organize more satisfying and coherent readings. That is no small contribution. Of course, authors will use their lives, themselves, their conflicts, consciously and unconsciously, in their work, at varying distances from their core conflicts. How unconscious conflicts influence and are expressed in creative writing remains to be explained.

I disagree with those psychoanalysts who assign priority to psychoanalysis as capable of organizing readings of texts around central unconscious fantasies (involved in a compromise formation) as the surface of a text (see chapter 6 in this book). To my mind, readings of texts have to be coherent, consistent, comprehensive, meaningful, and enrich the reader's experience and understanding of the text. Identifying an organizing unconscious fantasy may or may not provide the most persuasive reading of a text. Other readings may be more satisfying and persuasive. I do not assume that literature, or its surface, is a compromise formation.

The idea of compromise formation is a central one in contemporary psychoanalysis. Many clinical phenomena can be understood more richly when viewed as compromise formations (e.g., varieties of transference and fantasies about the self). Brenner's (1982) clinical perspective on compromise formation has been very helpful. However, regarding everything, including art and literature, as compromise formations does not make much sense to me. At the least, viewing literature as a compromise formation omits both what is outside conflict and the creative nonconflictual uses authors can make of their stable compromise formations. It is unwarranted to assume that unconscious conflict is the central motive force for creative writing. A more balanced and complex approach would assume that creative writing involves multiple aims, needs, and desires, some of which are and some are not still embroiled in conflict.

If literature is not reduced to a compromise formation, then the task is not necessarily to discern a central conflict or unconscious fantasy within (or behind) it. Identification of a central conflict and the uncon-scious fantasy involved in a text is only *one of the ways* in which a text can be read. To assume, as many psychoanalysts have done, that texts are indeed organized by conflict and fantasy does give a privileged posi-tion to psychoanalytic readings. Even the search for conflict and uncon-scious fantasy does not necessarily lead to agreement as to how to des-ignate *the* conflict and fantasy. Analysts reading texts, as in their clinical work, will often not agree on what is at issue.

I also disagree with the attempt to identify the author's unconscious fantasy and with the belief that what organizes a text best does indeed represent the author's conflict. Instead of this assumption, an open, nondogmatic approach to applied psychoanalysis would have to present convincing evidence that would connect organizing themes in texts with organizing themes in the author's life, and demonstrate that a major function of the writing was to master this conflict and *especially* that these themes provide a cogent reading of the text. Baudry (1979) advocates using biographical data about the author to support the crit-ic's reading of the text. Rosenblatt (1938:117) argues that "to derive an interpretation of a text from the author's life or stated intentions is . . . critically indefensible."

I agree that the author we seek is present within and through his texts and that that is how we readers experience him. The author does not need to be objectified apart from his work in order for a psycholo-gy of author, text, and audience to be formulated. Rather, we seek an intersection between these three participants, one that is subjectively created by the reader in collaboration with author and text during the reading experience. Although my view is that the real-life author's intentions cannot be established from his psychobiography, I do believe such psychobiographies can make literary interpretations more cogent and convincing.

Any literary interpretation must be judged primarily by literary stan-dards rather than by appeal to outside authority or "objective facts." Such standards can be of correspondence, intent, and coherence (Kris and Kaplan 1948) or coherence, consistency, comprehensiveness, and "conformity with refined common sense" (Schafer 1980:83). It will most likely be beyond the ken of applied psychoanalysis to demonstrate that a major function of the writing was to master a particular conflict. Priority would still be given to that interpretation that generates the most persuasive *literary* reading (cf. Fish 1980). And the most persua-sive literary reading may or may not include psychoanalytic metaphors!

Holland (1982) and Schwartz (1982) emphasize that psychoanalysis contributes to literature only as it contributes to the understanding of people rather than of literature per se. The people to be understood are writers, readers, and characters. Schwartz asserts that the psychoanalytic critic, in contrast to other critics, "seeks to represent the text by representing an absent author, by constructing an authorizing consciousness." Esman (1982) disagrees with Schwartz's emphasis on the communicative function of the text, preferring to view the text primarily as an aesthetic object.

Gorney (1980) quotes Green (1975), in order to emphasize the "reciprocal intersubjective nature of analytic discourse," as saying "the patient's aim is directed to the effect of his communication rather than to the transmission of its content." I would point out that this may be one aim of the patient and that for certain patients at times the effect on the analyst may be more important than the content related. At other times and for other patients, no psychoanalyst would ignore the multiple aims of the patient's communications, including their thematic content, wishes, defenses, transference meanings, and so on. I would expect that the more intense are a patient's or writer's feelings of isolation, loneliness, neglect, and depression, the more he may need to elicit intense responses from the other in order to bring both of them to life. In that case the balance of focus for psychoanalyst or critic would be tilted from content or form to effect.

Should psychoanalytically informed literary criticism move beyond helping readers understand their own affective responses to literature, and if so, where to? Should psychoanalysts attempt to contribute to an understanding of the text or of the author, and if so, how do they do this? The arguments turn in opposing directions. On the one hand, it is argued that careful understanding of the complexities of the reader's responses to the text clarifies the text. Further, that it is not necessary to worry too much about the author's "intentions" because we can assume that our responses correlate with certain strategies of our own in the reading experience, strategies of the text, or strategies of some construct of the author.

At the same time, it is acknowledged that the literary community does want to know, as a legitimate area of inquiry, what the real-life author intended; that within certain limits of probability, this can be ascertained. Studying ourselves, our own subjective reading experiences, we are on safer, more familiar ground. Freud (1907) warned us that when we attempt to interpret a literary work, we may find only "what [we are] looking for and what is occupying [our] own mind[s]" and attribute this to purposes unintended by the artist (p. 91).

Even if psychoanalysts can help readers to understand how reading a text affects them, how do we then proceed to distinguish intentional from unintentional effects, and to decide whose intentions these are? We certainly know from the consulting room how often our own driven needs, wishes, defenses, and transference and countertransference distortions disturb our work. Reading may offer us a little more protection in that we are not directly confronted with the needs and feelings of another live human being. On the other hand, alone with the text, we are freer to abandon controls, to immerse ourselves in fantasies and longings, less restrained by the pressures of reality and our task of helping a patient to understand himself.

The problem in reader-response criticism is how to use the reader's responses selectively and effectively so as to organize a more vital and complex reading than would result were the reader to disregard his own struggles during reading. The danger is always of subjectivism but not in the sense of missing the flesh-and-blood author's intentions or of an idiosyncratic reading not shared by other readers. The danger is of generating readings that are unconvincing, irrelevant, and uninteresting. But this is the problem with all interpretation, whether the reader's own subjective contributions are acknowledged or disclaimed. All critics must draw on their own subjective responses during reading, but for most this remains unacknowledged or undisclosed.

The proponents of "transactive criticism" have approached the problem of methodology in literary criticism with several points: all responses and all interpretations are subjective, reflective of the critic's own personal needs; the search for convergence in thematic meanings serves to reduce the critic's own anxiety; all subjective responses have "value" but some provide us with a better "fit" (Holland 1975:269) for interrelating and understanding a work. This last point allows such literary criticism to be shared usefully between critics for opening further, amplifying, and enriching one's own responses and understanding.

The criterion of value in a psychoanalyst's responses (within his own mind) to a patient always requires sorting out which responses within the analyst have little to do with the patient's own current conflicts and more to do with the analyst himself. It centers on the usefulness of the analyst's responses and understanding for enabling the patient to so understand himself that he becomes capable of change. How can this apply to a psychoanalytic understanding of literary relationships? How are we to take the leap from the characters, the text, and our own complex responses, to make assumptions about any author's psychological needs? This has to be the central problem in attempting a formulation of a psychology of the relationship betwen author, text, and audience.

When we attempt to use our own subjective responses to a text in order to "understand" text and author, there is certainly the risk that we will discover only what is present within ourselves. What we would hope for, like Gorney's (1980) idea of a dialectic of coauthorship, would be to discover within ourselves, as we confront text and author, "resonances" with the author. It may be that we can only find in an author's text, or a patient, what is also operative and available to consciousness within ourselves. Our motivation for understanding a literary text and its author is certainly not to assist the author with change. At times our predominant motivation may be further self-understanding by examining someone else and his creative product.

All of us, literary critics and psychoanalysts alike, have our own inner needs to understand and interpret. We persist with this regardless of "collective value." The "collective value" in providing formulations of an author's psychology may be, like the value in understanding responses to the content of the text, that it frees other readers to respond more fully and more complexly to his works. It may, however, have paradoxical inhibiting effects on readers as well as on the author. For example, Sartre (1952) may have helped Genet to understand himself but he may also have interfered with Genet's creativity. We hope that the effort to formulate the psychological relationship between author, text, and audience with greater sophistication, clarity, and complexity may aid understanding of creative efforts and the creative process.

We would expect that all behaviors, including writing, can be adapted to serve those needs that are most pressing. My assumption as a psychoanalyst is that when basic needs are intensely driven they will predominate in whatever behavior we examine, including writing. I would expect further that the level of object relationship as well as the *functions* of the object would be *somewhat* similar in the author's relationship with an audience, imaginary and real, as with other people in his life. It may be safer, nevertheless, to express such needs of an object within the fantasied relationship between author and audience, obscured by illusion and expressed through fictional characters within the medium of a literary text. Direct expression of such needs to other living people may create much greater risks, making the author feel much more vulnerable. Writing produces permanent changes. Each written work itself is permanent, indestructible, a testament to the author's creativity, and, if he is successful, the author's identity can be concretely transformed by his writing.

Gorney (1980) suggested that the evolution in literary criticism from textual criticism to an intersubjective dialectical relationship has parallels in psychoanalysis in a move away from exclusive focus on the patient's internal conflicts toward a newly creative experience with the analyst. I would shift the emphasis. Experience with "the widening scope of psychoanalysis" (Stone 1954) has required that psychoanalysis attend to the adult derivatives, manifested in conflict, of incompletely mastered early childhood developmental tasks. The functions the patient requires of his object, including his analyst, are of critical importance in such work.

This emphasis on unresolved early needs expressed as current conflict via the medium of a relationship with another who is vitally needed by the subject is an approach I have used in my reading of writers in this book. In this context, effect on the other, that is need of him, *may* have greater motivational significance than the expression of conflictual themes within the content and form of the dialogue. Both the relationship with the other (reader, characters) and the fantasy content of the story are aimed especially at managing what is most threatening to the author. For the authors considered in this book, rage, destructiveness, and need are most especially threatening.

Similar to my approach in this book is the trend in certain recent psychoanalytic writings on creativity that has emphasized the need for an intense, supportive relationship with another living person required by certain artists during a period of creativity. This has been described by Meyer (Panel 1972) as "secret sharing" or by Kohut (1976) as a "transference of creativity." Kligerman (1980) described Melville's "transference relationship" to Hawthorne and Hamilton (1980) noted the prominence of transference manifestations in Eugene O'Neill's correspondence with Beatrice Ashe. S. Weissman (1990) has recently described an intense supportive relationship between Coleridge and Wordsworth, from which both men drew deeply in their creative work, as well as in the rest of their lives. De Levita (Panel 1972) suggested that study of the artist's relationship to his audience when compared with his actual relations with love objects might clarify "the infantile situation in which the turn to what could be called the precursors of later artistic creativity took place" (p. 26). De Levita pointed out that examination of an artist's letter writing would be an excellent way to approach this since "at least one person of the audience as the addressee is named." I agree with de Levita that it would be fruitful to contrast the needs expressed in the artist's relationship with his audience with supportive literary relationships with living people, as through the study of correspondence (see chapters 4 and 5 in this book).

All of these approaches emphasize the artist's intense needs of another person, conceptualized predominantly as preoedipal narcissistic needs. However, to focus exclusively on the narcissistic tensions and on the imbalance that results during creative activity as does Kohut (1976), valuable as this is, misses the dynamic conflicts involved in creativity (see Kligerman 1980) as well as the needs served by the creative activity itself. An overidealization of creative activity may ensue, as it does, I think, in Kohut's (1976) approach. I disagree also with Kohut's (1976) claim that the "transference of creativity" does not "predominantly involve the revival of a figure from the (oedipal) past which derives its transference significance primarily from the fact that it is still the target of the love and hate of the creative person's childhood" (p. 820). To my mind, the audience for whom we write, and the people to whom we look for sustenance while we create, are never divorced from our unresolved needs for specific people from our childhood (i.e., parents) who are colored by our loves and hates and by the values and images we attribute to them.

Part One

SAMPLE READINGS: AUTHORS AND READERS

Chapter 2

THE AUTHOR AND HIS AUDIENCE: JEAN GENET'S EARLY WORK

This essay was stimulated by Khan (1965) and Bach and Schwartz (1972), who suggested the existence of a writing perversion that certain gifted authors can substitute for perverse sexual behavior. Implicit was the hypothesis that the relationship between a perverse writer and his audience may approximate a perverse sexual experience. I came to this work through my psychoanalytic teaching and writing about perversion in which I became intrigued by the relationship between artist and audience, a relationship relatively neglected in psychoanalytic studies of art. In order to investigate Genet's relationship with his audience, I decided to observe my own emotional responses to his writings, using myself as reader, audience, and psychoanalyst. At this point I had not yet learned about reader-response criticism. Once I did, I was rapidly led into the complications and concerns about methodology and aims that exist in contemporary psychoanalytic literary criticism.

I refrain from speculation about the actual Jean Genet in that I am more interested in attempting to construct an imaginary author/narrator with whom the reader contends in this writing. The relationship between narrator/author and reader is examined by a study of "the reading experience" of the works and the fantasies of the narrator/author I have constructed. I am less troubled than Booth

(1979) over whether the "implied author" is compatible with established biographical facts about the author. On the other hand, I do believe that what is known about an author *may* help to make literary arguments more persuasive. Reasonable standards for interpretation, such as those offered by Kris and Kaplan (1948) of correspondence, intent, and coherence, are more important than biographical reconstruction.

My material here is based on the early works of Genet: *Our Lady of the Flowers* (Notre-dame-des-fleurs [1943], to be abbreviated here as *OLF*), his first novel, written entirely in prison; *The Maids* (Les bonnes [1947]), his second play; and *The Thief's Journal* (Journal du voleur [1948], here designated as *TTJ*), an autobiography. I have chosen three different literary forms—novel, drama, and autobiography—in order to explore several forms of relationship between narrator/author and reader or audience. I argue that the relationship between narrator/author and reader is central to these works, more important than any specific content or fantasy elaboration. I also argue that the narrator/author seeks to engage and force his reader into an intensely responsive relationship, representative of that of loving parent and child, whose task is to provide him with affirmation, admiration, and acceptance. To establish my thesis, I intend to demonstrate that psychological meaning can be reasonably attributed to the narrative point of view of these works.

The Real-Life Genet: Some Background

Jean Genet wrote *Our Lady of the Flowers* in Fresnes Prison at the age of thirty-two. He was awaiting trial for theft at which he feared he would receive a ten-year sentence. Prior to this novel he had written only a few poems, which critics have regarded as crude. Considering his extreme emotional deprivation and the fact that he received little formal education, Genet's literary accomplishment is remarkable. Born illegitimately in the public maternity hospital of Paris, he was abandoned at birth by his mother; his father was unknown. Raised in a public orphanage until he was seven, he was then placed with a peasant foster family in the Morvan, a rural region of France. There is suggestive evidence (*TTJ*, p. 224) that Genet may have been accepted as a replacement for the foster parents' dead daughter. This may have interfered with the care he received and have added to an identification with the dead and the feminine. At age ten, Genet was branded a thief by his foster parents; this concretely labeled him an outcast, no doubt intensifying his feeling of being a bastard. His writings, and the meager factual information available about Genet, suggest that he never felt loved and accepted. At fifteen he was sent to Mettray Reformatory, most likely as punishment for theft. Unfortunately, as with the rest of Genet's biography, there is little reliable information about this incident and Genet's self-revelations are contradictory. However, in *Miracle of the Rose* (Miracle de la rose [1951]) Genet says (p. 225) that what led him to Mettray was the unprovoked gouging out of a child's eye. Is that fact or fantasy? Although Genet's works abound with sadistic, destructive images, there is no evidence that he actually engaged in such acts.

After Mettray, he briefly joined the Foreign Legion, then lived as a vagabond, homosexual prostitute, smuggler, and thief, and was often in and out of prison. Sartre (1952) says that at the age of sixteen Genet had the opportunity to learn from a professional songwriter. In fact, it is not known how he gained his impressive knowledge of language, art, and literature. Genet jokingly says he learned the art of browsing in bookstores by pilfering valuable books. He claims to have written *Our Lady of the Flowers* on the brown paper convicts were given to make paper bags. When his manuscript was confiscated, he rewrote it from memory on notebooks purchased at the prison canteen. How he smuggled the novel out of prison and had it printed is unclear. After publication of his first novel, Genet was adopted by a group of French writers. In 1948 a number of them, including Sartre, Cocteau, Mauriac, Gide, Mondor, and Claudel, successfully petitioned the president of France, Vincent Auriol, to pardon Genet, who faced life imprisonment for his tenth criminal offense. Genet the petty criminal was transformed into Genet the poet.

The Reading Experience of Genet's Early Work: A Sampler

Our Lady of the Flowers is dedicated to the memory of Maurice Pilorge, who, as the reader is told on the very first page, "killed his lover, Escudero, to rob him of something under a thousand francs, then for his twentieth birthday, they cut off his head, while *you* will recall, he thumbed his nose at the enraged executioner" (emphasis added). On this first page, the reader is also told the author is writing this book in honor of the crimes of three murderers and one traitor. The very first sentence contains a substitution of the reader for the narrator, representative of many similar shifts to follow: "Weidman appeared before *you* in a five o'clock edition, his head swathed in white bands, a nun and yet a wounded pilot fallen into the rye one September day . . . " (emphasis added). The tension between narrator and audience is kept taut by repeatedly calling attention to the fact that he is the writer and that "you" are the reader. The reader feels shocked by the suggestion that he, like the narrator, spends his time idealizing murderers. This engages the reader in the narrative and connects reader and narrator more intimately, while making the reader want to protest and disclaim the identity with the narrator that has been conferred upon him. Without doubt, the author/narrator is also evoking his own personal version of the prevalent contemporary critical principles of subjectivism, uncertainty, relativism, and indeterminacy.

On the fourth page "you" become part of the narrator's masturbatory fantasies, as he offers to caress the reader's prick and even boasts and recalls that this has already happened. The reader is startled, confused, wants to protest, perhaps is even titillated with such offers of phallic worship. But just as you feel this, the narrator jostles you again. Perhaps this is all make-believe, perhaps he is only playing with you. The final orgasmic image of this scene evokes religious adoration, sainthood, confusing the reader about the level of illusion to which the narrator has now moved. Then again, as narrator and reader are ascending heavenward, the narrator shakes you once more, reminding you in the next paragraph that he is telling you practical and important details of his prison life.

The narrator becomes the barker for a carnival sideshow, seductively offering to gratify the reader's most perverse fantasies once you enter into his world. These asides put the reader in his place and emphasize his dependence on the narrator. The arrival of Darling Daintyfoot, a pimp, is grandiloquently announced; the narrator interrupts the description to interject (*OLF*, p. 70), "which *you* can only imagine" (emphasis added). He rhapsodizes, "I was his at once, as if" and again interrupts, "who said that?" before completing the thought, "he had discharged through my mouth straight through to my heart." The narrator again invites the reader into his bed, encouraging the reader's jealousy and lust. Simultaneously, he rams your perverse curiosity down your throat.

The narrator of *Our Lady of the Flowers* describes his writing as an interlude between masturbating; he says he is reporting his masturbation fantasies. However, he drives home to the reader that he is unable to cope with his severe depression, fears of madness, isolation, loneliness, and vulnerability, when he is alone with his fantasies and with his masturbation. He needs the reader's enthusiastic participation. At this point it is ambiguous whether the narrator longs for imaginary readers or believes he is soon to acquire actual readers. He tells us that he knows that his imagination is lovely, but he feels insubstantial, inconsequential and remote, lost in his daydreaming. His fantasies lack credibility for him, even when he tries to vitalize them by masturbation; alone, he is unable to feel better about himself. The reader is invited to draw nearer as friend, lover, and healer. Genet writes (*OLF*, p. 132):

> My mind continues to produce lovely chimeras, but so far none of them has taken on flesh. Never. Not once. If I now try to indulge in a daydream, my throat goes dry, despair burns my eyes, shame makes me bow my head, my reverie breaks up . . . The despondency that follows makes me feel somewhat like a shipwrecked man who spies a sail, sees himself saved, and suddenly remembers that the lens of his spyglass has a flaw, a blurred spot—the sail he has seen.

He adds (*OLF*, p. 138):

> In the evening the preliminaries of sleep denude the environs of my self, destroy objects and episodes, leaving me at the edge of sleep as solitary as I was one night in the middle of a stormy and barren heath. Darling, Divine, and Our Lady [his characters] flee from me at top speed, taking with them the consolation of their existence, which has its being only in me, for they are not content with fleeing; they do away with themselves, dilute themselves in the *appalling insubstantiality of my dreams* (emphasis added).

In writing he seeks experiences in which the word (*OLF*, p. 178) "ceased to be word and became flesh."

The mood of *Our Lady of the Flowers* is one of depression. The narrator talks about suicide. All this is frightening and convincing to the reader; so are the images of madness. Village, the handsome black murderer, has been painting tiny lead soldiers in his cell—they take over (p. 189):

> One morning, after waking up, he sat down on his bed, looked around the room, and saw it full of stupid-looking figurines that were lying about everywhere, as mindless and mocking as a race of fetus-

es, as Chinese torturers. The troops rose up in sickening waves to attack the giant. He felt himself capsizing. He was sinking into an absurd sea, and the eddies of his despair were sucking *me* into the shipwreck. *I* grabbed hold of a soldier. They were all over the floor, everywhere, a thousand, ten thousand, a hundred thousand! And though I was holding the one I had picked up in the warm hollow of my palm, it remained icy, without breath . . . The little soldier whipped up a swell that made the room pitch (emphasis added).

The change of pronoun plays with uncertainty between object and subject and allows the reader to identify more closely with the narrator. But it is experienced as if the narrator were losing his grasp on reality, alarming us. The narrator then immediately transforms this image of impending madness into one of sexual dizziness, orgasm. Perhaps he was only being carried away by passion rather than madness. It is characteristic of each of these three works that negative, dangerous images of self and object are transformed by sexual seduction and poetry into exciting and beautiful counterparts. Sexual feelings are used to still pain, to make unpleasant reality illusory, and to dominate and control others.

The narrator is anxious about his forthcoming trial. As he reveals this (p. 189), he quickly shifts to describing himself masturbating, as if that will change what is real for him. The trial scene at the conclusion of *Our Lady of the Flowers* seems to lessen the narrator's anxiety through the mastery involved in writing about it. The psychiatrist's report about the defendant reads "unbalanced . . . psychopathy . . . schizophrenia . . . unbalanced . . . equilibrist" (p. 295). "Equilibrist" is then defined as "one who balances himself in unnatural positions and hazardous movements, as in rope dancing." This describes well how the narrator attempts to master his frightening feelings within the text by going right to the edge of the abyss, looking down, then reminding himself and the reader that this is all illusory and under the narrator's full control.

The narrator continuously proclaims how important his audience is for him. He writes (*OLF*, p. 212): "I feel such a need to complain and to try to win a reader's love!" And in (*TTJ*, p. 207):

By the gravity of the means and the splendor of the materials which the poet used to draw near to men, I measure the distance that separated him from them . . . By the gravity of the means I require to thrust you from me, measure the tenderness I feel for you. Judge to

what degree I love you from the barricades I erect in my life and work
. . . so that your breath—I am corruptible to an extreme—may not
rot me. My tenderness is of fragile stuff.

Again, in (*TTJ*, p. 268): "I aspire to your recognition, your consecra-
tion."

That the narrator "thrusts" his reader away while craving his presence seems apparent from almost any page of Genet's writing. Images
of the ugly and despicable, represented as beautiful, shock and confuse
us. The reader is dazzled and surprised by the narrator's sudden turns
and the unexpected and unusual transformation in his images. The
reader continually loses his footing, not knowing what to believe, what
is real and what is illusory, what is evil and mean and what is good and
valuable. Just as one feels this, the narrator introduces a dialogue with
the reader warning the latter how treacherous he can be while offering
to rescue the reader. The narrator reminds the reader of the latter's
dependence on him, his helplessness in the narrator's world, and pro-
tectively offers to sit close beside the reader and guide him.

When the narrator has revealed tender feelings, when he seems to
become more gentle and caring, and the reader relaxes his guard and
enjoys himself, then he pulls himself and you up short. The reader continually feels manipulated as he is invited into the narrator's finely crafted poetic images, only to be ultimately frustrated. For example, the
aging Divine, the drag queen who is losing her charm and lovers, meets
the "Archangel Gabriel," who is supportive and accepting. Divine
(*OLF*, p. 160) "swooned with love like a nymph in a tree" at Gabriel's
potency and passion with her; "Divine's eyes became brilliant and her
skin suppler." Then Gabriels's role is reduced to "fucker," whereupon
we are told: (*OLF*, p. 161) "Then he died in the war."

The narrator reminds the reader, that he, not you, is creating the
poetry. This is his world, not yours. You are an invited guest and if you
want to find your way in it, you need him to direct you; otherwise you
will become lost in a labyrinth. Think, for example, of Stilitano (*TTJ*,
p. 265), humiliated and trapped in the "crystal prison" of the Palace of
Mirrors, unable to find his way out of this game of glass, some of it
transparent and some mirroring. Occasionally he would see his own
reflection; sometimes he would see others beyond the glass. Since the
narrator keeps inventing and changing the images, there is no way for
the reader to find his own way. Yet the narrator keeps taunting the
reader with possibilities of sharing in the creation of the poetry, only

then to emphasize his own central role as author. He writes (*OLF*, p. 109): "Here are some "Divinariana" gathered expressly for you. Since I wish to show the reader a few candid shots of her, it is up to him to provide a sense of duration, of passing time, and to assume that during this first chapter she will be between twenty and thirty years of age." It is emphasized that this is an impossible task for the reader. Or again, the narrator introduces Darling and Our Lady and tells the reader (*OLF*, p. 134):

> I leave you free to imagine any dialogue you please. Choose whatever may charm you. Have it, if you like, that they hear the voice of the blood, or that they fall in love at first sight, or that Darling, by indisputable signs invisible to the vulgar eye, betrays the fact that he is a thief... Conceive the wildest improbabilities. Have it that the depths of their being are thrilled at accosting each other in slang. Tangle them suddenly in a swift embrace or a brotherly kiss. Do whatever you like.

The reader becomes annoyed, wishing that the narrator would proceed without so many interruptions, and by the teasing implication that the reader also is homosexually aroused by the characters, and even more by the narrator himself.

A character in these works always remains intermediary between self and not-self, never clearly becoming another separate three-dimensional (literary) person, with his own destiny, nor yet fully the author. Unlike *Our Lady of the Flowers*, in *The Thief's Journal* and *The Maids*, the narrator no longer reminds his readers that the characters are figments, representing himself; but they still are. They are depicted more realistically but they never take on their own literary life. A number of critics (especially McMahon 1963) have commented on the increased confidence and audacity that lead Genet to describe characters more objectively in his later works. This is only partly true. Characters may have the external trappings of real people, but inside they are hollow, or one finds an image of the author himself mocking the reader. Even Armand, in *The Thief's Journal*, with his tolerant acceptance of people others treat with contempt, seems to be only a wish, the embodiment of an ideal. The reader too is denied his independent existence; the narrator repeatedly demonstrates this. The technique, whereby the narrator threatens to turn the novel into a drama that can be replayed or directed further into a number of different versions, elevates the narrator to off-stage omnipotent master. Reader and characters are reminded (*OLF*, p. 136): "however rigorous the destiny I plot for you, it will never cease to be—oh, in the very faintest way—tormented by what it might also have been but will not be because of me." When the reader is cautioned not to believe the authenticity of the characters or the narrator's self-revelation, this too is double-edged; the narrator imposes on the reader the latter's experience of not knowing what to believe.

The narrator emphasizes his difficulty tolerating the independent existence of others. When another can make his own autonomous responses and movements, the images the narrator superimposes on him are destroyed and he feels himself crumbling. For example, he writes (*OLF*, pp. 302–03):

> In each child I see—but I see so few—I try to find the child I was, to love him for what I was . . . I saw myself in his face, especially in his forehead and eyes, and I was about to recognize myself completely when, bang, he smiled. It was no longer I, for in my childhood I could no more laugh, or even smile, than in any other period of my life. When the child laughed, I crumbled, so to speak, before my very eyes.

Other people should exist as the author's creations, born from his rib or feces, as living characters of his imagination. He writes (*OLF*, p. 238):

> Solange had become like one of those chilled excrements which Culafroy [representing the author most directly] used to deposit at the foot of the garden wall among the currant bushes. When they were still warm, he took a tender delight in their odor, but he spurned them with indifference—at times with horror—when they had too long since ceased to be part of himself . . . Solange was no longer the chaste little girl taken from his rib.

The narrator describes his search for a smile in the eyes of others that he himself has evoked; he becomes affronted and outraged that responses in the eyes of others are not under his control. The description in *Miracle of the Rose* (p. 255) of the narrator/author gouging out the eye of a child, fits this theme.

Words become things, metaphors become reality with the narrator/author's incantations and transformations. He says that he is trying to turn the word into flesh and to gain our assent for this. His words come alive by their brilliance and intensity, as do his images by their unusual, abrupt, and startling turns; the vile and loathsome become poetry. This engages the audience and leads us to concentrate on the narrator/author's poetic gift for magical transformations. For example, the narrator greets the reader, at the beginning of *The Thief's Journal,* by announcing (p. 9) that "convicts' garb is striped pink and white." He tells us there is a close relationship between flowers and convicts, and then proclaims: "The fragility and delicacy of the former are of the same nature as the brutal insensitivity of the latter." He will portray a convict by "so bedecking him with flowers that, as he disappears beneath them, he will himself *become* a flower, a gigantic and new one" (emphasis added). He turns convicts and flowers, word and image, into each other. He forces us to acknowledge his skill in making us believe in his images, which are contrary to our values and expectations. Our values are turned upside down; gold becomes shit and shit becomes gold.

In the trial scene at the end of *Our Lady of the Flowers,* the made-up names of the drag-queens and pimps are stripped away. He writes (p. 291): " the little faggots from Pigalle to Place Blanche lost their loveliest adornment, their names lost their corolla, like the paper flower that the dancer holds at his finger tips and which, when the ballet is over, is a mere wire stem. Would it not have been better to have danced the entire dance with a simple wire?" The writer convinces us that indeed it was these characters' names that made them sparkle. He jars us with his contradictions, while persuading us there is an underlying synthesis within the contradictions that converts nonsense and parody into poetic truth. To a degree, this is true for the expected "aesthetic plasticity" of all poetry; but here the striking contradictions, which can be synthesized, call attention directly to their creator. Genet writes (*OLF*, p. 228): "It is customary to come in drag, dressed as ourselves." Or here is Sartre's favorite example of such whirligigs (Sartre 1952:508–10): "The gardener is the loveliest rose in his garden."

Stilitano, the one-armed pimp in *The Thief's Journal* is often pictured with a gob of spit at the corner of his mouth. The narrator rhapsodizes over the loveliness of this image. Is he really trying, as he claims, to turn spit into pearls? After a while, the reader too is able to picture Stilitano with his gob of spit, to feel that the image fits very well: that's Stilitano, that's how one remembers him. Grudgingly, the reader acknowledges the aptness of the narrator/author's idiosyncratic and repelling images.

My reading of these three early texts of Genet's is that the narrator/author's vigorous efforts, conscious and unconscious, to engage the reader, should not be dismissed merely as an aspect of contemporary literary technique and style. Nor would I say that Genet primarily sought to identify with other contemporary authors. In reading these works, the relationship between narrator and reader is situated actively in the foreground rather than as the background upon which a story is told. This has been documented by the excerpts I have quoted from the texts. At issue here is the interpretation of this aspect of the narrative point of view.

Scholes and Kellogg (1966) have argued that the narrative point of view of the novel is not an aesthetic or psychological issue but relates to a shared perception of reality between author and reader. They stress cognitive and epistemological factors in the determination of narrative point of view. Rose's (1980) psychological aesthetics also emphasize "a theory of reality and perception rather than one primarily related to motivation" (p. 10). Rose here overly restricts motivation to drive discharge, whereas his actual aim is to discuss the role of motivation within perception and the relation of the self to external reality. Rose argues that the aesthetic experience assists the audience with newly creative integrations between subjective and objective. It could be claimed with little difficulty that Genet attempts to guide himself and his readers through internal and external chaos and to help himself and his readers to feel less depressed, vulnerable, and insecure. Or it could be argued that Genet tries to create his own dilemmas within the audience as if to infect us with what he hates and fears most in himself. To some degree these motivations are present within all of us and will contribute to all authors' unconscious needs of their audience. My argument is that in these early texts of Genet's, the pattern of relationship between narrator/author and reader must be considered in detail rather than taken for granted as the vehicle for the work, i.e., possessed of meanings common to contemporary (experimental) literature.

I have organized the strategies I have encountered during my readings of these texts into a coherent whole, which I have then symbolized and personalized as "the implied author" of these works. My implied author is preoccupied with the closeness and responsiveness of his audience. He seeks to establish a controlling relationship with his audience that is deprived of its own independent responses, unable to make a move without him. The audience must be near at hand, but not close enough to restrict his control and domination. He attempts to seduce and arouse his audience, alternately repelling and shocking us, carefully manipulating our feelings to just the optimum pitch. It is in Genet's dramas that this becomes clearest: the audience is attacked, forced into submission, with the demand that even in the face of this aggression, we admire and applaud, love and forgive the author, even feel guilty ourselves and make expiation for his sins. Affirmation and acceptance must be forced out of an audience against its will. He turns our world upside down, exposing the illusion in our reality, the blindness in our vision, the evil in our goodness, the hatred in our love. "Genet" attacks the reader for having neglected him. In his literary creations, he externalizes and concretizes an aggressive struggle between himself and the other, symbolically represented as mother. We are repeatedly confronted with the angry, aggressive demand that we celebrate the author's creativity to compensate for past neglect.

"A child is being murdered" is a central theme and complaint in these works of Genet's, as in Sade's (see Bach and Schwartz 1972). Ernestine, the mother in *Our Lady of the Flowers* had tried to murder her child (who most directly represents the author in the novel), as her child later arranges the death of another young victim. Child murder here refers to abandonment and neglect, to the murder in childhood of what are potentially the most valuable aspects of oneself. The murder is associated with intense helplessness, rage, and the inability to communicate his needs to others, as illustrated by another scene of eye gouging. Alberto lay prostrate (*OLF*, p. 284) "with a dagger stuck into his eye . . . as he could not make it visible to people's eyes, he had to transport it into himself . . . [The country people] did not understand the meaning of the slowness of his walk, the bowing of his forehead, and the emptiness of his gaze."

To resume his development, "Genet" must turn death into life, give birth to himself anew, become his own creator with the audience-mother as midwife. For him, creativity and self-recreation proceed hand-in-hand. *Our Lady of the Flowers*, the beginning of Genet's creativity, opens with the death of Divine (Genet), whereupon her struggle for life begins. Turning death into life is a major theme throughout Genet's work. The magical transformations in the images represent rebirth, while the audience validates this myth.

Paradoxically, these writings contain no female characters who are appealing as mothers or women. Rather, the world of the imagination is portrayed as a man's world, in which women are irrelevant or can be replaced by men, as demonstrated by the author's fascination with female impersonation. Two formulations about sexual sadism are rele-

vant here: "active negation" of the mother (Deleuze 1971); and,
defense against helpless dependency on a dangerous maternal imago by
emphasis on oneself as creator and omnipotent director of his own
world (Socarides 1974). The characters in these works may turn to men
for nurturance but, unable really to trust and need others, they remain
hungry and discontent. The reader is touched by the narrator, when
the narrator notes twice as an aside in *Our Lady of the Flowers* that two
of the characters, Darling and Our Lady, are father and son, without
knowing so; they become lovers.

With repulsion or admiration, the audience is forced to respond to
Genet, thus demonstrating his ability to elicit response from those who
are potentially unloving and unresponsive. That the audience is awed
by the magic of his words and images confirms his grandeur and his
ability for omnipotent manipulation. The audience is to provide him
with affirmation of his existence and value, to admire and encourage
him, to support his self-esteem, which he had been unable to do alone.
Genet has told us seductively that his fantasy constructions, being only
words and not flesh, lacked credibility for him. They missed the warm
breath of a loving parent—the task the audience has been elevated to
undertake. He needs tangible, concrete ways and experiences for
restoring faith and belief in himself. He must grab hold of the other's
intense response in order to trust and believe in its authenticity, so he
can nourish himself. The audience's response must reassure Genet that
he is not vile, loathsome, destructive, and deserving of the contempt of
his conscience and of others. He has shown us the worst qualities in
himself and convinced us they are poetry. Hence, he is worthy of being
loved. He, like everyone else, wants to be loved and accepted, as he tells
us, but he judges himself unacceptable, fears being so to others, and is
afraid to allow himself genuine needs for other human beings.

The narrator (*OLF*, p. 293) tells his audience that he wants them to
confer a new destiny upon him, to "elect him" to greatness. He says
(*TTJ*, p. 99) that in writing "his secret history, in details as precious as
the history of the great conquerors . . . it was therefore necessary that
these details make me out to be the rarest and most singular of characters." His "secret glory," "a poem written only for himself, hermetic to
whoever did not have the key to it" (*OLF*, p. 294), becomes the public acknowledgment of greatness when the author becomes famous.
The narrator makes this connection (*OLF*, p. 294) when he moves
from describing his self-created glory to telling about the augury that
"ennobles" him: a fortune-teller in a fair-booth assured him that one

day he would be famous. He uses this as others would use family ties, traditions, a mother's love. This will provide him with more substantial roots than the connection he plays with: that his name means broom-plant, native to French soil (*TTJ*, p. 45).

By his constant preoccupation with destruction and murder, "Genet" reveals his fearfulness of his own destructiveness toward others and himself. He needs to idealize destructiveness, to enact it as theatrical ritual and ceremony, obscured by illusion and imposture, to reassure himself against the destructive dangers in himself or in the other. Nobody has been destroyed if it can be affirmed both that death is the precondition for life and that evil is virtue and the material for poetry. Hatred and destructiveness are transformed into (recreated as) sexual arousal and passion or the poetry of drama. When his dramas are enacted on stage before a large audience, "Genet" gains concrete reassurance that murder destroys neither self nor object. It is only a ritual! Moreover, it is one that affirms his greatness and creativity rather than his evil. The connection of the divine magic of creativity with the miracle of rebirth also affirms that destruction is never final.

To counter depression, lack of vitality, and fears of his own destructiveness, "Genet" seeks concrete representation for himself and the characters of his imagination. He must demonstrate their continued existence. This he seeks in the written word, in black and white, from the audience's intense responses, and from the impersonation by living people of his characters. If he can establish, once and for all, his creative omnipotence, then he is beyond the terror of destruction, the danger of his own or his characters "crumbling." He gives himself a concrete form via his works; by creating them he has actually given birth to something indestructible. He ends *Our Lady of the Flowers* playfully, by leaving us with the image of the outline of his penis on the paper. *The Thief's Journal* concludes with the narrator regarding his book as his "Genesis" and his "commandments." Each, together with the collusion of his audience, imaginary and real, provides indestructible, irrefutable testimony that their author is a poet and creator rather than a devil and a destroyer. If he can create beauty from inner evil, he cannot be all bad; there must be redeeming goodness within him, which the audience must acknowledge. We are to reassure him (as he tries to reassure himself) that his shit, piss, semen, sweat, snot, as well as his selfishness, greed, hunger, exploitation, murderous hatred, and aggression are not only not bad but are the very stuff from which beauty and virtue are created.

Baudry (1979) suggested, somewhat like Sartre, that Genet may have despaired of having good, meaningful relationships with real people. If that is so, Genet's books may have represented a substitute object for him, or at least an affirmation that some part of himself was alive. I think that Genet's despair was not so total as to exclude the hope that others would respond to him. Genet does seem to treat his book as the only living part of himself, his penis. His dilemma is that he is forced to make himself feel more alive and authentic, less depressed and insubstantial. He does this however he can, including a relationship with an audience that is to some degree despairing and dangerous. He does not feel lovable nor can he take for granted that the audience will respond lovingly. He must force them under his own control, or at least under the illusion of such control, to respond to him; however, he is confident of his evocative power.

It may be that different authors in different texts allow the reader to participate in varying degrees of collaborative coauthorship. All interpretation involves a subjective reformulation or re-creation of the author's text. I have been arguing that "Genet" in the texts under discussion attempts to impose on the reader certain feelings, states of mind, and ideas that allow for little flexibility in the reader's experience. It may be that the enjoyment of such works requires that the reader allow himself to submit to the author's manipulations without too much distress or protest. Alternatively, if the reader can identify with the author and his intentions, he can become engaged in the work. In this type of writing, the implied author seems unwilling and unable to allow the reader, or the characters, truly to participate on their own as collaborators. The reader (as well as the characters) is denied his own independent existence because of the limited range of responses to the narrator's offerings. Like Sade, "Genet" revels in the total domination of his characters, showing us that they are creations of *his imagination*, so that he can do as he pleases with them.

Iser (1978) and Fish (1980) point out that stated intentions establish expectations in the reader, draw responses, are part of the reading experience, and are neither to be believed nor used as the basis of interpretation. Similarly, Rosenblatt (1938) argues that texts are not to be interpreted from biography or the author's claims. Baudry has argued that, on the contrary, biographical data about the author can be used to support the critic's reading of the text. The fact that the narrator/author tells us something about himself does not by itself directly reveal something about him. This is certainly the case with an author such as Genet who is so deceptive and contradictory. Scholes and Kellogg (1966) point out that one function of an unreliable or semireliable narrator in modern fiction is to have the reader participate in the artistic creation. The reader must struggle to understand what the narrator cannot fully grasp. Scholes and Kellogg emphasize that this device is in keeping with a contemporary epistemology of relativism and uncertainty. The question for this book then becomes: how does my fantasied construct of the implied author of these works correspond with his stated intentions and available biographical data? My view is that a more convincing reading of the implied author is produced when that reading is supported with (psycho)biographical facts.

My thesis is at variance with Sartre's (1952) claim that Genet's early writing often only served Genet as pleasurable masturbatory fantasies, autistic reveries, or as a self-focused attempt at rehabilitation. My construct does fit Genet's statements about himself, which Sartre affirmed, that Genet has difficulty tolerating the independent existence of others. Sartre argued in support of the thesis of an essential, intended relationship between Genet and his audience. My fantasied construct of the implied author of the works under discussion has seductive, controlling, and possibly sadistic qualities similar to those found in structured perversion. Nevertheless, I must remind you that I have sought a cogent reading of these texts rather than a psychoanalytic understanding of the real-life author. Whatever similarities there may be between implied author and the flesh-and-blood author may be fortuitous.

Thus, I conclude that the implicit hypothesis of Khan (1965) and Bach and Schwartz (1972), that the relationship between a perverse writer and his audience may approximate a perverse sexual experience, can guide readers toward a useful reading of the author's texts but that it should not be taken literally. Eschewing biographical reconstruction, where the relationship between narrator and reader is so obviously central to a work and overshadows plot, themes, and characters, the reader must understand this relationship and determine its psychological significance and functions during the reading experience. The narrator/reader relationship should never be reduced merely to psychological factors no matter how prominently those factors appear. A fantasied construct of the implied author of a work is an organizing strategy for interpretation of the work, not of the real-life author, however similar the implied and real-life authors may seem.

By his writing, Jean Genet succeeded in transforming himself from an outcast petty criminal into a celebrated poet, adopted as an object of veneration by a distinguished group of writers as well as by the general public. Genet and Sartre both remarked on the therapeutic efficacy of Genet's writing. Genet's autobiographical *The Thief's Journal* (1948) surprisingly reveals little about Genet that cannot already be learned from his earlier work. The tone has become more intellectual, abstract, argumentative, explanatory. He claims that by giving song to his life, he is providing it with an order it never had; i.e., he is rewriting his past. He says, and Sartre concurs, that he is struggling to understand himself. Genet stresses that he has ceased idealizing others, including criminals, and has begun to work at changing himself and setting his own values. *The Thief's Journal* often reads like Sartre's study of Genet, even though the latter was published subsequently; still Genet and Sartre had spent much time together before the autobiography was published in 1948. The narrator has become less seductive toward the reader and, at times, less appealing. By then Genet had already become well known in French literary circles and regarded himself as a poet. His narrator seems less profoundly depressed, more confident of his own creativity and of his ability to engage the audience. With the production of his plays (*Deathwatch* and *The Maids*) in 1947, Genet quite literally had accomplished his avowed goal of turning the word into flesh: living people play the roles he invents in the scenes he creates, while an audience watches, responds and, at times, is even part of the drama. Genet wrote (1963): "The actors' function is thus to don the gestures and costumes which will enable them to show me to myself, and to show me naked, alone and in the joyfulness of solitude."

Chapter 3

LOUIS-FERDINAND CÉLINE'S *CASTLE TO CASTLE*: THE AUTHOR-READER RELATIONSHIP IN ITS NARRATIVE STYLE

The author-reader relationship in this work is examined by a study of my own feelings and responses in readings of the novel and the fantasies I have needed to construct of the author-narrator. Use of this construct allows the reader to focus a psychoanalytic perspective on the psychological interaction between himself and his fantasied concept of the author-narrator for the purposes of identifying some common, universal contributants to the wishes to write and read. I will argue in this work of Céline's that the reader's need to create his fantasy of the author-narrator has been shaped (consciously and unconsciously) by this "author-narrator" so that the reader will attend to the author's craft and presence. It should be borne in mind that this does not attribute artistic or psychological *intentions* to the "flesh-and-blood author."

Who Is Céline?

Céline's writing is particularly suitable for such investigation because there is much careful, self-conscious attention given to style and effect;

the act and art of literary creation and of communication with the reader stand out sharply; the author/reader relationship is so prominent within the text and during the reading of all Céline's novels, and it has such emotional impact on the reader. In 1957, when Céline's novel *Castle to Castle* (D'un château à l'autre) was published, the author had been, according to his biographers, depressed, withdrawn, bitter, and disappointed with the lack of attention his earlier writings in the fifties had received (*Feerie pour une autre fois* [1952]; *Normance* [*Feerie pour une autre fois II*] [1954]; *Entretiens avec le Professeur Y* [1956]). *Castle to Castle*, well received by critics and public, helped to restore Céline's literary eminence. *Journey to the End of the Night* (Voyage au bout de la nuit, 1936) and *Death on the Installment Plan* (Mort à crédit, 1936) had won considerable critical acclaim, especially because of the innovations and imaginativeness of his narrative style. Céline's three anti-Semitic, collaborationist pamphlets (*Bagatelles pour un massacre* [1937]; *L'école des cadavres* [1938]; *Les Beaux Draps* [1941], among other writings and actions, first infuriated much of France and then, after Céline's trial as a collaborator, led to his being ignored, as if he were already dead.

Accurate biographical information about Céline is not available. Here are some facts: Born Louis-Ferdinand Destouches in 1894 in a suburb of Paris, he was raised in Paris; he died in 1961. He was wounded in action during World War I; one arm and both eardrums were injured so that Céline was afflicted with permanent tinnitus, some hearing loss, and chronic insomnia. He derived his pseudonym from his mother's given name, Louise-Céline. He offered financial reasons for this name change, but said (Thirer 1972:224–25): "No one would come looking for me behind a feminine name." He was married three times, the first two marriages being relatively brief. After a few months of medical practice, Céline left his second wife and young daughter for a position with the League of Nations that allowed him to travel widely. Céline's dissertation for his medical degree, *The Life and Work of Semmelweis* (La vie et l'oeuvre de Philippe-Ignace Semmelweis, 1818–1865), which was awarded a medal for excellence by the medical faculty, was more remarkable as a literary than as a scientific work. Semmelweis discovered the contagious nature of puerperal fever and advocated handwashing to reduce its spread. His ideas were not accepted, he was persecuted, became psychotic and died of a self-inflicted wound—all important themes in Céline's later writing.

Céline's biographers suggest that he had great difficulty with intimacy, that he needed women who would tolerate his sexual involvement with their girlfriends. He would enjoy watching a girlfriend sexually involved with one of his male friends or with another woman. Céline wrote about himself (McCarthy 1975:46): "A voyeur certainly and an enthusiastic consumer a little bit . . . I do not consume much, alas, concentrated as I am on my terrible work . . . I have always liked women to be beautiful and lesbian—very nice to look at and not wearing me out with their sexual demands."

The portrait painted of Céline by his biographers is of a depressed, angry, provocative, irritable, difficult man who needed others to respond and pay attention to him. Often, he seemed to provoke angry responses in others; he said that was his goal. It is thought that he needed to emphasize his independence and self-sufficiency in order to conceal how sensitive and needy he was about people's acknowledgment and admiration of him. His image of himself and of his characters as tormented victims has been stressed, as has the apparent self-destructiveness manifested by his collaborationist pamphleteering, in some interviews, and in newspaper writing.

Reading *Castle to Castle*

I find, not surprisingly, that my feelings change with each reading of *Castle to Castle*. At first I found myself responding with my own concerns about survival, feeling anxious and gloomy in response to the narrator's complaints about his aging, his waning literary abilities, and his medical practice. At certain points I found the novel oppressive and tedious, with its depressive pall and endless complaining. I felt the narrator's dialogues with the reader were angry but boring harangues, and I was very much relieved when the narrator would suddenly change the technique and the pace and move more passionately into a story. But I was frustrated trying to orient myself as I suddenly felt confused about what the narrator was describing. Were these real events, hallucinations, distorted memories, fantasies? Did it matter? Was he stressing their symbolic meaning? Did the narrator want me to feel confused, and so forth? The narrator's and the character's helplessness, passivity, and anxiety in a menacing, chaotic world made me anxious, helpless, and angry—angry at their situation and angry at the author for putting me through this. I struggled to guess how much in the novel had really been experienced by the author and how much was fantasy. During later readings, I was much less concerned about the reality of the scenes or with trying to determine whether it had really been like this for Céline during World War II. I was also less pained by my own anxious and depressive feelings, more comfortable with surrendering myself to Céline's imagination and my own, less in need of grasping at reality and facts. Characters portrayed as powerfully sadistic made me uncomfortable, while I remained aware that they never surfaced fully as three-dimensional literary people. They remained caricatures of the traits or gestures connoted; this tended to make them less menacing than if I had been confronted with real (literary) people. On further readings, less uncomfortable, less troubled about the reality of the images, I enjoyed the narrator's depictions of his strange characters.

I feel lonely reading this novel, as I do with Céline's other novels. Other than the narrator, there is no character with whom I would wish to spend time. And it seems to me that this is also true for the narrator, and not for this novel alone. Critics of Céline's earlier works seem to have been relieved to identify a few characters as warm, positive human beings. My own reading of most of Céline's early characters (e.g., Sgt. Alcide or Molly in *Journey to the End of the Night*) is that there is considerable irony in the rendering of the apparent selflessness of such characters and little indication within the novel that any positive relationship will endure. I find myself thinking of the author rather than the narrator, imagining how lonely he must be. What stands out to me is that I keep thinking of Céline, looking for him, wanting to discover something positive, something beautiful to fill the empty space I keep discovering. At such points, I usually become aware of the orchestration of the novel. I concentrate on its aesthetic form: its rhythm, tone, mood, the pace and variations in the imagery, the language, its sounds and evocativeness. I move from feeling directly affected by the novel to perceiving the author's style, feeling pleased and relieved to discover its beauty, order, and purpose amidst the apparent chaos of the plot. This gives me a more positive sense of the author's presence—I enjoy him and his imagination and creativity within the vacuum and chaos I have felt within the novel.

With each reading, the discrete scenes in *Castle to Castle* feel more amusing, more playful, more fanciful; the kaleidoscopic variations from scene to scene, image to image, fascinate me more. I find myself wanting to repeat the pleasure of feeling thrown from one seemingly (un)stable image to another, of enjoying losing my bearings and being carried away by the narrator's imaginative twists and turns. Just as I feel myself gaining some security and stability within the novel, I lose it. But as I become more accustomed to this happening repeatedly, I come to expect and delight in this. I know by now that within this novel, I can never feel myself in a stable position for very long. I know too that once I begin to be annoyed and bored with the repetition or the narrator's laments and griping, with the oppressive slowness of the pace, the pace, tone, and mood will soon shift, and a new scene will abruptly displace the other. Céline is sufficiently talented in playing his self-conscious, back-and-forth conversations with the reader, his moving and jostling the reader about and directing the reader's attention to the creative process that I do not become bored with concentrating on the process of the novel's construction. I no longer want to be transported into a story that is complete in itself. I, as reader, find myself directed, dramatically and skillfully, through a fun-house of the author's visions. Céline's aesthetic order, the beauty of his literary creativity, stands in sharp contrast to the depressing meaninglessness of interactions between people.

Céline on Céline

Céline said that he intended to have the kind of effect on his readers that I have experienced, indeed that this was the aim of his art. He professed to be a stylist rather than a purveyor of ideas, like, for example, Sartre or Camus. He sought, he claimed, to reintroduce feelings into literature. He wrote (Thomas 1979:84): "the language was dried up, I'm the one who has brought back emotion into the written language! . . . (. . .)to rediscover through writing the emotion of the *spoken word!*" And: "Emotion is hard to catch, fleeting (. . .)evanescent! (. . .) not to be seized, the bitch, by just anyone . . . years of desperate work, austere, monastic labor in order to seize it." About his well-known use of slang (of the poor, the underworld, the army, the sea), Céline wrote (Thomas 1979:85): "Slang is a language of hatred which enables you to stun your reader . . . to destroy him! . . . he's at your mercy! . . . completely shaken! . . . slang's a marvelous spice! . . . but a whole meal of spice only makes a miserable lunch." Céline professed that he wanted to treat his readers like subway passengers, whom he would hurl in a dreamlike, nonstop passage to the end (Thomas 1979:88): " in a dream! . . . not the least halt anywhere! . . . on to the end! . . . with full emotion . . . start to finish." Formal sentences are replaced by Céline's famous three dots that permit rhythmical pacing (Thomas 1979:88–9): "its firmly fixed rails! . . . I hit them bloody hard! . . . no more of them! . . . its nicely elongated sentences . . . no more of them! . . . its style, as it were! . . . I deform them in a particular way, so the passengers are in a dream . . . so they won't notice . . . spellbound . . . magic . . . violence too." "My three dots are essential! (. . .) To lay down my emotive rails (. . .) my rails won't hold firm by themselves! . . . I have to have sleepers! . . ." (Matthews 1978:227): "All the passengers loaded in, shut in, locked up! . . . All in my emotive train! . . . No fuss or bother! no question of them getting out!"

The effect Céline seeks is for the reader to feel certain (Matthews 1978:223) "that someone is reading to him in his head! . . . in the privacy of his nerves! (. . .) someone playing as he likes for him on the harp of his own nerves."

The reader's experience is similar to that proposed in Artaud's theory of drama, in which the audience is to be forced to break through its defensive facade in order to experience feelings and to see the world with greater clarity. People need to be helped to rediscover the emotional side of life that has been lost: the body and sensuality, rhythm, movement, dance, "lost verve" (a favorite phrase of Céline's), beauty, enthusiasms. The content of a novel is less important than the manner in which the tale is told. Intellect clouds emotions and can only be revived once emotions are restored to life. This is probably expressed most eloquently in Céline's last collaborationist pamphlet, *Les Beaux Draps* (1941), where it is presented as part of a call for a new moral order with a refocusing of educational goals. Céline's novels, however, hardly seem to contain a therapeutic goal for the reader.

Céline claimed that the more animosity he could arouse in his readers, the more certain he could be of the (financial) success of his novels. "I suggest, I incite, I titillate. I do everything possible." About an interview published in *L'Express* after publication of *Castle to Castle*, Céline expressed delight that readers were outraged. He confessed (McCarthy 1975:274) that he had put on a performance "like a pig wallowing in its filth." His praise of Hitler and Darnand was intended to display his full "disgustingness." Unfortunately, he joked, he hadn't elicited enough angry letters of protest. As Céline wrote in a 1957 letter (McCarthy 1975:277, quotation "a"): "When you don't have the strength you have to play the clown." In published interviews from the last four years of his life, Céline was predictably outrageous, playing his role to the hilt. When asked why he wrote, he answered (McCarthy

1975:277, quotation "b") that he wanted to "make the others seems unreadable."

There is certainly a literary tradition in which the writer is shown working at his novel; among a number of authors, one thinks of Sterne, Gide, or Genet. Indeed, a central feature of the contemporary experimental novel involves variations in narrative technique (see Scholes 1979). The central theme in *Castle to Castle* (and *North* [Nord, 1960] and *Rigodon*, 1969), however, is that the narrator is an aging and failing writer, flaunting his lack of interest in continuing the present novel. He writes, he says, only to pay the gas bills. It will therefore be necessary to determine, through a close examination of the text, whether psychological meanings can be attributed to the literary relationship between author and reader beyond the construction of a compelling novel or antinovel.

The Narrative Style of *Castle to Castle*: A Sampling

Céline begins *Castle to Castle* in an intimate, confidential tone:

> Frankly, just between you and me, I'm ending up even worse than I started . . . Yes my beginnings weren't so hot . . . I was born, I repeat, in Courbevoie, Seine . . . I'm, repeating it for the thousandth time . . . after a great many round trips I'm ending very badly . . . old-age, you'll say . . . at sixty-three and then some, it's hard to break in again . . . to build up a new practice . . . I forgot to tell you . . . I'm a doctor . . . A medical practice, confidentially, between you and me.

It is as if Céline is himself inviting the reader into his confidence, telling about his current concerns, as to some degree, he is. In this novel the narrator and the author are not clearly differentiated. Unlike the earlier novels the narrator is not usually referred to here by name. When he is, he is usually called "Céline"; only a couple of times is he referred to as Ferdinand. The confidential tone between narrator and reader has a bitter, complaining, wronged quality. But it is tempered by a grotesque hyperbolic style that makes it fanciful and, at times, amusing. The narrator throws the information at the reader that Céline has been tried for treason, treated as a pariah, or worse still, ignored. The reader becomes representative of the France that refuses to welcome Céline back and, therefore, needs to be chided, coaxed, and persuaded. A few pages later (p. 5) the narrator says, "I'm repeating myself . . . You can never repeat too much for the stubborn (. . .) Some people can't stand the idea that there should be people from Courbevoie . . . my age, too, I repeat my age . . . I'm repetitious? . . . doddering and repetitious? It's my right." The narrator attacks and expects to annoy the reader.

The narrator's references to Céline's other writings emphasize that a novel is now being written, that there is a live and distinguished author nearby. His publisher taunts him : "Make them laugh! You used to know how. Can't you do it anymore?" Or: "Céline, you're washed up! . . . You owe us enormous sums of money, and you've got no more verve! . . . Aren't you ashamed of yourself?"(p. 14). This also may represent a parody of the way that Ferdinand's parents in *Death on the Installment Plan* attack and shame him. As the narrator complains about his present situation, he interrupts to address the reader: "And in the meantime, while you're thinking it over, if you'd buy one or two of my books, it would be a help." Whereupon he playfully erases it: "Never mind about that" (p. 11). Céline so exaggerates the criticisms of himself as a man, writer, and physician that they become ridiculous and the reader becomes more interested in how this is rendered within the text. The narrator keeps giving intimations of what will soon emerge in the novel only to bring the reader up short by making him wait and haranguing him further. Leitmotifs of Siegmaringen appear early in the book, becoming more and more persistent before the setting of the novel does in fact shift to Siegmaringen (in reality Sigmaringen), Germany, 1944. After the first reference to Siegmaringen, with the implication that the narrator has lots of juicy gossip to tell about important people who were there, he interrupts: "But one fact remains . . . that my books don't sell any more . . . so they say . . . or not much . . . that I'm outmoded, senile! that's hogwash! a put-up job! . . . their idea is to buy it all up from my widow for a song! . . . sure . . . I admit it, I'm getting on!" (p. 17).

Similarly, the hallucinatory-lyrical episode of Charon's bateau-mouche "La Publique," perhaps the most famous passage in the novel, is preceded by a number of references to Charon and how he will destroy the "me-me-ism" of Céline's enemies. As the narrator begins to work this up into an exciting attack, he comes to an abrupt halt: "But back to my story . . . now and then, I've got to admit, some stubborn bastard manages to discover me in the sub-basement of some storehouse under a pyramid of returns . . . oh, I could easily get used to the idea of being the scribbler that nobody reads any more . . . rejected by pure, purified Vrance! . . . oh, I could be perfectly happy about it . . .

but there's the question of noodles" (p. 19).There is a teasing irony here in that just as the narrator is about to tell a story, he returns to the "story" of his laments. This emphasizes the reader's dependence on the narrator. As Céline points out in *North* (Matthews 1978:190), the reader is never to forget that it is "me there telling you the story I could shut up too."

A brief dialogue with a publisher illustrates Céline's ability to maintain a comic perspective on his own bitterness as well as to engage the reader with the author's creative struggles:

> "Recapture your humor, Céline . . . if only you'd write the way you talk! what a masterpiece!" "You're very kind, Gertrut, but take a look at me! just take a look!" I calm him down. "Look at the state I'm in . . . I can hardly hold a pen." "No, no, Céline . . . you're full of vigor . . . the best age! . . . take Cervantes! . . . I'm not telling you anything new." That's the dodge all publishers pull when they want to stimulate their old nags . . . they tell you Cervantes was a stripling . . . at eighty-one! "And disabled worse than you, Céline!"   (p. 40)

The novel is punctuated with asides to the reader such as: "I see that I'm boring you" (p. 56) or "Damn . . . I'm digressing . . . I'm getting you mixed up" (p. 82). As the narrator begins setting the scene for the Charon's boat episode by connecting it with his childhood memories of boat rides on the Seine, he suggests he is writing a personal letter to the reader. Interweaving childhood memories with his present-day medical visit to his one remaining dying patient leads to the uncertainty of whether he is really seeing Charon's boat or whether this is a hallucination (caused by senility, insanity, or fever). The narrator seems to head off the reader's objections by acknowledging: "But say, I'd better go easy, I'm forgetting about you . . . telling you stories of childhood . . . I didn't go down there to get you mixed up . . . I'd better watch my step" (p. 86). The narrator struggles with his inability to differentiate reality from fantasy but this is so presented as to keep the reader mixed up, to emphasize that the reader cannot count on the reliability of the narrator. Perhaps most important, the reader is being encouraged to relax his guard, to let himself be guided into the narrator's own personal fantasy world, told that he need not struggle so to hold onto his own bearings—a hopeless task in any case. The reader is relieved that the narrator is finally beginning to tell "the story."

"The story" mixes together, as if time could be arrested, as it seems to be within the narrator's imagination, death and life, past reality and imagined present fantasy, violence, persecution, and helplessness—all balanced by the power of the writer's creative imagination. The pace is quickened, the narrator begins to throw the reader about more abruptly now; this is startling but welcome. Hints become more frequent that the reader will soon hear about Siegmaringen, that the reader needs to hear this to understand what has been happening until now. The hallucinatory episode is terminated, and present reality is reestablished with the appearance of the narrator's wife and dog. The reader must acknowledge his indebtedness to the narrator's skill in orchestrating his story: "I'm sorry . . . let's get down to brass tacks . . . these things . . . I've got to tell them . . . with my pen . . . not just any old story . . . at random . . . This story by my own hand . . . the document!" (p. 107). The narrator has an attack of fever, a frequent ploy of Céline's, which allows entry into the recesses of imagination and memory without the reader's worrying too much about the structure of the narrative. Again, the narrator parries the reader's objections to the stylistic devices: "There, there . . . I'm playing around . . . looking for effects . . . I'm going to lose you" (p. 110). The narrator's emphasis on "exactitude" in his memories is playful; he is imploring the reader to listen carefully. The narrator is much less concerned with reminiscing about the past than with using elements from the past around which to construct images, to tell a story, to be listened to, to live within a world that he himself can shape and direct, a world his readers will acknowledge as aesthetically valid. There is not much that is sustaining about the narrator's past memories except for his own refashioning and presentation of them. "The true artist creates himself," says Céline (McCarthy 1975:253).

It feels as if the slow-paced, despondent narrator needs his fever to boil him up, as he claims, in order to tell his tale with more animation; this is precisely what happens as the pace quickens, as the narrator seems to recover his "verve" and "humor." Mood, tempo, punctuation, words capture the reader in the procession and feelings of the abruptly changing scenes. Shit overflows the toilets and hallways; an insane surgeon is operating without anesthesia on Céline's bed; the narrator asks for help. Instead he is handed his own death sentence, proclaimed by the French Resistance. The narrator apologizes for shocking the reader and takes him back to the present reality of the narrator being ill, confusing him a little more, referring to the writing process: "they (publishers) wait for the work to come in! . . . fever or no fever! . . . "How you coming, clown? . . . how many pages?" (p. 175).

Some of Céline's critics have taken his rendering of sex in *Castle to Castle* too literally as portraying only his contempt for women, or for people generally. His presentations of people lusting in the chaos of war are poetic; they are choreographed, as Céline can do, like ballet, with emphasis on movement, rhythm, intensity (for examples, see p. 184).

The Psychology of the Author-Reader Relationship in *Castle to Castle*

To my mind, Céline's conversations with the reader are dramatically effective in engaging the reader in the narrative, with Céline and his writing. They are also effective in accomplishing Céline's avowed goal of making his reader feel intensely, of obliterating the distance of literary artificialities, of restoring "verve" to written language. These conversations help the reader to identify with the author, to experience the latter's memories and fantasies more directly as his own. They successfully meet the reader's objections, guiding the reader to trust the narrator, relax his guard, and enter into the fantastic nature of this novel. The disruptions in the narration of a fixed story strengthen the notion that there is not a stable, fixed reality that is dependable—a common twentieth-century theme, especially of Céline's. Subjective and objective are not clearly distinguishable, nor are author and reader. The story the reader is now reading is still being written or it has just been finished; the outcome, rather the next scene, is always in doubt. Nothing can be taken for granted as fixed and finished.

Scholes and Kellogg (1966) argue that the narrative point of view of the novel is not an aesthetic or psychological issue but rather relates to a shared perception of reality between author and readers. They stress the influence of cognitive, epistemological factors in the determination of narrative point of view. Thus it could be said that Céline shares with his readers a view of the world as subjectively and objectively chaotic. That is unobjectionable. Rose's (1980) psychological aesthetics also emphasizes "a theory of reality and perception rather than one primarily related to motivation." However, Rose here overly restricts motivation to drive discharge, whereas his aim is to discuss the role of motivation within perception and the relation of self to external reality. One could make a strong case that in *Castle to Castle* the author seeks to reorient himself within a subjectively and objectively chaotic world, to attempt to heal himself, to enhance his self-esteem, and to offer such opportunity to his readers. My position is that, additionally, narrative point of view does have a psychological dimension that involves shared needs between author and readers.

The self-consciously radical disruptions of the narrative process are also intended to advance Céline's claim that he is at the forefront of avant-garde writers, that he is unique. Similarly, Céline's narrative is comprehensible to the reader only to the degree that author and reader accept a common set of conventions about the novel; to subvert the novel's narrative form requires first that author and readers acknowledge their mutual understanding of narrative form (see Culler 1975). Given the literary efficacy of Céline's narrative art, to what degree does this style of conversation between author and reader serve the author's own psychological needs? Does Céline use this technique to gain recognition from a public that ignores or rejects him? What does this author seek from his readers?

Even if there were accurate biographical information, psychological interviews with Céline that established that in 1957 he was severely depressed, paranoid, bitter, and found involvement with other people difficult, would this help provide answers to these questions? Would it reveal what the author's intentions were in his writing or even how he conceptualized his narrator's intentions? Although my view is that it is not possible to establish the real-life author's intentions from his psychobiography, I do believe that that psychobiography can make literary interpretations more cogent and convincing. Any literary interpretation must be judged primarily by literary standards rather than by appeal to outside authority or "objective facts." Such standards can be (Kris and Kaplan, 1948) of correspondence, intent, and coherence or (Schafer 1980:83) coherence, consistency, comprehensiveness and "conformity with refined common sense." Many of Céline's critics and biographers have dealt with this differently, emphasizing that the narrators in his novels represent exaggerated and distorted aspects of his actual personality rather than the man himself.

Certain reading of certain writing, to some degree all reading of all writing, creates a space in which the reader feels the need to place an imagined writer. This fantasy construction of "the author" primarily serves the reader's own needs, not the writer's. For some writing, as I am arguing about Céline, the space in which the reader feels the need to create his fantasy of the author, has been deliberately shaped (consciously and unconsciously) by the "author-narrator." Earlier in this chapter I have described how much of a lonely vacuum I have at times felt reading Céline's novels and how much I have then wanted to locate and know the author. This lonely, negative sense of something missing is created within the reading experience of the text by its chaos and evanescence, the lack of relatedness and three-dimensional (literary) quality of the characters, who themselves are unappealing or even repulsive as people; also by the abrupt twists and turns in the narration, the reader's inability to read on his own without the narrator's intrusive mocking of the reader's helplessness and reversals of the "story" to himself and his own story. The aesthetic form of the narration, its rhythm, tone, mood, pace, changes, language, and sounds seem to dominate the reading experience. This disrupts the reader's contented immersion within the plot, tending to make the novel "unreadable"; this emphasizes that something is missing that then paradoxically can be filled in by attention to the aesthetic pleasure afforded the reader by the beauty, order, and purpose of the narrative form and by the search for an author behind the narration.

What I mean by "space" is precisely this vague but obtrusive and consistent awareness that something is missing that needs to be filled in. It is to be filled in by attention to form and to an author standing behind the narrator. I am not referring to transitional space in Winnicott's (1967) sense, although absence and presence and search for another are involved. The author, whom I construct in fantasy, fits a space the author-narrator has opened up, but he primarily fits my own needs. Although this should conform to a psychobiographical portrait of Céline, this is not the same as attempting to discover Céline's intentions. I have constructed a reading fiction of the author; I have not attempted to psychoanalyze the real-life Céline.

Green (1978) speculated, as a theoretical point without reference to a specific text, that every writer is involved with a dialectic of the absence and presence of the reader. Influenced by Winnicott's (1967) concept of "potential space," Green conceived of both writing and reading as "the capacity to be alone in someone's presence" (p. 228). In my reading of *Castle to Castle* I emphasize that the author's fantasy of the reader's presence has been made explicit within the crafting of the novel. Unlike Green, I do not take for granted that writing/reading, for all authors and all readers, is primarily motivated by later attempts to reexperience the mother's presence.

My argument that the lonely space I feel reading this novel leads me to focus on the novel's form and the fantasied presence of the author is in sharp contrast to Holland's (1968) early attempts to differentiate form and content in literature. He suggests that form is used to defend against dangerous fantasies within the content of the work. Attention to language, rhythm, sound, form "attenuates or thins out our emotional response" (p. 136). My position is that all of these "formal" techniques heighten the reader's affective experience in *Castle to Castle*. I do agree with Holland that "arty" techniques "call attention to themselves," " focusing our attention on "the logic of the techniques themselves" (p. 150). But I think it is simplistic to claim that this serves only to "manage content." Following Holland's earlier position, it could be argued that my attention to form, and my search for the author's presence during my reading of this novel, defend against my own lonely, anxious and depressed feelings. That is certainly correct. Additionally, I think it is also valid that the fine artistic construction of this novel makes it likely or inevitable for readers to have experiences similar to mine and that this also serves certain needs of the "author-narrator."

I can say the following about my fantasied author of *Castle to Castle*: He wants me, as reader, to pay particularly close attention to him as a creative artist. He at times is afraid that I will not be responsive and attentive, or that others have not been. He then seems angry and attacking. When he seems more confident of my interest in him, we both seem relaxed and involved together. He seems to keep wanting to surprise, startle, shock, in order to maintain his reader's interest, and to keep attention focused on the creative process and on the narrator himself. I experience the narrator's contempt and rejection of living people as if he were simultaneously inviting me to abandon such interests and to turn to a literary relationship with him as a substitute. It seems that the only beauty to be found is within his own writing. There is a desperate quality to this, as if he must persuade himself of its validity and as if he had to convince others so that they will want to read his works. Art does not seem to be an approach to life as much as a substitute for it; literary relationships seem superior to live relationships with other people. Yet, the only moving literary relationship is between the narrator and his reader, rather than between characters within the text. This may indicate that the author cannot tolerate his characters having their own literary life or that his relations with others, including fictional characters, remain despairing. I would doubt the complete validity of the latter hypothesis because of the way I feel engaged by the narrator.

He may seem mistrustful and angry at times, but he usually seems confident that the reader will become taken with him and his writing. I suggest that an emotional vacuum has been deliberately shaped within the reading experience of the text so that the reader (who responds to Céline's work), in his lonely, anxious, and depressed mood, will seek the author's presence.

Slochower (1946) argues that the negativism in Céline's language and style should be viewed as an ironic dialectic that indicates cravings for love and acceptance by the very exaggeration of destruction and rejection in these images, metaphors, and tone. I wholeheartedly concur with this. To a degree, however, this is more transparent in Céline's earlier novels than in *Castle to Castle*. Slochower's "response" is, I think, quite similar to mine in that he is drawn in, finding the positive behind the negative, feeling an intense needy demandingness for acceptance by the author-narrator. Where we differ is in my hesitation to attributte such intentions to the flesh-and-blood Céline, preferring to confine my interpretation to the reading experience of the text. I believe the search for the author's real intentions to be an objectivist illusion. I would prefer to illuminate the text and my readings of it than to psychoanalyze the author. As I have noted, my reading of *Castle to Castle* has changed with further reading, with my own struggles with the text, and with further reflection. That is inevitable. I have sought to organize and integrate these varied responses and readings into a coherent and persuasive reading. I think it is better not to ask which responses and which readings did the actual author intend. The reading experience of a challenging and difficult text has to vary, be contradictory, always complex and uncertain. I have been presenting some of the intermediate steps during my reading experience that lead to the formulations I make.

I have speculated that the degree of collaborative coauthorship that an author allows his readers *might* reflect the level and functions of the author's relations with objects. My own reading experience of Céline's *Castle to Castle*, not too dissimilar from what I describe about my experience of Jean Genet's early writing, did not leave me much freedom to imagine and create along with the narrator. It was impossible to anticipate where he would move from page to page. Although the asides with the reader established an intimate mood, I felt myself controlled by them, as if the narrator were intruding into my own thoughts, my objections to his writing. The narrator seemed afraid to leave me on my own very long as I read the book. That the reader is encouraged to be mistrustful of the narrator seems to derive from the author's mistrust of his readers. The reader's task here seemed to be to provide the author, under the latter's control, with affirmation of his creative talents, by responding intensely to him and to his pessimistic picture of life. By agreeing that beauty is to be found in literary creativity, the reader is confirming the author's own value, superior to his apparently pervasive self-contempt.

Scholes and Kellogg (1966) suggest that one function of an unreliable or semireliable narrator in modern fiction is to have the reader participate in the artistic creation. The reader must struggle to understand what the narrative chararacter cannot himself fully grasp. Scholes and Kellogg connect this device, which they understand within the narrative point of view of the novel, with a contemporary epistemology of relativism and uncertainty. What I would stress about my reading of Céline's *Castle to Castle* is that the reader is not free to participate together with the author in the novel's creation. At most the reader can puzzle about the veridicality of the narrator's fantastic images and their relation to the author's autobiography. The reader is left helplessly dependent on the narrator's unfolding of his own imagination. This adds to the reader's awareness of the form and the narration of the novel and the presence of the author in creating it. I am arguing that the only room left the reader's creative imagination is the fantasy construction of the author and the desire for his presence; and, even with this, the reader is not free but, at least for certain susceptible readers, has been moved into a position where this becomes inevitable. Scholes later (1979) suggested that those contemporary novels that stress the form of the work "assert the authority of the shaper" (p. 3). I imagine that the "implied author" wished in creating *Castle to Castle* that the reader continually desire and be aware of the author's presence and creative power.

Does the degree of an author's preoccupation with his readers within the text reflect the degree of his need for their involvement with him? I do not know the answer to this question but I would guess that it may, and that it does for Céline. I would assume that an author who felt himself to be acceptable and lovable, would be less concerned with the continual presence of another person, imagined as his reader. If such an author were able to take for granted the presence of an audience, which I assume to be at least an unconscious need of every author, he might be able to leave his fantasied readers implicitly in the background of his work. Then he would not have to evoke their presence continually.

In my study of Genet I suggested that effect on the other (the reader)—that is, need of him—has greater motivational significance than the expression of conflictual themes within the content and form of the dialogue. I understood this within the perspective that unresolved early needs are expressed as current conflict via the medium of a relationship with another who is vitally needed by the subject. I suggested that it may be safer to express intense needs of an object within the fantasied relationship between author and audience, obscured by illusion and expressed through fictional characters within the medium of a literary text. Direct expression of such needs to other living people may create much greater risks, making the author feel much more vulnerable. In *Death on the Installment Plan* (1936), Ferdinand does allow himself some comforting and nurturance from Uncle Edouard, who I must acknowledge is a positive character. What is sad, however, is that Ferdinand cannot hold still long enough to relax and enjoy this human warmth. It is present like a light attracting a reluctant moth; as Ferdinand says, "I like you fine, Uncle . . . But I can't stay . . . I just can't." In *Castle to Castle* the expression of warmth to the narrator is presented as surrealistic farce, as when Orphize, the filmmaker, cajoles that Céline shouldn't be depressed, that he has friends in France who admire and love him.

If Céline cannot believe in or accept the love of other people, what then does he crave from his reader? One literary critic (McCarthy, 1975) referred to Céline's pervasive need to affirm his existence in the face of serious doubts about it. This critic was convinced of the degree of Céline's depression, fears of annihilation, and emotional detachment from other living people. He suggested that what Céline needed from his audience, from all of France, was vigorous response of any kind, although enthusiastic praise, despite Céline's denial, was what he sought. Although I cannot evaluate the accuracy of this statement about Céline the man, it is congruent with my fantasy of the author-narrator of *Castle to Castle*. The narrator's irritating bragging that he is the contemporary author most responsible for infusing the novel with life, despite the irony and sarcasm in the statement, is experienced by the reader as if a precocious child were angrily demanding the recognition and attention he craved. Through all of Céline's writing runs the angry complaint that virtually nobody has been willing to appreciate the author's own unique needs and abilities. Charon will "knock the me-me-ism" (p. 18) out of everyone when he gets ahold of them. The narrator jokingly refers to his own self-absorption here but the interpretation is implicit that this is derived from the failure of other people to acknowledge the author. That is what the reader cannot fail to do: he must pay homage to the author, acknowledging the unique skills and talents of this tormented genius.

Chapter 4

FREUD AND FLIESS: A SUPPORTIVE LITERARY RELATIONSHIP

*Das beste, was Du wissen kannst,/Darfst Du den
Buben doch nicht sagen (The best that you know, you
must not tell to ordinary men)*
—Goethe's *Faust*, part 1, scene 4

The psychoanalytic prototype of the supportive literary relationship (see chapter 1), negotiated largely through letter writing, is that of Freud and Fliess. There has been debate in the psychoanalytic literature, although surprisingly little given the importance for all psychoanalysts of the Freud-Fliess relationship and of Freud's early creativity, about the meanings and functions of Freud's relationship with Fliess. A supportive literary relationship will be regarded here as the vehicle through which creative writing is focused upon to provide one or both participants with badly needed "support." I will delineate how this is negotiated through a letter-writing relationship. My emphasis will be on how a dependent relationship with another (an audience of one) serves a writer in the early stages of his creativity, before he feels secure enough about himself to write on his own. The model of the Freud-Fliess relationship and of the reader's relationship with Freud will lead to consideration of certain issues in the contemporary psychoanalyst's creativity.

My reading of these letters will certainly not be naive.[1] That would

1. A number of valuable suggestions and criticisms made by Roy Schafer, Ph.D., in his discussion of an earlier version of this chapter, read to the Association for Psychoanalytic Medicine, New York, October 6, 1981, have been considered.

be impossible. What reader-response criticism has conveyed most emphatically is that all readings are informed, biased, and subjective. This is best acknowledged and clarified for oneself and one's own readers and critics. Thus you should know the following: my interest in this study derived, in part, from my own wishes and conflicts with writing and creativity. Studying Freud's use of a supportive literary relationship helped me to get at aspects of similar needs in myself. There is nothing new or unusual in this. Psychoanalysts have long turned to Freud in order to understand themselves better. Freud himself gave us the model in these letters of creativity and self-understanding moving hand-in-hand. Freud made explicit what most of us hesitate to acknowledge—that our writing has to relate to our own subjective wishes and conflicts, at least to a degree. More public consideration of the conditions, conflicts, and needs with which writers create will help to demystify creativity.

You should bear in mind the temptation to move from a fantasied construct of the "implied author" of these letters to statements about the flesh-and-blood Freud. The urge to do so about Freud, our psychoanalytic progenitor, is great indeed. No matter how I word my statements, I am not referring to Freud but to a "Freud," my own personal fantasy construct for the purposes of this study. Obviously others already have and will continue to invent different "Freuds" congruent with their—disclosed and undisclosed—intentions and needs. Although it is difficult for psychoanalysts to resist the temptation to psychoanalyze the author (Green 1978), I will, as far as possible, restrain my speculation about underlying motivations and conflict in this "Freud."

Regarding letters as literary texts requires that they be separated from biography and from the author's stated intentions. How Freud himself would have interpreted these letters is not relevant to the task at hand. However, in my "Freud" construct I do aim for consistency with the psychobiographical real-life Freud.

For psychoanalytic biographical interpretation, Mack (1980) stresses that autobiographical documents such as memoirs and diaries should be examined in terms of their purposes, functions, and intended (imaginary and real) audience. Thus Schreber's *Memoirs* (1903) read differently if the imagined future readers by whom the author wishes to be judged and vindicated are considered. For whom were the Freud-Fliess letters intended?

I shall assume that it is not possible to give a definitive answer to this question and that that is in the nature of a letter-writing relationship. That is, the addressee invariably comes to stand for more than himself as a single distinct person in the here and now. This makes the psychoanalytic study of the reading experience of correspondence potentially valuable. It further supports the distinction between the biographical study of letters and the psychological study of letters as texts.

As a seventeen year old, Freud (E. Freud 1960:4) wrote his friend, Emil Fluss, "you have been exchanging letters with a German stylist. And now I advise you as a friend, not as an interested party, to preserve them—have them bound—take good care of them—one never knows." In 1885, Freud wrote (E. Freud 1960:140–41) his fiancée, Martha Bernays, that he had almost completed a task "which a number of as yet unborn and unfortunate people will one day resent . . . they are my biographers . . . we have no desire to make it too easy for them. Each one of them will be right in his opinion of 'The Development of the Hero,' and I am already looking forward to seeing them go astray."

Freud had just destroyed his notes of the preceding fourteen years, including letters, scientific excerpts, and manuscripts. We know from Jones (1953) that Freud destroyed Fliess's letters to him and that he insisted that Marie Bonaparte destroy his own letters to Fliess, which Madame Bonaparte had purchased from a bookseller. These had been sold by Frau Fliess, who herself was well aware that Freud preferred their destruction. I submit that all that can be concluded from these points is that the addressee was not, in fantasy, delimited totally by one single actual live person in the here and now. This is not predominantly an issue of Freud's ambition, grandiosity, or even accurate self-assessment but rather an issue concerning the nature of a letter-writing relationship.

As discussed in chapter 1, De Levita (Panel 1972) suggested that examination of an artist's letter writing would be a useful approach to a study of the artist's relationship with his or her audience since (p. 26) "at least one person of the audience as the addressee is named." To my knowledge, the only psychoanalyst besides de Levita who has attempted to place the study of letter writing within the broader context of the literary and psychological phenomena that occur during and as a result of correspondence, has been Erikson. In his review (1955) of the Freud-Fliess letters, Erikson described extended correspondence as a "rituel à deux." Correspondence, according to Erikson (p. 2), "develops and cultivates particular levels of mood, selected confessions, and habitual admissions, it is apt to indulge in plaintive comparison with the

unseen recipient's person or fate, and in expressions of hopes for a
reunion; often it invites some kind of mutual *correspondence-transfer-
ence*" (emphasis added). Erikson points to varied meanings of mail and
claims that "much of the passion of intellectual intimacy and much of
the mutual aggrandizement" of the Freud-Fliess letters are common to
nineteenth-century intellectual correspondence. Erikson does not document this nor does he distinguish between common and distinguishing features of these letters. Erikson introduced the concept of a "correspondence personality," which is the biographical counterpart of the
psychological-literary construct of the "implied author."

What is distinctive about letters as a literary form is precisely the fact
that an audience of one is named and addressed, although absent.
Absence and presence, whatever varied meanings they may have for a
given correspondent, are far more accentuated in letters than in any
other literary form. The letter writer announces her wish for connection with her correspondent while acknowledging their separation. In
order for the letter writer to obtain the emotional response she wants
from her correspondent, she must arouse reciprocal wishes in the latter. As distinct from talking on the telephone, the letter writer is less
hindered in the fantasies of her partner that she can summon up. Telephone conversation provides immediate feedback to correct transference fantasy distortions, which is not the case with correspondence.
The tangible, lasting property of letters, unlike telephone conversations, may serve varied psychological functions in being available for
rereading (such as denial of separation, reassurance of one's value, love
worthiness, and so on.).

Scholes (1977) noted that literariness requires tension between
communication with others and a self-referential "emphasis on its own
formal structure" (p. 108). The communicative function of correspondence should not be emphasized so exclusively that the literary function of letters is ignored. The letters of a well and classically educated
writer reflect her knowledge of and identification with her literary traditions and her pleasure in creating the letters as aesthetic objects. Since
communication through correspondence, unlike in person or by telephone, requires intensity of expression so as to engage, affect, and convey meanings, Schafer (1981) suggests that letters "invite a shift toward
hyperbole and more or less extravagant metaphor in order to try to
make sure that certain points are heard as intended." From this Schafer
concludes that judging the intensity of the letter writer's affective states
may be very difficult and that one may tend to exaggerate them. The

dialectic between the reader's absence and fantasied presence contributes to the writer's greater freedom to express what might not be said in person, as well as the pressure to convey and incite affective meanings in his or her reader. I would argue that Schafer's insights demonstrate the usefulness of constructing a coherent reading of letters around the literary concept of the "implied author" rather than attempting to reconstruct the writer's actual intentions and his psychology.

Much of the debate about the Freud-Fliess letters simply ignores what Erikson has underscored about the meanings to be attributed to Freud's personality. This is not surprising on two counts. First, this has become a common psychoanalytic approach to literary criticism. Second, Freud has such significance and transference valence for all psychoanalysts that it is almost inevitable that psychoanalytic writing about these letters would become polarized between idealization and debunking (see Kohut 1976). An early, acrimonious example of this polarization is the debate between Suzanne Bernfield and Edith Buxbaum published in 1952, following publication of Buxbaum's (1951) paper interpreting aspects of Freud's neurosis from these letters. Scientific method was less at issue than was the proper regard for "The Hero." Eissler's (1964) thoughtful and uplifting review of the *Letters of Sigmund Freud*, entitled "Mankind at its best," although inspiring is, I consider, overly idealized. Kohut (1976) suggests that it may be impossible for the current generation of psychoanalysts to arrive at a balanced appraisal of Freud.

The Reading Experience of the Freud-Fliess Letters: A Sampling [2]

The letters begin on November 24, 1887, in Jones's (1953) translation, with the salutation "Esteemed Friend and Colleague." Rather than attempt to reconstruct how a nineteenth-century German reader of these letters would have experienced them, which would be a misleading and distorted reading according to a number of contemporary critics (see especially Gadamer 1975), let us together, you and I, see how we feel as readers. This first letter continues intimately and

2. This study was done before publication of *The Complete Letters of Sigmund Freud to Wilhelm Fliess, 1887–1904*, ed. by J. M. Masson (1985). Revisions will be indicated in chapter 7.

seductively, indicative of what was soon to follow (p. 51): "I must start with the confession that I hope to remain in contact with you, and that you left a deep impression on me, which might lead easily to my telling you frankly in what class of men I place you." The second letter, a month later, adds, "I still do not know how I managed to rouse your interest . . . But I am delighted all the same. So far I have always had the luck to choose my friends among the best of men, and I have always been particularly proud of my good fortune in that respect . . . I hear about you from time to time—mostly wonderful things, of course." In letter 4 Freud writes, "the magic of your prestige cannot be transferred," while in letter 6, disappointed about being unable to meet Fliess in Berlin, the writer says, "I feel very isolated, scientifically blunted, stagnant, and resigned. When I talked to you, and saw that you thought something of me, I actually started thinking something of myself, and the picture of confident energy which you offered was not without its effect . . . for years now I have been without anyone who could teach me anything." Jones (1953:296) translates this more poignantly as "without a teacher." In letter 13 (July 10, 1893), when Freud had been using the familiar *Du* instead of the more formal *Sie* for about a year, he refers to their "partnership."

As the writer announces his ability and confidence to write on his own about the neuroses, he seems to need to soothe and console the reader (p. 76): "In saying this I am not dissolving our partnership. In the first place, I hope you will explain the physiological mechanism of my clinical findings from your point of view; secondly, I want to maintain the right to come to you with all my theories and findings in the field of neurosis; and thirdly, I still look to you as the Messiah who will solve the problem [birth control] I have indicated by an improvement in technique."

In June 1894 Freud writes, "Since my scientific contact with Breuer has ended I have been thrown back on myself alone, why is why it goes so slowly." In an unpublished letter a month later (Jones 1953:298) we read, "Your praise is nectar and ambrosia for me." The following year we find (p. 181), "This separation and letter-writing is a great trial, but there is no help for it." Soon after, Freud writes (p. 119) about his consuming passion, his hobby-horse, his tyrant: "in his service I know no limits." This tyrant is psychology, he says (p. 120): "during recent weeks I have devoted every free minute to such work; the hours of the night from eleven to two have been occupied with imaginings, transpositions, and guesses, only abandoned when I arrived at some absurdity, or had so truly and seriously overworked that I had no interest left for the day's medical work."

The feminine creative metaphor is introduced on June 12, 1895, with reference to the Project (p. 121): "saying anything now would be like sending a six-months female embryo to a ball." The burden of writing is superhuman so that Freud (p. 121) "must treat that mind of mine decently, or the fellow will not work for me"—hence cigar smoking instead of abstinence. What Freud is creating is intended primarily for Fliess (p. 123): "The only reason I write to you so little is that I am writing so much for you." While describing how well he writes (see pp. 129–30), Freud says, "If I could talk to you about nothing else for forty-eight hours on end the thing could probably be finished." He ends this excited, enthusiastic letter, "You will not have any objection to my calling my next son Wilhelm."

New Year's Day, 1896, is celebrated with a letter to Fliess (pp. 140–41), "to shake your hand across the few kilometers between us." "The thought that we should both be busy with the same work is the happiest that I could have just now," the writer says. Freud wishes to arrive at his original ambition of philosophy, while his friend in parallel studies physiology. I was startled to find that the editors omitted a moving passage from this New Year's Day letter, which Jones (1953:298–99) provides:

> People like you should not die out, my dear friend; we others need the like of you too much. How much have I to thank you in consolation, understanding, stimulation in my loneliness, in the meaning of life you have given me, and lastly in health which no one else could have brought back to me. It is essentially your example that has enabled me to gain the intellectual strength to trust my own judgment . . . and to face with deliberate resignation, as you do, all the hardships the future may have in store. For all that accept my simple thanks.

The following month the writer again exhorts his reader to share in a mutually strengthening twinlike relationship (p. 157):

> Criticism will not affect you any more than Strümpell's criticism affected me . . . I am so sure that we have both laid hands on a fine piece of objective truth, and we can do without recognition from strangers (strangers to the facts) for a long time to come. I hope we shall make still more discoveries and go on correcting our own mistakes before anyone catches up with us.

Freud writes (p. 158) after praising a draft of Fliess's, "I read it through the first time as if it had been intended for me alone." The tandem movement of writer and reader is again expressed (p. 161): "If we are both granted a few more years of quiet work, we shall certainly leave behind something which will justify our existence. That feeling strengthens me against all daily cares and worries." When his father is nearing death (pp. 168–69), Freud writes, "I am in a rather gloomy state, and all I can say is that I am looking forward to our congress as to a slaking of hunger and thirst. I shall bring with me nothing but a pair of open ears, and shall be all agape."

New Year's greetings of 1897 are similar, if two days late (pp. 182–83):

> We shall not be shipwrecked. Instead of the passage we are seeking, we may find oceans, to be fully explored by those who come after us; but, if we are not prematurely capsized, if our constitutions can stand it, we shall make it. *Nous y arriverons.* Give me another ten years and I shall finish the neuroses and the new psychology; perhaps you will complete your organology in less time than that . . . no previous New Year has been so rich with promise for both of us. When I am not afraid I can take on all the devils in hell, and you know no fear at all.

The twin passage motif is sought again (p. 211): "We share like the two beggars one of whom allotted himself the province of Posen; you take the biological, I take the psychological."

The wish to create on his own is increasingly more strongly conveyed to the reader, from beginnings such as (p. 214) "the old, unjustly despised technique of exchanging ideas." A letter of October 15, 1897, begins (p. 221), "My self-analysis is the most important thing I have in hand." This seems to contrast with the previous feeling that the relationship between the writer and reader had been preeminent. In contrast to earlier pleas for support and encouragement from Fliess, Freud writes on October 31, 1897 (p. 227): "I have a reassuring feeling that one only has to put one's hand in one's own store-cupboard to be able to extract—in its own good time—what one needs." Freud writes that he has become interesting to himself, since he has been studying his own unconscious in his self-analysis. Freud here refers to a line from Goethe's Faust (part I, scene 4), which he uses again in these letter, in *The Interpretation of Dreams*, and when he received the Goethe prize: "*Das beste, was Du wissen kanst,/Darfst Du den Buben doch nicht sagen* (The best that you know, you must not tell to ordinary men).” This is used in the context of the writer's confronting what he formerly dared not face and his conflict about sharing his self-knowledge with others. The more general appeal of this line to the writer may involve the reader's role in formulating his ideas, in creating his written work with the supportive presence of a special, chosen other before these ideas can be promulgated.

The shift in the writer's ease of creating on his own is vividly conveyed (p. 244): “I am deep in the dream book, writing it fluently and smiling at all the matter for 'headshaking' it contains in the way of indiscretions and audacities . . . Self-analysis has been dropped in favor of the dream book.” A month later (p. 248), in contrast, the reader is called closer: “My freshness for work seems to be a function of the distance of our congresses.” Similarly, in the next letter (p. 249), the reader is told, “You must not refuse the duties attached to being my first reader and supreme arbiter .” The writer's manner of creating now changes in a way that should be reassuring to all who are struggling to create (p. 258): “It [a chapter of the dream-book] was all written by the unconscious, on the well-known principle of Itzig, the Sunday horseman. 'Itzig, where are you going?' 'Don't ask me, ask the horse!' At the beginning of a paragraph I never knew where I should end up.” Later (p. 307) Freud indicated another change in his way of creating: “If the sexual theory comes up, I shall listen to it.” The editors contrast this with what Freud wrote to Abraham in 1914, that he now went forward to meet his new ideas instead of just waiting for them to come to him.

Betwixt ambivalent feelings toward Fliess and their overt disagreements, Freud writes seductively (p. 272): “So you see what happens. I live gloomily and in darkness until you come, and then I pour out all my grumbles to you, kindle my flickering light at your steady flame and feel well again; and after your departure I have eyes to see again, and what I look upon is good.” Two letters later we find: “You can have no idea how much your last visit raised my spirits. I am still living on it. The light has not gone out since; little bits of new knowledge glimmer now here, now there, which is truly refreshing after the comfortlessness of last year . . . I need you as my audience.”

As the writer discloses more intense angry feelings, he seems to struggle with separating himself from his own “shackles” (a frequently repeated image) to the reader (see e.g., p. 285). Still he emphasizes how comforting he finds (Erikson 1955:15) “the self-assurance of your judgments.”

The written work is often linked in these letters with pregnancy and childbirth accomplished with the reader's active participation, as here (p. 313):

> I heard with great satisfaction that your interest in my dream-child is unabated, and that you lent your hand to stirring up the *Rundschau* and its indolent reviewers . . . I have now come down on the side of being very grateful to you for standing godfather to it, and of thinking it good and sound. It has been a consolation to me in many a gloomy hour to know that I have this book to leave behind me.

The writer refers to his feminine longings for the reader overtly in a well-known line (p. 318): "[T]here can be no substitute for the close contact with a friend which a particular—almost a feminine—side of me calls for." Eissler (1971) suggests that "*etwa feminine*" is more accurately translated as "as it were, feminine," since *etwa* combines "probably," "perhaps," and "as it were."

The Forms of the Supportive Literary Relationship

It is well-known how skillful Freud was in his scientific writing at engaging his readers, raising their objections, establishing a dialogue with them, guiding them effectively and elegantly towards Freud's points of view. Here we need only acknowledge that the writer, in the passages I have quoted from the correspondence with Fliess, succeeds admirably at engaging the reader. In these letters the reader is drawn in by flattery and praise, by the personal importance the writer attributes to him, that his continued presence and encouragement are required by the writer to counteract the latter's depression, loneliness, flagging self-confidence, and hesitation with his ideas and their written expression. This is seductive and appealing to the reader, who is given a central inspirational role in the writer's creativity. From what is known about Fliess, this way of relating to the reader should have been effective with him. Most prominent in these letters are the relationships between writer and reader and the writer's creative work, his tyrant. Psychology, the tyrant, drives the writer to create between eleven and two after a long day's work; it requires some mildly painful discomfort and considerable gratification.

The rest of the writer's and reader's lives, including other people and the satisfactions they provide, pale in comparison to writing and the correspondence relationship between writer and reader. It is remarkable in this version of these letters how little the writer tells about the other important people in the writer's life. This intensifies the literary relationship, making further creative writing contingent on continued impassioned correspondence. From the many examples quoted, it can be seen that passion is an outstanding feature of these letters. The intensely passionate relationship between writer and reader has been expressed in two predominant modes: a twin motif and a passive, dependent, feminine form. In my reading, elements of idealization of the reader are overshadowed by this sense of twin, parallel, equal accomplishment and importance. To debate whether this represents idealizing transference or twinship transference would do violence to the text. We would do better to confine ourselves to noting that these letters urge the reader to share in a passionate twin relationship, in which each is to urge the other on toward more ambitious and greater creative achievement. Creative work on one's own is described as too difficult, depressing, or demanding. As the writer begins to create more confidently, easily, and fluently, unsupported by the other, he first apologizes to the reader and keeps the latter connected in parallel with him. Only later does the writer exhibit his exhilaration and pride in his more private work, accomplished unaided. The reader is initially asked to tolerate, approve, and admire him. Finally, the writer is able to unshackle himself to a degree from needing the reader to provide him with enthusiastic response. The shift from a close bonding with a twinlike reader toward a more confident, contained, capacity for solo creative writing is very obvious.

The passive, dependent, feminine form in which the writer offers himself to the reader is evident in the passages I quote, where the reader is asked to fill the writer's emptiness, to kindle his flickering flame, to keep his light burning, to participate in and watch over the birth of the created works, to be near at hand so the writer can feel signs of life again. I noted the writer's explicit statement that his need for close contact with the reader derives from an "as it were, feminine" side of himself. Creativity is here equated with fullness, vitality, fertility, pregnancy, and birth. The lonely, depressed, flagging writer must be inspired, filled, brought to life, kindled by the praise and devotion of the reader. The writer of these letters comes across to us as lonely, depressed, insecure, and needy. The reader has been passionately engaged to provide intense responsiveness, friendship, love, encouragement, admiration, and praise.

The Functions of the Supportive Literary Relationship

Psychoanalytic authors disagree as to how much of the neurotic part of his relationship with Fliess Freud was able to resolve through his self-analysis. All agree that Freud, after he completed *The Interpretation of Dreams*, was less idealizing, more overtly critical of and less dependent on Fliess than he had been previously. Although self-criticism and doubt are still reported after completion of *The Interpretation of Dreams*, the author is convinced of his monumental achievement. It could be that appreciation of what he had been able to accomplish helped to secure the author's confidence in his own creative ability. The alternative argument would be that his self-analysis had helped to free him of neurotic impediments to confident solo creative work. These explanations are not mutually exclusive. What I am after is a correlation between changes in the correspondence relationship between Freud and Fliess with changes in the created product.

Psychoanalysts take for granted that Freud's theory building and introspective self-understanding went hand-in-hand, especially during the Fliess period and Freud's "official" self-analysis. To the degree that this is accurate, this should have helped to secure his confidence in his ability to draw on himself creatively. That is, what he could comprehend about himself, once he, like Oedipus, could understand his own resistances against self-knowledge, could become the stuff from which to understand the psychology of others. This may well have been a powerful motivation for systematic self-exploration, in addition to the wish for relief from mental suffering. From this perspective, Freud needed a relatively nonneurotic patient to confirm the general applicability of his findings with his analysands. Freud eagerly solicited dreams from relatives, friends, and colleagues, as well as from himself, to be understood and used as examples. Becoming his own patient offered him exactly what he needed.

The first such reference in these letters dates from September 23, 1895, when Freud wrote: "A dream the night before provided me the most amusing *confirmation* that the motivation of dreams is wish-fulfillment" (emphasis added). The interconnections between Freud's self-analysis and his analysis of patients are well known, of his using each to facilitate the other. For example, when in May 1897 Freud had a sexual dream about his oldest daughter, he interpreted this as a wish for validation of the paternal seduction theory of the etiology of neurosis. Here Freud keeps considerable distance from the central affect of his dream experience. It has been suggested that Freud's initial position in favor of the seduction theory—blaming the father—derived in part unconsciously from the secrecy regarding his father's marriages (the most recent evidence is that Freud's father was married three times) and in part from primal scene trauma (the family living in one room in Freiberg until Freud was three). Not only does Freud's self-analysis allow him to recognize conflicts in himself but he shifts in his interpretation of dreams and other data toward emphasis on the centrality of the subject's affective experience. The themes in which this was elaborated are familiar: ambition, death wishes against one's parents, oedipal rivalry, incestuous longings for the parent of the opposite sex, anality, greed, hunger, separation, and so on. A broader way to organize the shift is in terms of increasing tolerance of conflict over (including guilt at) hostile aggression. We can witness the author becoming increasingly more capable of experiencing and expressing angry feelings with greater directness, less need for defensive distortion. Nevertheless, conflict about hostile aggression persists throughout these letters. Psychoanalysts emphasize Freud's recognition of the persistence of infantile conflicts. Schur (1972) suggests that Freud, to a degree, protected himself from his current conflicts with Fliess by interpreting (especially dreams) backwards to childhood. That is, a contemporary analyst regarding the Freud-Fliess relationship as a self-analysis with Fliess as the predominant figure for transference elaboration, would recognize defensive operations in Freud's shifting the focus predominantly to the past away from the here-and-now.

Changes in the Correspondence Relationship— Changes in the Creative Work

Freud's shift in the relationship with Fliess can be organized in terms of conflict between dependent submission to an idealized authority and the capacity to tolerate angry, critical feelings without undue self-criticism, depression, doubt, and indecision. Of course, Freud had not yet formulated the dual instinct theory. But whatever one calls the dangerous dark side that Freud was exploring within his patients and himself, from a contemporary position it is possible to see the role of hostile aggression, even in sexual conflict. Within these letters we see a substantial change from a seemingly dependent position in which the other's approval and encouragement seems crucial; the other must be regarded as substantially similar to the self; and the self's inner affective experience must be kept at a distance. As the writer becomes better able to tolerate what is present in himself, he becomes clearer about himself and others. He then seems less urgently driven to maintain the connection with the other and seems more confident about what is in himself and the creative uses he can make of this. Even at the end of the relationship with Fliess, however, Freud writes of his craving for a close male friend and the wish that the friendship with Fliess could have continued. The defensive requirement against direct experience and expression of anger persists. I agree with Schur (1972) that Freud displaced his criticism from Fliess onto Breuer (a common motif in these letters) in the unpublished passage from the letter of August 7, 1901, which Schur provides (q.v.).

Freud learns through his relationship with Fliess and his self-analysis that hypocrisy, absurdity, and humor are interrelated modes for defended expression of anger. He then makes central use of these in the dream and joke books. Absurdity in dreams in the dream book is reached through connection with Freud's hostile feelings about Fliess in his own absurd dreams. "Absurdity in dreams! It is astonishing how often you appear in them. In the *non vixit* dream I find I am delighted to have survived you" (letter 119, September 21, 1899). In his associations in the dream book, Freud progresses from self-reproach and guilty overconcern to underlying anger and competitiveness. The connection between angry feelings toward Fliess and the understanding of hypocritical dreams was made explicit by Freud (1900:145):

> While I was engaged in working out a certain scientific problem, I was troubled for several nights in close succession by a somewhat confusing dream which had as its subject a reconciliation with a friend whom I had dropped many years before. On the fourth or fifth occasion I at last succeeded in understanding the meaning of the dream. It was an incitement to abandon my last remnants of consideration for the person in question and to free myself from him completely, and it had been hypocritically disguised as its opposite.

The reference was to Fliess.

The Irma dream (July 24, 1895), although referred to, is not present in these letters. Schur (1972) is persuasive that Freud was here dealing (unconsciously) with hostile, critical feelings toward Fliess, immediately related to the latter's surgical mistreatment of Emma, another patient, and to Fliess's grandiosity. In the dream book, Freud acknowledges wishes to ridicule others so as to exculpate himself. The critical affects are, however, kept away from Fliess, who is here regarded positively. However, the emphasis in Freud's presentation of the Irma dream in the dream book and in his references to it in these letters is on his excited discovery of systematic free association to the manifest dream elements. Freud had found that this was the pathway to dream interpretation through access to the latent dream thoughts and the dream work. Hostile, deprecatory tones seem present even in some of the writer's early teasing exaggerations of the reader; for example, see letters of January 31, 1895, or October 9, 1896 (Schur 1972:107). The first direct expression of anger at Fliess in these letters occurs on April 28, 1897, in association with the "Casa Secerno" dream. Freud writes: "I felt a sense of irritation with you, as if you were always claiming something special for yourself; I criticized you for taking no pleasure in the Middle Ages," On July 7, 1897, referring to the beginnings of his self-analysis, Freud writes: "Something from the deepest depths of my own neurosis has ranged itself against my taking a further step in understanding of the neuroses, and *you* have somehow been involved [emphasis added]. My inability to write seems to be aimed at hindering our intercourse."

Angry, critical feelings are involved in the dream about Freud's childhood doctor in Freiberg (October 15, 1897) as well as in the dream "My friend R. was my uncle" (March 15, 1898). In writing about these dreams, Freud did not associate to Fliess directly. He did, however, tell the latter he hoped he would not disapprove of the feelings Freud revealed in his associations to the latter dream in the dream book manuscript. By July, 1899 (letter 10), Freud expressed directly to Fliess how oppressed he felt by the latter's superiority and his "shackling life with numbers and formulae." In the next letter Freud wrote: "The ancient gods still exist, for I have bought one or two lately, among them a stone Janus, who looks down on me with his two faces in a very superior fashion." As I have already noted, Freud had written about his ambivalence at feeling dominated by a tyrant, usually identified as psychology. Numerous times he referred to feeling unsure of himself when reading the extensive literature on dreams, established by the gods to discourage new understanding. And Schur (1972) points out the one reference in these letters to Fliess as Freud's demon. There is conflict here between dependent submission to the authority of another and angry feelings toward this tyrant, with wishes to invest this authority in oneself instead.

Early in 1900 (letter 131) Freud writes that he will not meet with Fliess, announcing clearly his understanding of his need to struggle on his own with his neurotic conflicts. He had become aware that transference wishes prolong psychoanalytic relationships, with the likely implication that this was relevant to his relationship with Fliess, which needed resolution. Freud had by then been able to formulate clearly that neurotic symptoms are compromise formations between the repressed and a repressing force. He connected the repressing force with guilt and emphasized that the need for punishment relates to angry and aggressive wishes. Freud's self-reproaches in these letters typically involve (excessive) criticism of the form (less often of the content) of his writing. Even when his new understandings are profoundly significant, he tends to criticize the poverty of their aesthetic expression. Freud oscillates between the need for Fliess to counter Freud's own excessive self-criticism and the growing and persistent conviction that Freud himself had indeed already made a profound contribution to psychology.

Thus I have been linking Freud's creativity with his self-discovery of what was present in himself. As he could become less fearful, critical, and accepting of the dark side of himself, even viewing that as the pathway to creativity, he could become more confident of himself and of what lay within him. He then, to a degree, was less needy of the protection, approval, and assurance offered by a supportive relationship. It seems likely that Freud's self-analysis helped him to tolerate his own angry, aggressive feelings better. The contribution of Freud's monumental discoveries toward helping him to tolerate, without substantial intrapsychic working through and change, the dark side of himself should not however be discounted; that is, a creative writer, or psychologist-explorer, who is able to utilize what is troublesome and conflicted within himself so as to create a significant or beautiful work must thereby be reassured about himself. What seems evil cannot be only bad if it can be drawn upon to create what is good. The turning point may be when the creative worker can affirm for himself the value in what he has created. That Freud could proclaim what he found in himself was, to a degree, present in everyone, would have offered a similar reassurance against anxieties and guilts. The creative artist, too, uses himself or herself to create a work having general significance beyond his or her own personal concerns. This similarly is reassuring that what is present within oneself is universally valid for everyone.

From Freud and Fliess to the Present-Day Psychoanalyst/Writer's Creativity

Kohut (1976) argues that a writer's idealization of creativity, and a psychoanalyst's idealization of Freud, interferes with creativity and leads instead to tradition-bound writing, which at best may be regarded as productive rather than original and inspired. I agree with Mahony (1979) that Kohut contradicts himself when he then claims that creative people more commonly seek idealized rather than mirroring objects. I also agree with Mahony that Kohut's assumption that creativity and transference neurosis are necessarily incompatible should not be taken for granted. From the model of Freud and Fliess, for certain creative analysands, the transference relationship with the analyst might aid, or "support" creative work. In any case, one would expect that multiple, complex meanings and functions would be served by creative work during psychoanalysis, including transference meanings and resistances in relation to the person of the analyst. Kohut claims that (1976:813) the "energic drain," anxiety, and possibly other unspecified factors that occur during creative work lead to an enfeeblement of the self that is repaired by the search for a self-object relationship providing vitally needed affirmation or strength. Kohut then interprets Fliess as representing for Freud an idealized archaic omnipotent figure, required primarily for Freud's creative accomplishments rather than as the transference object for Freud's self-analysis. Most other psychoanalytic authors have emphasized the opposite achievement, that is, that Freud's self-analysis required the (distant) presence of Fliess and then led to the breakthroughs in Freud's creativity.

It would be incorrect to regard a supportive literary relationship as serving *only* to assist creative writing. Creative writing itself, including an imagined relationship to potential (imaginary and real) readers, can serve to negotiate many of life's difficulties. It is more accurate to think of a supportive literary relationship as the vehicle through which creative writing is focused upon to provide one or both participants (since this may be very unequal) with badly needed "support." The enthusiastic responsiveness of the reader is used by the writer to alleviate loneliness, depression, self-criticism, and insecurity, as well as to handle certain conflicts specific to ambition and creativity. I have particularly emphasized how a supportive literary relationship can be used to reassure writers against what they dread most in themselves—their angry, aggressive feelings. One function of the supportive literary relationship then is to assist the writer's transformation of the dreaded dark side of himself or herself into the creative work. This is not to imply that creativity simply is a transformation of unconscious content. Nothing of the sort! But I am focusing upon how a supportive literary relationship helps writers to draw on what they fear in themselves so as to be able to use this creatively. Thus a supportive literary relationship functions like any other highly dependent relationship, especially for reassurance, containment, and protection against (anxieties and guilts related to) one's feared destructiveness, which cannot be integrated and managed alone (see Coen 1992). In this model, creative work reassures writers that they can contain what they fear within themselves and that they are not all bad. Magical, defensive confusion between oneself and one's creative product helps to reassure the writer against the dread of total inner badness. "If what I create is good, then I *am* good." On the other hand, such confusion between self and product leads to self-attack and depression, when the writing is not good enough.

The creative twin motif, of writers working in tandem or collaboratively, helps the fledgling writer to feel less lonely, vulnerable, anxious, guilty, grandiose, excessively competitive, ambitious. There is a similar other with whom to share these burdens and terrifying pleasures. I have emphasized how Freud needed to attribute to Fliess (to create in a "Fliess") what was initially difficult to acknowledge uniquely about himself; he needed to share such strivings with another. I have then traced his gradual unshackling from the need for a supportive literary relationship.

To a degree, Kohut (1976) is correct that original work draws on grandiose strivings, of daring to go where others have not, and is, therefore, frightening. Freud's fondness for the quotation from Faust ("The best that you know, you must not tell to ordinary men") expresses well this need for someone else with whom to share the arrogance of one's most original thought. The grandiose arrogance in creativity also involves competitiveness and destructiveness with one's forebears and contemporaries in daring to be original, different, better. Successful creative writers do not, however, no matter how much of a genius they are, break with tradition. Rather they must be able to assimilate what is most valuable within their tradition while daring to transform or transcend it. For example, the most radical innovations in literary technique take for granted the writer's and reader's knowledge of the history of forms against which the present innovation is to be contrasted and understood. Within psychoanalysis, too, the creative writers who will make significant lasting contributions are continually involved in a dialectic of accommodating themselves to their tradition while seeking to revise some of it. Excessive hostility and competitiveness—which cannot be acknowledged and managed—with what has been traditional usually leads to inadequate comprehension and assimilation of the traditional, leading to tendentious rather than valuable criticism. Thus, unlike Kohut (1976), I would argue that creative psychoanalysts are involved in a vital and potentially adaptive dialectic between grandiose and idealizing trends. It is to be hoped that their own destructiveness is sufficiently well managed that they do not need to idealize others excessively, surrender to them, or to feel terrified by their (temporary) wishes to be The Hero or The Heroine, which have become integrated as one aspect of their creativity. Returns to studying Freud and his contributions should help psychoanalysts to understand themselves and their field by promoting a healthy respect for our progenitor and his struggles and by neither excessively idealizing nor excessively debunking him.

Eissler's (1971) distinctions between talent and genius are another way of formulating similar issues. Eissler differentiates the genius such as Freud, who discovers new paradigms that reorganize a science, from the talented worker who makes new and creative uses of the genius' new paradigms. Others less idealizing of creativity would argue that the acceptance of a given paradigm reflects the current needs of an interpretive community as expressed in communal assumptions, agreements, and interpretive strategies. A paradigm, like an interpretation or idea, cannot be created free from and prior to these. Paradigms reflect our approach to interpretation, our needs, biases, fears, fantasies, defenses, adaptive solutions, and everything else we bring to attempts at understanding. Eissler's (1971:293) felicitous phrase, "active passivity," refers to the adaptive, creative use Freud made of passive experiences and longings. Eissler speculates that the genius is better able to use his own maternal elements than is the merely talented person. What Eissler emphasizes most about the genius such as Freud is the accessibility and ability to utilize those aspects of oneself, ordinarily conflicted and in disharmony with one's predominant self-conceptions. Whether a "conflict-free synthesis" (Eissler 1971:295) is required, as Eissler claims, may be less at issue than the ability to draw on all of oneself, including what is ordinarily dissociated, and to use this as the stuff of and pathway toward creativity. The synthesis we imagine may be more in our experience, or our fantasies, of the created work than in the creator.

The moral for contemporary psychoanalysts and writers from a reading of the Freud-Fliess letters is a familiar one, which, nevertheless, needs emphasis and repetition. This book is an attempt at understanding ourselves, the current generation of psychoanalysts and writers, and our dilemmas, rather than guessing at what Freud really needed and got from Fliess. With this intention I have constructed a reading of these letters and constructed a fantasy image, an "implied author," a "Freud" to serve these purposes. This "Freud" gives us the model that self-questioning and self-understanding is the way (and the content) toward creative thought and work. That "Freud" subjected himself and the relationship he required with "Fliess" to scrutiny and tolerated the existence of painful contradictory feelings and wishes in himself, especially the dependent, feminine, angry, and aggressive, is remarkable. Our contemporary parallel is to examine the conditions, conflicts, and needs with which present-day psychoanalysts and writers create, to make this more public, in order to help demystify creativity. "Freud's" legacy, that self-understanding and responsible self-revelation are a cornerstone of psychoanalysis, needs to be applied to how creative psychoanalysts and writers create, and how to encourage and develop such talent. What "Fliess" did for "Freud," or better what "Freud" let himself do in relation to "Fliess," can be a model for the development of talent, if not of genius, in both psychoanalysis and creative writing.

Chapter 5

WHY IS SADE ANGRY?

It is not surprising that the Marquis de Sade's writing (letters and fiction) reveals very little tenderness, caring, or concern, given or requested. The reader expects expect rage, destructiveness, hatred, sadism, sexual exploitation and domination, murder. He never disappoints! Yet, despite his intense denial, he was human, and human needs somehow must be acknowledged. Sometimes, when he felt safer *or* very threatened by loss, neglect, and helplessness, he could express tenderness and the need for affection. This chapter will examine Sade's shifts in the display of vulnerability and need in his letters and in his fiction. Bear in mind of course that I have constructed a "Sade" who fits the implied author of these writings and who is congruent with the historical Sade. This chapter emphasizes how "Sade" attempts to manage both destructiveness and need within dependent literary relationships, and demonstrates how Sade's writings are fertile ground for exploring the author-reader relationship.

Bach and Schwartz (1972) are the first psychoanalysts, to my knowledge, to elaborate a writer's (Sade's) fantasied relationship with his readers. This is a concept by which I have been strongly influenced (see also chapter 1). They speculate that one aim of the Marquis de Sade's writing in prison was its effect on imaginary readers. Bach and Schwartz suggest that in writing *The 120 Days of Sodom* in prison Sade sought to shock and devastate his readers so as to affirm his grandiose self and to counter his fears of annihilation. Their emphasis is not literary but psychoanalytic, and draws especially on what were at that time fresh ideas about pathological narcissism (Kohut 1971).

They speculate that Sade wished to overwhelm his readers with feelings of horror, disgust, and outrage, thereby exercising the sadistic power through which he affirmed his grandiose self, and consequently aggrandizing himself. Imaginary readers are "both his mirroring audience and his victims" (p. 470). Through the "brilliance, intensity, and sensation" (p. 470) of his fantasies, Bach and Schwartz suggest, Sade sought to evoke vivid affective reactions in his characters and in his readers. These authors concentrate predominantly on their understanding of what Sade sought within the text itself rather than with his imaginary audience. That is, drawing on the ideas of Heinz Kohut (1971), they emphasize Sade's delusional attempt within the text to validate grandiose self-images and idealized object-images, as defenses against psychotic fragmentation.

Khan (1965) earlier notes connections between writing and perversion. Khan suggests that the confessional quality of writing by certain perverse authors approximates dreaming or hallucinating more than organized ego activity. None of these psychoanalytic authors, however, describe how they process their own feelings and reactions to reading Sade. As a result of their omission, I have long felt tempted to explore Sade's writing for myself. In what follows, of course, the reader of a letter and the reader of a book are not to be equated. (I have discussed the psychology of letter writing in chapter 4 of this book.) However, to the degree that an author seeks to establish an intense, intimate connection with his imaginary reader, fiction writing may tend to resemble correspondence. This chapter explores "Sade's" uses of his readers, through fiction as well as through correspondence.

Bach and Schwartz begin their article with the most tender and moving passage from Sade's published letters (translated into English). Theirs is a wonderful introduction because it captures the reader immediately in the paradox of Sade the fiend longing for maternal love. The reader, in vain, searches these letters for more of this—it is not to be found. At most, Sade, writing from prison, is at times seductive toward his wife; but much of this seems intended to manipulate her into more strenuous attempts to free him or to send him money or goods. He is manipulative with his mother-in-law and with his attorneys. Sade's letters are bitter, attacking, and, especially, self-justifying. This is not only or primarily to obtain his release from prison. For that, he would have done far better to have acknowledged, at least partially, some wrongdoing, some remorse (which early during his imprisonments, he was, at times, able to announce). Certainly Sade felt enraged and wrongly treated by his repeated and prolonged imprisonments (often in solitude), in an era in which debauchery was tolerated in others of his rank. Sade (*Justine* 1791:611) actually tells his readers how much he wants to provoke them into acknowledging him as one of those

> perverse writers whose corruption is so dangerous, so active, that their single aim is, by causing their appalling doctrines to be printed, to immortalize the sum of their crimes after their own lives are at an end; they themselves can do no more, but their accursed writings will instigate the commission of crimes, and they carry this sweet idea with them to their graves; it comforts them for the obligation, enjoined by death, to relinquish the doing of evil.

Although in letter 1 (Lély 1966:33–35), Sade attempts to move his mother-in-law, who is largely responsible for his imprisonment, to seek his release from prison, his imagery in his suicide threat is similar to the imagery he evokes later in the same letter about Laura (p. 34): "My mother calls out to me from the depths of her womb: I seem to see her open her bosom once more to clasp me to it—the only refuge I have left. It is a comfort to me that I shall follow so closely, and my last wish, Madame, is that you should have me laid beside her." Images of clinging and attachment are clear here, even as he interrupts his harangue, in a letter (Lély 1966:52–53; letter 4, February 17, 1779) to his wife, to tell about his pleasure in reading Petrarch and in Laura. "I read it slowly for fear of having read it. Laura turns my head; I am like a child about her; I read her all day long and at night I dream of her." Then he tells his wife his dream, allowing himself to place her in a maternal position. Laura/mother invites him to join/merge with her (p. 53):

> It was about midnight. I had just fallen asleep with her Memoirs in my hand. Suddenly she appeared to me . . . I saw her! The horror of the tomb had not impaired the brilliance of her charms, and her eyes had the same fire as when Petrarch celebrated them. She was draped in black crêpe and her beautiful blond hair floated carelessly above it. It was as if love, to preserve her beauty, was anxious to soften the lugubrious effect of the mourning in which she appeared before my

eyes. "Why do you moan on earth?," she said to me. "Come and join me. No more ills, no more sorrows, no more trouble in the vast spaces I inhabit. Have the courage to follow me there." At these words I flung myself at her feet and said, "O mother! . . . " And my voice was choked with tears. She proffered a hand which I covered with tears; she too shed tears. "When I lived in this world which you hate," she added, "I used to enjoy looking into the future; I extended my posterity as far as you yourself but never saw you so wretched." Then absorbed in my *tenderness* [emphasis added] and despair, I threw my arms about her neck to hold her back or follow her and water her with my tears, but the ghost had disappeared. All that remained was my grief. "O ye who travail, here is the way / Come to me if there is no other." (Petrarch, Sonnet 59, in Italian in Sade's letter)

He then proceeds to write *tenderly* to his wife. The reader is touched and relieved that the writer is able, at least briefly, to seek solace as he draws the reader closer. The reader may be tempted to cling to such moments of tenderness when he has to contend with the writer's more usual rejection, torture, and control of the reader. Sade's reader wants to reassure himself that Sade was, indeed, human and at least temporarily capable of giving in to genuine human needs of others, including his readers. I suspect that one biographer of Sade, Lély (1962), exaggerates Sade's capacity for tender concern in order to avoid the full emotional impact of Sade's destructive exploitation of others. Another biographer, Thomas (1976), is somewhat less idealizing of Sade.

Sade had been arrested on February 13, 1777, by *lettre de cachet* and within two days was in a cell at the fortress of Vincennes. His tender dream of Laura occurs, as Bach and Schwartz point out, on the second anniversary of his incarceration and close to that of his mother's death. He falls asleep with his uncle's *Notes for the Life of François Petrarch*, which confirmed that Petrarch's Laura (to whom Petrarch expressed adoration in his poetry) was Laura de Sade, née de Noves. The Marquis de Sade (as had his ancestors) made much of this. In 1792 the Marquis arranged to have the remains of Laura de Sade moved to a church on his own estate, after the revolutionaries had destroyed the church in Avignon where she had been buried. Another Laura, Laure de Lauris, enters his desires, as his mistress, whom he had wanted to marry, although both fathers were opposed. Shortly before his marriage to Renée de Montreuil, Sade writes Laura de Lauris on April 6, 1763

(Lély 1961:37–40), pleading, attacking, and threatening that she must be his.

Thus, Sade the fiend was also a romantic poet, longing, at times, in the safety of his imagination, for an idealized love. It is not known whether Petrarch actually succeeded in loving his Laura in person. She is known through Petrarch's writing. More than four hundred years before Sade dreams of his Lauras, Petrarch writes, in his manuscript of Virgil (Lély 1961:10): "I first set eyes on Laura, famous for her virtue and long sung in my poems, in the flower of my youth, in the year of our Lord 1327, on April 6th, in the morning, in the church of St. Claire in Avignon." It is touching that Sade can allow himself, at times, such tender longing, to identify with Petrarch's (poetic) adoration of Laura, to crave the love of a four-hundred-year-old-spirit, even though such fantasy love (poetry) is safer than risking more direct expression of need with available living people. Sade's writing, unfortunately, so seldom reveals him as a romantic poet. There are so few times when Sade's readers can relax and enjoy warm human relatedness, even sexual desire for another whole but separate person.

Some Background

Sade was born, June 2, 1740, in the home of the head of the younger branch of the ruling Bourbon family, to which Sade's mother was related by marriage and in whose household she was lady-in-waiting. The son of this royal family, Prince Louis Joseph de Bourbon, four years older, became the playmate of the young Marquis. Sade's father, the Count de Sade, also from a distinguished family, had a military and diplomatic career. He has been characterized as distant and emotionally uninvolved. The parents apparently spent much time apart; after 1760 Sade's mother lived in a Carmelite convent. In *Aline et Valcour*, an autobiographical novel, Sade explains the origins of his grandiosity (Lély 1961:25):

> Allied through my mother with all the grandest in the kingdom, and connected through my father with all that was most distinguished in Languedoc—born in Paris in the heart of luxury and plenty—as soon as I could think I concluded that nature and fortune had joined hands to heap their gifts on me. This I thought because people were stupid enough to tell me so, and that idiotic presumption made me

haughty, domineering, and ill-tempered. I thought that everything
should give way before me, that the entire universe should serve my
whims, and that I merely needed to want something, to be able to
have it. I will relate only one incident of my childhood to convince
the reader how dangerous were the notions which, with such utter
folly, they allowed me to foster.

As I was born and brought up in the mansion of the distinguished
nobleman whom my mother had the honor to serve, and who was
approximately of my age, the family made every effort to bring him
and me together, so that by reason of our having known each other
since infancy I might enjoy his support at every turn in my life; but
such was my impetuous willfulness, in my utter ignorance of this
scheme, that the day came when in our boyish games I took offense
because he would not give way to me in something, and still more
because—no doubt with very good reason—he thought himself justified by his rank in what he did. I replied to his obstinacy by hitting
him time and again; nothing could stop me, and it was only by force,
indeed, by quite violent means, that I was finally separated from my
opponent.

The following should be added to what the Marquis confesses: his
mother had asked the servants, who represented the godparents (the
father was out of the country at the time), to have him christened Louis
Aldonse Donatien. Instead he was named Donatien Alphonse François.
The name, Louis, first name of the Bourbon kings, Sade would not
relinquish so easily. There are multiple examples of his signing his name
with "Louis." Further, the Prince de Condé died shortly after the birth
of the young Marquis, while the Princess of Condé died the following
year, leaving the orphaned prince, at least initially, to be raised by the
Countess de Sade. Sade continues his confession (Lély 1961:25–6; letter of August 16, 1744): "About this time [he was four years old] my
father was employed on some diplomatic mission and my mother trav-
elled to join him . . . I was sent to my grandmother in Languedoc and
her blind affection for me fostered all the defects I have just confessed."
Lély suggests additionally that the Marquis's five maternal aunts may
have contributed to spoiling their only male descendent. Perhaps too,
the Marquis's short stature (a little over five feet two inches tall) contributed to a compensatory grandiosity.

Exposure to his uncle the Abbé de Sade's libertinage, while being
raised by him between the ages of five or six and ten, may have con-

tributed to Sade's feelings of entitlement to being indulged. The uncle was imprisoned briefly when he was caught by the police with a prostitute and another woman. Between ten and fourteen, the Marquis attended a Jesuit school near the Condé Palace in Paris, for the sons of the nobility. At fourteen, he entered the Light Horse, a prestigious cavalry regiment, beginning his military career.

There is little evidence that Sade had much sustained involvement with his parents, with whom he lived only briefly. Sade claims that the first person who had any significant influence on him was a tutor at age ten! Although Sade emphasizes his own indulgence, it seems more likely that he needed to justify his bitter entitlement to be indulged. Sade seems to have been stimulated in the grandiose possibilities of what might have (should have) been his and fixed on these in his rage and deprivation. Watching the regal and selfish indulgence around him, together with the relative disregard for his own childhood needs, encouraged his grandiose entitlement and rage at his neglect and deprivation. His tender longings were ephemeral and ethereal; he could not count on being treated tenderly and lovingly.

Of course, a psychoanalyst is tempted to explain Sade's severe psychopathology as related to childhood trauma (neglect, deprivation, the teasing stimulation of watching others' self-indulgence). However, data about Sade's early life are quite meager. Recent psychohistorical writing (Ariès 1962; Hunt 1970; Marvick 1974) indicates that contemporary expectations of child rearing did not apply in early eighteenth-century France, especially among the nobility. Sustained tender respect, concern for, and nurturance of children seem first to *begin* to appear late in the eighteenth century. Neglect, deprivation, abuse, exploitation, domination, intimidation, and sexual overstimulation were not uncommon experiences for children in early eighteenth-century France. My hunch, however, is that Sade's experience was worse than the ordinary child of the nobility. What is more important, however, is that Sade, unlike some others (say Louis XIII, as described in Jean Héroard's seventeenth-century journal [Hunt 1970]) could *generally* sustain his rage, destructiveness, grandiosity, and sadism rather than yield to withdrawal, isolation, and depression.

How was Sade able to develop his sadistic perversion rather than succumb to depression and despair? Of course, any answer must be speculative and incomplete. Sade's letters make very clear that he struggled, especially through his writing, against surrender to hopeless despair and depressive immobilization. I would emphasize his turning to corrupt solutions in identification with corrupt, selfish, and (sexually) self-indulgent caretakers. This also provided him with a model of extractiveness and denial/destruction of reality, both of which are crucial for perversion. What the sources were for a perverse *sexual* solution are less clear. There was the influence of the debauchery around him, certainly by his libertine uncle, the Abbé de Sade, and by the nobility among whom he lived and whom he observed. One imagines this exposed the young Sade to considerable sexual overstimulation. Unfortunately, little is known about his sensual relationship with his parents; we do not know whether this might have been a source for the intense childhood sensuality that is so often the fabric out of which perversion is woven (Coen 1985).

Sade's life would have been very different had he been able to exercise some discretion and some greater control over his libertinage. His wife's feelings, needs, and pregnancies had little influence on the Marquis's behavior. Initially, his mother-in-law, Madame la Présidente de Montreuil, seemed willing to tolerate and obscure his exploits. The Marquis's seduction of her younger daughter and their joint travels, together with his other notorious misbehavior, lead her to obtain a *lettre de cachet*, which resulted in his incarceration for most of the period between 1777 and 1790. The evidence, although not clear enough, indicates that the Marquis de Sade was far less destructive in action than he was in his writings. Sade certainly was tempted to enact his perverse, sadistic fantasies but not to the relentless, repetitive degree displayed in his fiction, which demonstrates absolute domination over anything human in the other. He acknowledged sexual whipping of women, but insisted that they had agreed to this in advance; that he had administered aphrodisiacs to prostitutes that led to acute toxicity, probably because he misjudged the dose; that he kept young women at his secluded estate to use them in orgies, but insisted that they had agreed to stay with him. His denial of sodomy, punishable then by death, seems false. Rather, he seems to have taken part in anal intercourse with both women and men (at least his valet). He denied seducing virginal teenage girls, claiming that responsibility for this belonged to the madam who had supplied them. But then the Marquis was not good at accepting responsibility for what he did. He denied aborting pregnant women, that he was merely interested in learning how this could be done; he denied necrophilia—the bones in question were merely a joke, used in a sexual game; he denied sexual experimentation/vivisection; he even repeatedly denied authorship of his highly popular erotic/provocative novel, *Justine*. Who else could have written this?

Sade as a Writer: Tenderness and Imagination Fettered

During his imprisonment at Vincennes, the Bastille, and the Charenton asylum, the Marquis became depressed, enraged, and monumentally self-justifying. His letters and his fiction during this time are angry, attacking, destructive, vengeful. Later, while he was out of prison and living with Madame de Quesnet (after his wife had obtained a separation from him), his writing was less destructive and outrageous; he seems somewhat more content. In 1790 Sade, and other prisoners held by *lettres de cachet*, had been released from custody by a Decree of the Assembly. For example, the Marquis dedicates his 1791 version of *Justine* "To my dear friend" (Madame de Quesnet): "Yes, Constance, it is to thee I address this work; at once the example and honor of thy sex, with a spirit of profoundest sensibility combining the most judicious and the most enlightened of minds, thou art she to whom I confide my book" Even as Sade plays between virtue and vice in this dedication, he keeps Constance tenderly in mind. "I do declare, this woman is an angel sent me by Heaven," Sade proclaimed in 1799 (Lély 1961:322; letter of January 1791). His biographers (Lély 1961; Thomas 1976) indicate, if this is indeed accurate and not overly idealized, substantial change in Sade's attitudes and behavior once he began to live with Madame de Quesnet. Lély goes so far as to claim (without documentation, however) that Sade, now kind and adoring, no longer thought about other women.

In his letters from prison to his wife, Sade wrote at times in a seductive, knowing, possessive way, as if to emphasize the intimate bond between them. The threat of disruption of this bond, by unconcern, interest in another man, or separation, seemed very troubling to Sade. For example, he writes (Lély 1966:119; letter 14, June 1783): "I kiss your bottom and I am going—else may the Devil take me—to give myself a smack in their honor! . . . you have another very good way and warmth in the rectum which gives me a strong reason for agreeing with you. I am truly yours." Or again (Lély 1966:137–42; letter 19, November 23/24, 1783):

Charming creature, so you want my dirty linen, my old linen? Do you realize that this is not the last word in tact? You see how much I appreciate the value of things. Listen *my angel*, I have the greatest desire to satisfy you on this point, for you know that I respect *tastes and whims*: however strange they may be, I find them worthy of respect both because one is not master of them and because the oddest and most singular whim of all, properly analysed, always has its origin in some principle of delicacy. I will undertake to prove it whenever you like: you know that there's no one like me for analysing things. I have then *mon petit chou*, the greatest desire to satisfy you."

In each succeeding paragraph of this letter, Sade continues to address his wife as: "my little *Toutou*"; "O Joy of Mahomet"; "my turtle-dove"; "Celestial pussy-cat"; "fresh pork of my thoughts (I am very fond of pork and eat very little here" (note added by Sade); and so forth. He concludes: "Torch of my life, when will your alabaster fingers come like that and exchange Lieutenant Charles's fetters for the roses of your breast? Adieu, I kiss it and go to sleep."

Contrast this with Sade's intense jealousy of his wife in 1781 (Lély 1966:93–97; letter 9, c. August 15, 1781): "If Boucher [police clerk] does accompany you and you are dollied up like a tart as you were on the last occasion, I shall refuse to come down." Sade continues to harangue his wife that her dress has not been sufficiently modest:

If you are honest, I am the only person you should want to please; you will certainly never please me except by the appearance and *conduct* of the greatest propriety and the most perfect modesty. In short, I demand, as you love me (and I am surely about to see the proof; the thing I am asking of you cannot be refused without completely unmasking yourself, concerning your signs, your marks, and all your stupid mystifications), I demand then, I repeat, that you come in the dress which you women call "robe de chambre," [and so on] . . . I swear to you by all I hold most sacred that you will rouse my wrath to a pitch of fury and that there will be a furious scene if you deviate in the slightest from what I am prescribing. You should blush at failing to see that the persons who got you up as you were the other day inwardly jeered at you. Oh! they would certainly be saying: "the little marionette; how easily we do what we want with her!" Be yourself for once in your life . . . I will never forget an outrage and I shall not make any effort to take back a *possession* [emphasis added] which would have ceased to belong to me. The mere idea that a woman could think of any other man when in my arms has always revolted me, and I have always refused to see again any woman whom I suspected of deceiving me.

There is evidence that Sade's jealousy involved a former secretary of his (Lefèvre). An unpublished letter from the Marquise to the Marquis is covered with blood and angry jottings. The Marquis refers to the dimensions of Lefèvre's penis; to his wife's signature, he adds Lefèvre's name. The Marquis tore (thirteen times) a drawing of Lefèvre, stained it with blood, and defiled it with words. The Marquise de Sade in response, attempting to calm her husband, took a room in a nunnery! Sade wrote his wife (Lély 1961:242): "I dreamt of you much older than when I left you, before that visit of last July [1781], when you had a secret you had to tell me but about which you would never say any more; and you were constantly being unfaithful to me, in the full meaning of the term. I think I have dreamt that particular dream five hundred times." Additionally, he misinterpreted his wife's writing to mean that she was pregnant.

There seems to have been little reason to suspect the Marquise de Sade's behavior. Her letters to the Marquis emphasize her masochistic submissiveness, her willingness to tolerate his excoriations and demands of her. Sade wishes to possess his wife fully, her not to be an autonomous agent but to be under his domination, unable to have her own desires or to leave him. She is to be what he is not! She is to serve as the good part of himself, so that he can feel more acceptable while contemptuously denying any such need. Some of Sade's pathological jealousy seems to derive from his homosexual conflicts, as his biographer Lély (1962) suggests. His rivalry with other men and their penises seems obvious. His characters shift between wanting to dominate, seduce, and fuck other men and wanting themselves to passively be revitalized by another man's strength. In *The 120 Days of Sodom*, four powerful men (with obvious weaknesses), tolerate sharing control, possessions, and each other. That they do not seek to destroy each other, in this most destructive of novels, suggests an uneasy truce in the author/narrator's rage toward men.

What is most intriguing is why this pathological jealousy appeared when it did. Sade, and his characters, seem to (almost) continually maintain a defensive (narcissistic) avoidance of fully needing another. This would make it seem unnecessary for Sade to construct additional protection against intimate needs through construction of a compromise formation of pathological jealousy (see Coen 1987). *Unless*, of course, he were suddenly much more threatened by *feeling* his needs for his wife (and for strength and sustenance from a man)! This is plausible. Feelings of impotence and fears of loss and disintegration were then (1781) more intense in Sade's writings. Indeed Sade's reader feels the writer attempting to exercise his power and control over the reader, as he attempts to seduce, cajole, plead with, dominate, and torture the reader into submission and intense responsiveness.

A Sadian Primer: How to Manage Helplessness, Rage, and Need

Much of Sade's rage in his prison letters refers to his inability to compel others to attend to him, that he can be ignored or disregarded, and to the fact that others have the power to censure and punish his libertinage. His prison letters describe the awfulness of being imprisoned, enclosed in a small, cold, dreadful space, and his terrible isolation. Nobody listens to him; he feels unable to influence anyone; his requests go unheeded. When he is kept in solitary confinement, such feelings become intolerable, overwhelming. Seemingly despite himself, the Marquis addresses his need to talk to and to gain some comfort from others. He laments that he is allowed only ten minutes a day to talk with his guard when he is brought his food. After his release from prison, he describes his need to talk with people (Lély 1966:178; letter 18, end of May, 1790):

> Nevertheless company is necessary; I felt this during my long retreat and now that my misanthropy is leaving me a little, I feel the need to spread myself. The despair of never having been able to communicate my ideas for twelve years has resulted in such a quantity collected up in my head that I must "give birth," and I still find myself talking to myself sometimes when no one is there. I have a real need to talk; I was aware of this and because of it I see that the Trappist establishment would no longer suit me too well.

Enraged and depressed, he must demonstrate the opposite: not only can he affect others, but he is irresistible. The *120 Days of Sodom* especially emphasizes the author's power over his characters, and over his readers, to do precisely as he wishes with them. He revels in this illusory power to destroy ordinary values, to feel excitedly, superhumanly beyond such humble restraints. In his writing, he insists on his Caligulalike role (enraged, indulged, omnipotent child); whatever he wants, any whim or caprice, must be gratified. *The 120 Days of Sodom* is to demonstrate that Sade is master of the universe, of a universe that he can transform, as he wills. No one, character or reader, can resist. Everyone's autonomy is to be destroyed; no differentiation or separateness is tolerated. All is one and one is all!

The reader can respond with some interest and even some sexual curiosity and excitement to the initial scenes in *The 120 Days of Sodom*. *Some* sexual sadism can, indeed, be arousing. But the reader soon feels oppressed, bored, and tortured by the endless repetition and increasing destruction of human relatedness in the writing. It often feels as if the author rubs the reader's nose in the fact that the reader is not strong enough to tolerate imagining himself in the role of Sade's sadists. The author/narrator seems to revel in the reader's disgust and revulsion; intense response of any kind in the reader seems to confirm the author/narrator's power. The reader imagines that only his boredom and indifference would disappoint "Sade." But even when the reader feels bored and indifferent, he can imagine "Sade" contemptuously gesturing that the reader cannot stomach the author's tales.

Indeed, I failed in my earlier attempts to complete reading this novel. Only when I had become able to tolerate more fully my own sadism and destructiveness, could I then allow myself, at least partially, to resonate with these qualities in the author/narrator and in the characters and thus to finish reading this novel. Even so, I had to make a conscious effort to use my reading experience of *The 120 Days of Sodom* as a therapeutic exploration of myself in order to complete reading it. Reading the end of the novel was painful and unsatisfying; I longed to have finished reading it. The reading experience of colleagues (psychoanalysts and professors of literature) in a study group on psychoanalysis and literature was similar. All of them had considerable difficulty reading the beginning of the novel; none ventured beyond the required assignment!

Chasseguet-Smirgel (1978) compares *The 120 Days of Sodom* with *The Bible*; one denies differentiation, the other proclaims it. For Chasseguet-Smirgel, the inferior, illusory fecal penis is claimed, in the anal-sadistic universe of perversion, to be superior to the paternal phallus, which the child, pervert, or Sade feels he does not possess. This is exhibited and affirmed through such outrageous writing.

The need to undo and reverse Sade's awful helplessness and insignificance because of his imprisonment seems to be a major contributant, to the cloistered, dungeonlike images in his fiction. Chasseguet-Smirgel's (1978, 1983) suggestion is apt, that these dungeonlike pictures refer to the bowels and the anal sphincter. The *120 Days of Sodom* especially emphasizes the author's (anal) power over his characters— *and over his readers*—to move and eliminate them at will. Being locked away from the world, helplessly imprisoned, unable to resist, having to submit, losing autonomy, identity, and bodily integrity, not mattering, being interchangeable, exchangeable, shit, nothing, are all repetitive themes here.

Although psychoanalysts are familiar with such sadistic anal themes, they have not considered that the writing/reading experience can enact such conflicts. Of course, psychoanalysts would expect that any behavior, including writing and reading, could be infiltrated by one's predominant conflicts and adapted to deal with them. Here I am attending to the interplay between self and other, author and reader, as it seems to have become overtaken by malignant sadomasochism. It is as if "Sade" is trading places with his reader, so that the latter becomes the helplessly imprisoned, worthless one. There is so little imaginative space granted the reader in which he can join the author in envisaging what is to come next.

The reader feels the unrelenting oppression of the writer's insistence that he will carry out his writing experiment to the very end, cataloguing every variant of perversion as he proceeds. The reader will not be let off the hook when he feels like arguing with the author that we have already been through this type of perversion sufficiently. Just as the writer cannot gain release from imprisonment, especially solitary confinement, and from crippling depression, so too must the reader be endlessly bombarded by the writer's repetitive outpourings. Indeed, endless repetition, with so little variation during prolonged intervals, makes the reader feel helplessly shackled. The reader's angry protests of "enough already" seem to mirror the writer's impotent rage about mistreatment. But if the writer succeeds in convincing himself that he has indeed traded places with his reader, he may certainly feel better, as the reader feels worse. Then the writer has, in fantasy, escaped from his prison—both real incarceration and psychological fetters—by getting the reader (and the characters) to take his place.

Intense feelings of despair and immobilization seem to be countered by insistence on an omnipotent entitlement to dominate and extract sadistically from others whatever one needs. Paradoxically, this aspect of sadistic entitlement preserves object relations and self-esteem regulation in the face of tendencies to give up on human relations. It is as if the sadist continues to claim that others, having neglected and deprived him, are responsible for his plight and owe him care. For the sadist (not for his objects), this may be better than psychosis or despair. Put another way, "Sade" would seem to manage better when he can feel enraged, powerful, and effective with others than when he succumbs to helpless despair and isolation. Certain people, who find ordinary human relations so taxing that they tend to wall themselves off from their needs of others, do indeed feel better when they allow themselves to reconnect with another in a hate-filled bond (see Coen 1992; Gabbard 1991).

The Destructive Child/God; or, How Can You Stop Being Angry When Paradise Can Never Be Yours?

Comparison of Sade with the God of the Bible is apt in the perverse sense of the biblical God as the angry child, whose grandiose, omnipotent illusions have been sorely frustrated. The contrast between parental deprivation and neglect, and the regal, grandiose illusions of what could be, tends to be incendiary and even more enraging. Other deprived children surrender with less protest. Sade, of course, also struggles (usually successfully) against wishes to surrender. Sade depicts so many scenes of sadistic exhibitionism, of people forced to watch others get their pleasure. Sade, in life and in fiction, insisted on having what he wanted, regardless of who owned it or of what the consequences, to others or to himself, might be. Sade's chronic rage at the deprivations and frustrations of childhood led to endlessly, repetitive attempts to regain his *rightful*, grandiose place and to the fixation of his pathological grandiose, entitled self-image.

Sade's need and ability to incite and arouse others mixes with his grandiosity and destructiveness and, at times, with prescience about what can be effected. In 1792, attempting to protect his estate at La Coste from the zeal of revolutionary destructiveness, he writes to the President of the Constitution Club at La Coste (Lély 1966:180; letter 29, April 19, 1792):

> If they remove a single stone from the house that I own within your city walls, I will present myself before our legislators, I will appear before your Jacobin comrades in Paris and request that they engrave

these words upon it: "Stone of the house of the one who caused those of the Bastille to fall and which the friends of the Constitution wrenched from the house of the most wretched of the victims of the tyranny of kings. Passers-by inscribe this outrage in the annals of human blunders!

Delusional grandiosity? No, indeed! Sade seemed well aware that the only way for him out of prison, given that Paris was almost ready for insurrection in the summer of 1789, was to provoke the storming of the Bastille. On July 2, 1789, with an improvised loudspeaker made from a metal funnel, he shouted from his window to the crowd in the square below that orders for the guards to kill all the prisoners in the Bastille had been issued and were already being executed. He urged the crowd, which soon swelled, to quickly come to his aid. Appropriately worried by Sade's behavior, the government quickly moved him to Charenton Asylum. Unfortunately, when the Bastille was stormed *twelve days later*, Sade's possessions, including his manuscripts (fifteen volumes ready for publication), were destroyed. His scroll of *The 120 Days of Sodom* was not recovered during his lifetime. Sometime during the nineteenth century it was discovered hidden in a wall of the cell Sade had occupied in the Bastille. Surprising to us now, and even more remarkable in Sade's provocation of the storming of the Bastille, is the fact that in July 1789 the Bastille housed only seven prisoners!

Sade began his writing in prison. It is clear, by now, how he wrote to preserve his sanity, protect his self-esteem, and master his needs of others. Especially in *The 120 Days of Sodom* Sade seeks to squelch sentimentality, concern, and affection. Such emotions are punishable within the novel by death—they are to be eradicated, replaced by sensuality. One is not to care about others. Fathers may fuck or kill their daughters without compunction. Mothers are to be killed so as to be rid of them and to get their goods. One is to cherish his freedom at the death of a mother, not to mourn her loss for a moment. For example, in *The 120 Days of Sodom*, pp.293–94, the Duc says:

Does that mother of ours give us happiness in giving us life? . . . Hardly. She casts us into a world beset with dangers, and once in it, 'tis for us to manage as best we can. I distinctly recall that, long ago, I had a mother who aroused in me much the same sentiments Duclos felt for hers: I abhorred her. As soon as I was in a position to do so, I dispatched her into the next world; may she roast there; never in my life have I tasted a keener delight than the one I knew when she closed her eyes for the last time.

When a young girl, whose mother recently died, cries on hearing this speech, the Duc has himself frigged by an older woman so that his sperm ejaculates at the entrance to the girl's vagina. In *Justine*, Rodin describes what a father's regard should be for his daughter (p. 552): "I place roughly the same value (weighing the matter very nicely) upon a little semen which has hatched its chick, and upon that I am pleased to waste while enjoying myself. One has the power to take back what one has given; amongst no race that has ever dwelled upon earth has there been any disputing the right to dispose of one's children as one sees fit."

Sade explicitly (e.g., *The 120 Days of Sodom*, p. 532) recommends sexualization for dealing with pain:

> One has got to learn how to make the best of the horror; there is in horror matter to produce an erection, you see, and the reason there-of is quite simple: this thing, however frightful you wish to imagine it, ceases to be horrible for you immediately it acquires the power to make you discharge; it is, hence, no longer horrible save in the eyes of others. . . . Nothing's villainous if it causes an erection, and the single crime that exists in this world is to refuse oneself anything that might produce a discharge.

Or again, in *Justine* (p. 460): "There was nothing one ought not do in order to deaden in oneself that perfidious sensibility."

Here the reader may have mixed reactions. Sade has described, long before psychoanalysts wrote about sexualization or erotization, a technique for managing psychic pain. Emphasis on sexual excitement can indeed temper painful feelings. The reader may indeed wish to share with the author the powerful role of repetitively seducing others to avoid what is wrong within. Everyone uses sexualized defense at times; those who are more sadomasochistic or perverse do so more often (Coen 1992). Sade can indeed tempt his reader to follow him in glorifying such sexualized misuse of others. If the reader can relax, enjoy, and identify with some of Sade's perverse exploitation of others, he can more easily become absorbed in this writing, at least for awhile. Indeed, I believe that the universal (ambivalent) appeal of Sade's advocacy of sexualized misuse of others is a prime reason that Sade continues to be read. But it is very difficult for the reader to feel immersed in Sade's fiction, to feel carried away sufficiently actually to participate in Sade's imaginary world. Sade's writing is just too controlled; there is just far too little imaginative space available for the reader to meet and collaborate with the author in shaping this fiction. As a result, the reader feels subordinate to, and distant from, the author/narrator, who insists that he alone is the only important one in the reading experience of this writing. Additionally, since most people cannot enjoy the degree of Sade's sadistic destruction of human relatedness, he cannot easily be followed in such exercises. But I believe that the reader's greatest difficulty is that the writing consists of exercises of cataloguing fantasies and so is not a coherent imaginative novel in which the reader can abandon himself. Indeed, the reader wishes the author/narrator could let go of his intense control and abandon himself in his writing, so that the reader could feel more involved with the text and freer to feel involved with the imagined author. Sade just does not invite his readers' closeness, although he certainly does seem to crave it secretly.

One way Sade protects himself from yearnings for others, and wishes to surrender to them, is by his negativism, superiority, and contempt for everyone but himself. He needs to dissociate himself from what/who is available to him and from what is wrong: for self-definition, to enhance self-esteem, as a denial of craziness and helplessness (I cause/choose it myself), and to resist further surrender and regression. Also contributing is the defense against (unconscious) guilt manifested by his attacking everyone else and justifying himself.

To his wife, he writes (Lély 1966, pp.152–53; letter 22, 1783):

> O manufacturer of this evil little round ball, you who perhaps with one single breath set ten thousand million spheres like our own in the immensity of space, you whom the death of these ten thousand million would not cost even a sigh, what amusement you must find in all the imbecilities of the little ants with which it has pleased you to scatter your globes; how you must laugh at the King of Achem who whips seven hundred women and the Emperor of Golconda who uses them as a post-chaise and the *"homme noir"* who expects one to keep one's head when one spills one's sp—! Good night, my little wife.

The context for this is a diatribe against those who presume to judge Sade. He joins God in looking down contemptuously at those who foolishly pretend to uphold Christian morality.

Sometimes his self-justifications seem silly and totally implausible (see, for example, Lély 1966: 77; letter 7, February 20, 1781—the note in his wallet about how to abort a woman). He certainly is fascinated with the themes of pregnancy, birth, and abortion. In his "long letter" to Madame de Sade (Lély 1966: ; letter 7, February 20, 1781), he especially attempts to justify himself as a libertine not a criminal. He describes his kindnesses to others, as if that should be sufficient to demonstrate his worthiness. His self-criticism is really quite superficial. At least in these letters, he shows little overt guilt and responsibility for what he has done/felt. For example (Lély 1966:80; letter 7, February 20, 1781): "Here then is the letter; written as if I was on the point of death, so that if I should suddenly die before I have the comfort of taking you in my arms once more, I may with my dying breath refer you to the feelings expressed in the present letter, as to the last ones that a heart anxious to take at least your good opinion to the tomb will address to you."

Unconscious guilt and the need for punishment and containment are suggested by Sade's outrageous refusal to learn from experience and to modify his desires, so as to adapt to the reality of his world, thereby unconsciously (provoking) arranging for others to punish and regulate him; by his own need to be beaten; and by his and his characters' need for forgiveness and acceptance from others by getting others to participate in his orgies and to take on the burden of his (guilty) suffering—in effect by trading places with him. A predominant motivation in Sade's disguised pathological dependency may be a need for another to regulate and contain his destructiveness, so that he and his object world can survive. I suggest that this is an important goal of his prison writing; he seeks to enact a sadomasochistic dependent relationship with his imaginary readers. Alongside and under the obvious sadism is an intense dependent need for the reader to contain and absolve the writer's destructiveness, so that he can preserve his psychic world. Sade simultaneously seems to want to destroy everyone *and* to affirm and deny that self and other cannot live separately. Sade does not report genuine remorse. His bad feelings seem to function mainly for this more primitive self-regulation.

The other's unwanted and unexpected arousal, and thereby involuntary participation, may make the sadist feel accepted and forgiven. In Sade's fiction there are innumerable images of characters becoming sexually aroused and involved despite themselves. Note, for example, the many accounts early in *The 120 Days of Sodom* of monks delighting in initiating young girls into sexual arousal. The other is to exist solely to serve one's own needs, to relinquish her/his own. The child/god again becomes triumphant in insisting on his centrality, that he is indeed to run the show. Meanwhile, the other/parent is to respond, admire, love, gratify, forgive, obey. It is as if the sadist says to the other/parent, "Since you allow me to do as I wish with you, it must mean that all is forgiven, that you love and admire me." Intense response from the other includes negative reactions of outrage, disgust, and revulsion, which Sade's reader cannot fail to deliver. The reader cannot remain indifferent to the author/narrator but is compelled to respond vigorously, reaffirming "Sade's" power and authority. At least angry response from others, almost against their will, counters one's loneliness, isolation, and helplessness. Much of the repetition and progression of *The 120 Days of Sodom* demonstrates this by increasingly greater tyranny over others to the point of their destruction, interchangeability, nonexistence. Sade avers that the other's life depends on him just as his life, unfortunately, depends on the other.

Here is a relatively mild example (among many) from *Justine* (pp. 585–86):

> When five o'clock strikes, the Girl of the Watch promptly descends to the monk she serves and does not leave his side until the next day, at the hour he sets off for the monastery. She rejoins him when he comes back; she employs these few hours to eat and rest, for she must remain awake all night throughout the whole of the term she spends with her master; . . . the wretch remains constantly on hand to serve as the object of every caprice which may enter the libertine's head; cuffs, slaps, beatings, whippings, hard language, amusements, she has got to endure all of it; she must remain standing all night long in her patron's bedroom, at any instant ready to offer herself to the passions which may stir that tyrant; but the cruelest, the most ignominious aspect of this servitude is the terrible obligation she is under to provide her mouth or her breast for the relief of the one and the other of the monster's needs: he never uses any other vase: she has got to be the willing recipient of everything and the least hesitation or recalcitrance is straightaway punished by the most savage reprisals . . . at the suppers her place is behind her master's chair or, like a dog, at his feet under the table, or upon her knees, between his thighs, exciting him with her mouth; sometimes she serves as his cushion, his seat, his torch. . . . If they lose their balance, they risk either falling upon the thorns placed near by, or breaking a limb, or being killed.

Or (p. 635): "As of the present moment you inhabit the world no longer, since the least impulse of my will can cause you to disappear from it. What can you expect at my hands? Happiness if you behave properly, death if you seek to play me false."

An angry, hungry, urgent neediness precludes frustration, patience, and tolerance. In *Justine*, when an uncle of the Count de Bressac's dies, leaving him a considerable inheritance, Justine encourages him to wait for the death of his aunt rather than to poison her so as to acquire her money. "'Wait?' the Count replied sharply" (p. 523) "'I do not intend to wait two minutes . . . are you aware I am twenty-eight? Well, it is hard to wait at my age.'" Especially in *The 120 Days of Sodom*, perhaps because of the author's prison isolation, depression, and the danger of further regression into psychotic disorganization, there is a need for continual stimulation, contact, excitement, arousal, triumph, exploitation, domination. Other instances of his writings (letters and fiction) are less driven and intense; they are calmer and easier. The intensity of the need for the other, together with the dangers of loss, hurt, frustration, as well as of the wish for passive masochistic surrender, can lead to extreme denial, devaluation, dehumanization, and insistence on omnipotent control and manipulation of the other. One aspect of this urgent neediness is expressed sexually. The repetitive cataloging of what seems like every imaginable sexual desire, except for mutual loving and tenderness, encourages its readers to regard *The 120 Days of Sodom* as a textbook of the polymorphous perverse. Here, the author's intention does not seem to be primarily to share with his readers his own passions but to overwhelm and shock those readers, to trade places with them as he does with his characters. What seems most exciting to Sade is what is most forbidden and outrageous and what elicits the most intense response from his partners and himself.

Chasseguet-Smirgel (1978) proposes that Sade's excitement, and the excitement in sadism, is the anal-sadistic destruction of reality, and its replacement by the anal abolition of all differences. This is an important contribution. However, there is no reason to make this so concrete, as if everything else could be eliminated. Differences remain, and remain exciting and frustrating! Incestuous wishes (positive and negative) persist intensely in Sade; they are defended against by partial denial, devaluation, and destruction. To take but one example: in *The 120 Days of Sodom* the fathers delight in seducing their young daughters and marrying them. However, they then share their daughters/wives with their friends and insist that this father/daughter attraction is meaningless, easily dispensed with. But that is untrue. To dispose of their incestuous desires, the fathers must dispose of their daughters' attractiveness and ultimately of their daughters. The dangerous woman/mother must be tamed, reduced, or shunned, either by contempt, domination, or brutality or by turning away from her to men as sexually desirable. Fully allowing oneself to need and love a woman/mother seems to be the most dangerous relationship of all (Deleuze 1971; Socarides 1974).

Given the emphasis one expects to encounter on sadism in Sade's life and work, his fictional characters' relationships and his own (in his letters) lean more in the direction of hatred. Pao (1965) pointed out that a relationship "perpetuated" by hatred differs from a sadomasochistic relationship in that there is less libido tempering the hate. Pao especially noted the organizing, stabilizing function of chronic, hateful relationships and of feelings of hatred; hatred involves the ego's assimilation and attempted mastery of rage. In my view (Coen 1992), sadism may be regarded as an effort to manage rage and destructiveness by illusory transformation into an exciting sexual game (sexualization).

Sade needs to keep telling his readers that, since nature intends there to be destructiveness, it is not to be judged as bad. Instead it is to be enjoyed, to become the stuff of libertinage. The danger for Sade's characters is depletion, loss, abandonment, total destruction of needed objects, so that they are truly alone. At the end of *The 120 Days of Sodom*, not everyone has been murdered. Certain vitally needed people, such as the three cooks, must be preserved! Even Sade's most notorious libertines must know when to stop! Thus, there is oscillation in Sade's work between rage and destructiveness, hatred and sexual sadism. I suggest that when he (author/narrator) is best able to manage, his writing is calmer, easier, with aggression appearing mainly in the form of sexual sadism. When he is most threatened with being overwhelmed and unable to manage himself, his writing is urgent and frantic. Aggression then emerges more crudely as wanton destructiveness, in a blind-yet-systematic, rage-filled attempt to subjugate, reduce, and eliminate the hated but needed object. Then the self feels small and insignificant in relation to the overvalued powerful object by whom one is discarded or ignored. The enraged, impotent self denies and attempts to reverse this helplessness and bondage by attempts to seduce, exploit, dominate, denigrate, mutilate, or murder the object. To the degree that one feels unable to manage alone, the vitally needed object cannot really be gotten rid of, no matter how loudly one talks about murder. Such fantasies of escape from bondage by murdering the needed object, at some point, must be undone. There must be reassurance, through some intense (sexual) responsiveness, that the needed object survives. It is an illusion that one can murder (get rid of) such a vitally needed object. So long as the need persists, the internal presence of such an introject is keenly felt. External objects can easily, endlessly be replaced. The imaginary reader reassures the (destructive) writer that he has indeed not murdered his vitally needed object.

At times, Sade can let go of his vindictiveness, of his need to stay attached in a hateful relationship. He writes to his attorney (Lély 1966:185; letter 31, August 3, 1793): "During my presidency [of The Section des Piques] I had the Montreuils put on a recommendations for mercy list. I had only to say the word and they would have had a rough time. I said nothing; that's how I take my revenge!" Does he mean to deny his relinquishment of vengefulness in the very act of doing so? He tempers his reasonableness with competitive superiority and contempt for his tormentors. Lély (1962) points out that Sade's interventions, on behalf of a number of people who had been denounced as plotting against the Revolution, were probably responsible for Sade's arrest some months later. Sade's destructiveness, given the reign of terror in revolutionary France, seems at this point to have been well in check!

Hatred, and a focus on murdering the object one denies needing, can serve (Hill 1938; Pao 1965; Bollas 1984/1985), partly, as defense against dependency (especially wishes to be cared for and loved), passivity, and helplessness. As I have noted, Sade allows so little tenderness in his writing. Even while working so hard at inciting his readers, he does not acknowledge how much he craves their response. It is so refreshing when Sade, more undisguisedly, announces his human needs of others, contemporaries, characters, or readers. Similarly, his overdone libertinage attempts to conceal what he wants from others. It is not just to be sexually aroused around the clock, as he would claim. In certain respects (Margolis 1977; Coen 1981), it is less humiliating to view oneself as hateful, cruel, or thoroughly perverse, than to acknowledge one's childlike, irresistible hunger for others' care and concern.

When the author/narrator seems to feel most impotent and insignificant, *or* when he fears he will uncontrollably destroy his world, is when he seems tempted by the wish to surrender to an idealized/aggrandized other. Passive masochistic surrender offers the promise of a comforting, protective, containing parent, who will totally take over one's care and responsibility for one's global destructiveness. Note that passive masochistic surrender is not the same as despair in human relations, immobilization and giving up. Rather, it is another way to defend against these greater dangers. Although Sade can acknowledge some of his wishes for surrender to his Lauras and to death, he must deny this in relation to his captors (jailers, mother-in-law, France). He must repeatedly enact his wish to provoke others into being his tormentor/captor since he cannot acknowledge this wish. The ritualization and repetition of Sade's *The 120 Days of Sodom* seems to reassure the author/narrator against such wishes for merger. Here, intense feeling, sexual or angry, in the self or in the other, serves to counter the danger that one has ceased to exist. Rage and hatred then help to define boundaries between self and other (Epstein 1977), just as they help to energize the self rather than yield to despair and immobilization. Sade cannot dispense with a relation with a powerful other, who is to be responsible for him, even as he plays at reversing who is who in this game.

Perverse Writers Compared

Certain similarities should be noted in the fiction of other angry, perverse, provocative authors. Jean Genet (see chapter 2) and Louis-Ferdinand Céline (see chapter 3) similarly engage their characters and readers in a relationship marked by manipulation, control, domination, and mistrust. The other's (readers and characters) autonomy is to be denied. The author is to be responded to intensely—with excitement, admiration, or loathing—so that he can feel valued, affirmed, loved, significant. Neither characters nor readers are allowed to be on their own long enough to develop their own perspective. The author/narrator insists so on shaping and developing the characters' and readers' responses (to him) that there is little aesthetic freedom for anyone but the author. In this type of writing, the author seems unwilling and unable to allow the reader, or the characters, to truly participate on their own as collaborators. Each author revels in showing, to himself and his readers, that his characters are the creations of *his imagination*, so that he can mistreat them if he so chooses. In all of this writing, the characters may briefly turn to others but, unable really to trust and need others, they must remain hungry, discontent, and bitter. Tenderness, caring, and need are to be denied and eliminated, replaced by sensuality, excitement, and misuse of others. Like Sade, Genet began writing in prison, seemingly feeling depressed, angry, isolated, abandoned. It should be clear by now how useful becoming a writer can be for a creative prisoner. Céline's post-World War II novels were written when the author felt depressed, bitter, and withdrawn. Céline had been tried as a Nazi collaborator; an infuriated France ignored him as if he were already dead. Although not imprisoned, Céline, like Sade and Genet, felt shut away from the public acceptance he craved so intensely. The author creates his own fantastic (literary) world as a substitute for the despair and isolation of prison life; and he insists that his readers (imaginary and real) validate this. Similarly, he attempts to transform whatever is bad and worthless in himself into something irresistibly evocative and creative, either beautiful or repulsive. This is a major goal for Sade, Genet, and Céline. Each describes well how much he seeks to turn the vile and loathsome into poetry. He can dream of acceptance and rebirth as a valued, admired author. Such magical, grandiose wishes for transformation and adoration by the world help to counter the outcast author's self-hatred, loneliness, neglect, and despair. To the degree that he is successful as a writer, he realistically gains attention and fame, and even, to a degree, succeeds in transforming himself from an outcast into a celebrated author. Ultimately, however, disappointment must follow. Such grandiose wishes, which can never be fulfilled, offer the promise that now finally the writer will be endlessly loved and admired, in contrast to the felt deprivation of childhood and ongoing self-hatred. This attempt at a writing cure must ultimately fail. Only in part can the author play at turning what he hates in himself into the stuff of poetry; ultimately he cannot rid himself of his badness, his destructiveness, and his self-loathing, which can never be sufficiently camouflaged or transformed by his literary images.

The abandoned, enraged, helpless author/child succeeds in intensely engaging his characters and his readers, insisting on his being attended to, as if it were his right. Unlike Sade, however, both Céline and Genet easily reveal how much they crave the reader's (and the characters') affection. Often this is right up front, captivating, seducing, pleading, annoying, infuriating. At times, the negativism in the author's language and style, and an exaggeration of destruction and rejection in the images, draw the reader in. The reader, in seeking something positive behind the negative, discovers instead, right beside him, an intensely needy author/narrator, who demands his acceptance.

Tenderness and affection, even in writing, seem more difficult for Sade. It may be that these other authors (Céline, Genet) felt safer asking for caring from unknown, imagined others (readers, characters) in a fictional medium, obscured by illusion, than from people more directly available. Direct expression of such needs to other living people may create much greater risks, making such authors feel much more vulnerable. To a degree, they seem less despairing, although depressed, and less enraged than Sade, in that they can more easily trust their acceptance as writers. Somehow Genet, despite the horrors of his childhood and his imprisonment, unlike Sade, was able to believe that others would find beauty in his writing. At least, he can risk asking this of his readers.

Abandonment, neglect, helplessness, rage, destruction, and murder run throughout all this fiction. Each author seems to need to reassure himself that his own vileness is the stuff of beauty and creativity. No matter how much he emphasizes his badness, he cannot be all bad, not beyond acceptance and admiration as a talented creator. Unfortunately, Sade's literary skills are not remarkable. He is not as talented a writer as either Céline or Genet. His notoriety, his daring and ability to explore the perverse and outrageous, his need to shock and inflame, are what have immortalized him (as he predicted).

Despite all the apparent wildness and perverse sexuality in this writing, it lacks abandon. No one really allows himself to value and need another. There is no risking of intimacy, commitment, or love. Instead, people play at surrender to sensual excitement and to (Parkin 1980) masochistic enthrallment. The dangers are too great of needing others and of the intense wish to surrender oneself fully to the aggrandized power of another. Sade's writing is more cerebral, more controlled than Genet's or Céline's. The reader cannot immerse himself in Sade's writing the way he can in fiction by Genet or Céline. Sade seems to have been unable to allow himself to become lost in his reveries, not knowing in advance where they would take him. His writing thus must remain shallow, on the surface. This contrasts with the Laura dream and its narration to Madame de Sade, which displays imaginative abandon and verve, as Céline would say. It is as if Sade can almost never forget, even briefly, so as to be able to enjoy creating, his own psychological goals in writing. These so overwhelm his writing project that there is no room for literary play or the unfettered use of his imagination. His writing remains sterile, not affording him the rewards of an unpredictable immersion into his own literary imagination, which might have better countered the barrenness of his prison life. To do otherwise, a depressed writer would have to be capable of some optimism, in his imagination, that he could find good (new) things in himself and with others. To take such a chance, he would have to be able to bypass his rage, destructiveness, and mistrust. Sade seems to have been too angry and mistrustful, and probably not sufficiently talented, to have been capable of this.

Part Two

SAMPLE CRITICISM:
AUTHORS AND THEIR
CRITICS; CRITICS AND
THEIR CRITICISM

Chapter 6

SOME EXAMPLES OF RECENT PSYCHOANALYTIC LITERARY CRITICISM: AN ASSESSMENT

In *The Literary Use of the Psychoanalytic Process* (1981) Skura offers an integrated, hierarchically organized approach to reading texts that includes content, function, mode of representation, rhetorical function, and process. Hers is an ambitious project of formulating a psychoanalytic model for reading texts. Skura is especially good on the *processes* of reading, understanding, and criticizing. She takes a subjectively interactional psychoanalytic perspective that emphasizes ambiguity and challenges the ordinary assumptions about reading and meanings; she struggles with what to do with the reader's responses and with how the subjective reading experience is to be related to the text's meaning.

Skura's central contention for both psychoanalysis and criticism is that what is most important is continual examination of process—psychoanalytic process or reading process—as the overall framework within which the constituents (content, function, mode of representation, rhetorical function) are to be considered. I agree with her contention that the radical questioning of our assumptions in reading and the ability to shift levels and modes of reading in order to tolerate ambiguity, contradiction, uncertainty, and complexity lead to more interesting and better readings of texts.

But I do not agree with her application of terms from the psychoanalytic process to reading. For instance, she refers to the reader's struggle with the complexities of a text as "working through." I consider that "working through" is accomplished only if readers do in fact succeed in new mastery and integration of their own inner conflicts through reading a text. I would argue that this is rarely accomplished during reading, that more often readers stabilize themselves defensively by the illusion of having rid themselves of what has been troublesome within (see chapter 8 of this book). I agree with Skura that what psychoanalysis contributes most to applied psychoanalysis is not specific psychosexual fantasy content but a complex approach to understanding people and their conflicts. But I do not agree that reading literature is akin to the psychoanalytic process.

Skura writes (p. 272) under the assumption that the psychoanalyst and critic "both seem to feel that they understand what each other does and can do it better—at least for their own purposes." From that premise, she then assigns priority to psychoanalysis as having revised literary criticism. She is not alone. Among others, Murray Schwartz (1982) also contends that psychoanalysis has "lastingly unmasked critical privileges." At the same time, both these thoughtful writers reflect on the revised contemporary perspective toward interpretation within psychoanalysis, literary criticism, the philosophy of science, and the rest of modern scholarship. That is, psychoanalysts, critics, and scholars now study not just intrapsychic content or meanings objectively located within a patient or text but also the investigator's investigation of patient or text. What is proved is always only something consistent with our assumptions and our procedures. Uncertainty, indeterminacy, relativism, and subjectivism thoroughly permeate our contemporary epistemology. As we question ourselves, our assumptions, and our procedures, we naturally look elsewhere for more radical models with which to understand what we are doing. Thus, it is inevitable that psychoanalysts will turn to literary critics to aid their understanding of understanding (hermeneutics) and that critics will idealize psychoanalysis as capable of informing meanings. There will be less disillusionment for both psychoanalysts and literary critics if we are more candid about our uncertainties, dilemmas, and unrealistic wishes that idealized others from another discipline will relieve these, and if we then settle for a much more limited collaboration between psychoanalysts and critics.

This is my major objection to Skura's otherwise fine reassessment of literary criticism in relation to psychoanalysis. Unlike Skura's, my experience has repeatedly been that participants in interdisciplinary study groups on applied psychoanalysis observe that the psychoanalysts and professors of literature are each turning to the other for better understanding of what interpretation is about. The psychoanalysts want to learn about criticism and the literature professors want to learn about psychoanalytic meaning that will add new dimensions to texts. A distinguished psychoanalytic author confided to me that he learns more about the processes of understanding and interpretation from reading literary critics than from psychoanalysts.

If Skura's book is read within the perspective of the current situation extant within literary criticism and psychoanalysis—that each is seeking help from the other—a more balanced and fair appraisal of the current scene emerges. Skura presents a thoughtful, comprehensive overview of trends within psychoanalytic literary criticism, useful to both critics and psychoanalysts. She raises the well-known problems of applied psychoanalysis, but her considerations are uniformly thoughtful, complex, and interesting.

Skura's identification of common themes within the language, story, narration, and reader's experience of the text is well done. Her transference model of exchanges between author and reader through the text is presented in terms of the variety of relationships "presumed" by the text with the reader. I agree with her criticism of applications of Winnicott's (1967) concept of "potential space" to applied psychoanalysis as simplistic. Skura presents an interesting contrast between narrative over control and an "imaginative play space" in her reading of Dickens's *The Old Curiosity Shop*.

Skura follows Lionel Trilling in arguing that psychoanalysis has constituted poetry and allegory as natural and native to the human mind. The connection here is with dreaming and its mechanisms; condensation and displacement are then related to metaphor and metonymy. I do not agree that poetry needs such legitimization from psychoanalysis. The dream is no more native to human experience than the poem. The role of fantasy in literature and the differences between artistic creation and intrapsychic content remain unclear in Skura's analysis.

As a professor of literature, practicing psychoanalyst, skilled reader and critic, Mahony has by now become well known to psychoanalytic readers through his four books (1982, 1984, 1986, 1989) about Freud's writings (see chapter 7 in this book). In 1984, when the Interdisciplinary Colloquium on Psychoanalysis and Literary Criticism was established at the American Psychoanalytic Association, he preferred to replace the term *literary criticism* with the term *discourse*. In *Psychoanalysis and Discourse* (1987), Mahony explains the psychoanalytic and literary reasons for this preference, claiming that psychoanalysis is unique in the history of discourse in terms of a transformation of its varieties (expressive, aesthetic, rhetorical, referential). He applies careful attention and analysis of formal elements of style (expression) both to patients and to texts.

What is most interesting about this book is the path Mahony has followed to reach his recent Freud criticism. All but one of the essays in *Psychoanalysis and Discourse* were published before his four volumes on Freud (see chapter 7 in this book). The evolution of Mahony's writing demonstrates the integration of his separate identities as practicing psychoanalyst and professor of English. The reader can trace his increasing confidence in these disparate talents and his growing conviction and passion about his own creativity and psychoanalytic skill, which lead to greater ease and pleasure in writing. Thus, the most recently written essay in this volume, "Further thoughts on Freud and his writing" (1984), although familiar, is the most delightful to read. What I enjoy most in Mahony's writing is the passion with which he immerses himself in a text. He allows himself to resonate with the work in multiple, relatively uncontrolled (primary process) ways and then carefully subjects this to systematic analysis—and invites the reader to join him.

He practices criticism both as formal *explication de texte* and as psychoanalytic resonance with derivative elements, instinctualized and defensive, embedded within the text. I retract my earlier (1988) criticism of Mahony's play with phonemes as too speculative. He was then surprised that I was so standoffish. I have become convinced of the value of his responsiveness to the multiple meanings of words, embedded words, sounds, references, allusions, and puns. As a polyglot, he is especially skillful at tracing meanings in the original language of texts.

Translation and transformation are ideas and metaphors that run through all of this work, imbuing it with energy as instinctualized derivatives within the text reverberate with the reader's (Mahony's) unconscious. Mahony shows us that Freud understood *Überzetzung* as both translation of ideas and affects into words and of unconscious material into consciousness. Mahony then connects "translation," "metaphor," and "transference" etymologically (p. 44): "Translation' comes from the Latin 'carried across'; the infinitive of that most irregular verb is *transferre*, from which comes 'transference.' What's more, the Greek for *transferre* is *metaphorein*! On one level, consequently, metaphor, transference, and translation are identical." In his practical criticism, Mahony continually emphasizes these connections between translation, transference, and metaphor. They come alive as he illustrates the movement between and among the author's unconscious, the text, and the reader's resonating preconscious apprehension of the text.

Mahony seeks to reclaim the "linguistic freedom" of free association by emphasizing (p. 21) that the German *Einfall* "denotes a spontaneous and coincidental falling out into the open." He contrasts (p. 42) the verticality of the image of ideas emerging from the unconscious with Freud's description of the technique whereby "a patient falls into the trap" [*"Geht der Patient in die Falle"*] (1925, *S. E.*, 19:235). He finds (p. 24) the one time Freud (1906, *S. E.*, 9:109) suggests that "'the most important sign' of a connection between two thoughts is the length of the patient's hesitation between them." Like Sharpe (1940), Mahony connects bodily functioning with speech; having established this association, Mahony implicates all forms of expression with psychosexuality. Hence the analyst needs to facilitate the analysand's recognition of such self-expression in whatever ways the analyst can recognize, not only via speech.

By connecting psychic functioning with poetry, Mahony can combine psychoanalytic with literary critical techniques of investigation (cf. the different use made of this connection by Skura 1981). In German, condensation and poetry (*Verdichtung* and *Dichtung*) are clearly interrelated. He follows Jakobson (1960) in emphasizing the important role played in dreams by metaphor (similarity) and metonymy (contiguity). Lacan (1966) equated metaphor with condensation and metonymy with displacement. Further, metaphor is typical of lyric poetry while metonymy is characteristic of epic poetry (Jakobson 1960). Rosen (1967) noted that patients tend to free associate in either lyrical or epic style. It is especially through poetry that Mahony convinces me that I have not appreciated sufficiently the importance of sounds as a vehicle for conveying meanings in psychoanalysis.

Mahony's formalist analysis of the Irma dream is impressive in establishing a "homology between grammatical structure and semantic content" (p. 116). From the German, he demonstrates multiple visual, vertical, temporal, and pronominal shifts and emphases, not obvious in Strachey's translation, which connect further with Freud's guilt and his desires.

Chapter 7 in this book will introduce those unfamiliar with Mahony's books on Freud to processive writing and reading and the polyphonic quality of Freud's prose. Mahony is masterful in demonstrating the multiple levels of complexity in Freud's writing and in reading him. Mahony is also a good storyteller, as in his tale about Freud and Jung and the development of the International Association of Psychoanalysis and its parallel enactment (especially of competitive annihilation) in Freud's writing of *Totem and Taboo*.

In his chapters of literary criticism, Mahony displays his skill at close reading; he is a fine critic. My favorite of these essays is his comparison of Ben Jonson's two poems about the deaths of his young children: "On My First Son" and "On My First Davghter." From both content and the communicative structure of the latter poem, Mahony derives the poet's guilty sexual desires, including those toward his infant daughter. Mahony is especially good at identifying those aspects of literary style that are inconsistent, as a psychoanalyst would do with a patient, and then drawing inferences from these. He does this well with examples of syntactical inversion and ellipsis (omission of words) in Shakespeare's Sonnet 20, arguing that this furthers the anal erotic homosexual theme to be found in this sonnet. With Kafka's "A Hunger Artist," he highlights the author's skillful shifts between the particular and the universal in referring to the hunger artist. Mahony's ironic contrasts between the hunger artist and the dying Christ are well done.

The psychoanalytic profession is privileged to have a writer of Mahony's caliber, who is able to combine the skills and talents of clinical psychoanalysis and literary criticism, or as Mahony would say, discourse.

I agree wholeheartedly with *Reed* (1985) that the spirit of the psychoanalytic approach, as within the psychoanalytic situation, is more useful in applied psychoanalysis than is psychoanalytic theory. We agree in opposing dogmatism, certainty, and the search for single meanings in applied psychoanalysis. Opening questions, exploring ambiguities, uncertainties, and contradictions, lead to more satisfying readings of literature and art—and of analysands. Psychoanalysts, however, are not alone in such an approach, nor is it only the clinical psychoanalytic process that guides us toward such currently popular views of the complexities of the reading experience. Various literary critics (especially reader-response criticism) have emphasized the importance of paying careful attention to what the reader struggles with in reading a text— the difficulties, traps, frustrations, interruptions, etc. These must be somehow involved with understanding and interpreting texts. Psychoanalytic writers have pointed cautiously to certain similarities between the psychoanalytic situation and reading texts; in addition to Reed, Skura (1980) and I (Coen 1982 a and b; 1984) have taken such an approach. What we all struggle with—still—is methodology. How can psychoanalysis be used to read texts?

In contrast to Reed, I would not assign priority to psychoanalysis as capable of organizing readings of texts (around central unconscious fantasies involved in a compromise formation as the surface of a text), (see chapter 1 in this book). Identifying an organizing unconscious fantasy may or may not provide the most persuasive reading of a text. Other readings may be more satisfying and cogent. By now it should be clear that I do not assume that literature, on its surface, is a compromise formation. If literature is not reduced to a compromise formation, then our task is not necessarily to discern a central conflict or unconscious fantasy within it.

My view is that the identification of a central conflict and the unconscious fantasy involved in a text is only *one* of many readings that can be offered. To assume, as Reed does, that texts are indeed organized by conflict and fantasy does give a privileged position to psychoanalytic readings. Even the search for conflict and unconscious fantasy does not necessarily lead to agreement as to how to designate "the" conflict and fantasy. Analysts reading texts, as in practicing their clinical work, will often not agree on what is at issue. I concur with Reed's emphasis on the need for persuasive evidence for the hypotheses we formulate. Again, psychoanalysts and critics alike can heighten our awareness of the difficulties, complexities, and pleasures in reading texts.

I agree with Reed's emphasis that open exploration of texts is desirable and with the view that the clinical psychoanalyst attempts to tolerate and encourage ambiguity, uncertainty, contradiction, and avoid foreclosure. I do not agree that psychoanalytic theory is fixed and bound so as to mean precisely what it says. Nor do I believe that all psychoanalytic theory is a set of "verbal propositions which generalize phenomena originally discovered in other psychoanalytic explorations of individual utterance" (p. 237). I find G. S. Klein's (1976) division of psychoanalytic theory into a clinical and general theory useful. The clinical theory is derived from the psychoanalytic situation but is not just a secondary process translation of unconscious latent content. That is, the word does not just fix the unconscious fantasy. Clinical generalizations are not written encodings of unconscious fantasies. They are attempts to derive hypotheses from clinical data, which are heuristical-ly useful for more than one analysand. They are attempts at under-standing and interpreting, which ultimately have their value and valid-ity in their applicability to the psychoanalytic process. The correctness of psychoanalytic understandings is largely functional—based on their efficacy in furthering and deepening the psychoanalytic process, lead-ing to intrapsychic change. From this perspective, there is no way to use any aspect of psychoanalytic theory, general or clinical, dogmatically or a priori. Any hypothesis has to be tested in the clinical situation, or rather, has to be derived and based on the specific unfolding of this one particular psychoanalytic situation. Theories are hypotheses, whose usefulness depends on specific clinical data.

Formal criteria for the correctness of a psychoanalytic interpretation are really aesthetic criteria such as those offered by Kris and Kaplan (1948) (correspondence, intent, and coherence) or Schafer (1980:83) (comprehensiveness, consistency, coherence, and "conformity with refined common sense"). Formal criteria for the correctness of a psy-choanalytic interpretation apply at the time the interpretation is made. Functional criteria, of furthering the psychoanalytic process, can only be assessed later. Freud (1937), Kris (1951), Schafer (1976), Lipton (1977), Leavy (1980), Coen (1987), and others emphasize functional criteria for the correctness of an interpretation. I think that when a skilled psychoanalyst such as Arlow (1981) suggests that analysts do tend to know whether an interpretation is correct at the time it is prof-fered, he means that he can probably *predict* the effectiveness of an interpretation.

In Reed's reading of a poem by Mallarmé ("L'Après-Midi d'un Faune"), she demonstrates well the interconnections through the read-ing experience of wishes in sensuous and bodily desires in fantasy and in creative activity. This poem is a good exercise in reading literature because it informs us constantly that it is difficult to read, that it cannot be pinned down easily. The poem certainly evokes our difficulties with desiring another as we shift among lust for another real being, our own fantasies, our own creative activities, sexual union and masturbation, act, daydream, dream, and so on. Reed's attention to the connections between form and content in the poem is similarly helpful.

Thus, I agree enthusiastically with Reed's approach to the Mallarmé poem, except for her view of compromise formation. We agree that sig-nifiers have endless meanings, that the surface and depth of a text are to be played against each other, that the unreadability of a text leads us both to wish for certain meanings and to open up manifold, contradictory, unreconcilable meanings, and so forth. That a signifier has multiple meanings does not, however, necessarily mean that it is a compromise formation that expresses and reconciles a specific unconscious conflict. That perspective overemphasizes the role of conflict in creative acts; in Reed's model, it transforms a possibility into dogma. It would be much more interesting to attempt to assess the role of conflict in a given work, if that could indeed be done. And then, we would have to argue in whom this conflict exists—in the author, in the text, in its characters, in its narrator, or in its readers.

I certainly agree with Reed's emphasis on exploring contradictions in texts and in readers' and critics' responses to them. Her earlier work on Diderot (1982) is an interesting attempt to use the concept of parallelism to understand the contradictions in critics' understandings of a text. Reed's approach leads to interesting readings of texts although not necessarily to the author's unconscious fantasy. An open nondogmatic approach to applied psychoanalysis would have to present convincing evidence that would connect organizing themes in texts with organizing themes in the author's life, and to demonstrate that a major function of the writing was to master this conflict.

The eminent French literary critic and psychoanalyst, Julia Kristeva (1982), discusses abjection and horror in life, religion, and literature thoughtfully, especially drawing on the writings of Louis-Ferdinand Céline (see chapter 3 in this book). Kristeva argues that literature, especially modern "literature of abjection," has replaced, to a degree, religious ways of confronting and tolerating abjection. Literary style, its rhythm, music, tempo, beauty, transcends the powers of horror, surviving them, creating meaning out of contemporary meaninglessness. Kristeva does a fine, close semantic and literary analysis of Céline's style. Her readers should be aware however that Kristeva's style, as translated into English, often merely points to meanings or tersely asserts ideas as if they were universally accepted. As a result, this is a difficult book to read until the final six chapters, which draw on Céline's work and where the arguments are more fully elaborated.

Unfortunately, Kristeva's discussions draw on early Freud, notice Winnicott, and then rush immediately into criticism, leaning heavily on Lacan. Even worse, psychoanalytic ideas are used so abstractly and interpretations are, at times, made so certainly and exclusively, that the sensitivity, complexity, and thoughtful humility with which psychoan-

alysts interpret is lost. Of course, certain French psychoanalysts emphasize the obligatory role of the paternal phallus as symbol for differentiation from the maternal imago and the development of triangular
object relations.

Kristeva exaggerates the malevolent intentions of the primal mother
toward thwarting separation and individuation. As a result, abjection
largely becomes equated with maintenance of the boundary between
self and other [mother]. Although this is the most primitive issue that
must be repudiated as *abject*, many other meanings need to be attributed to what we regard as abject. Too many of humanity's unspeakable
horrors are here reduced to symbiotic wishes and fears, as dread of the
feminine and maternal. Nevertheless, Kristeva continually emphasizes
the aggression that underlies fear, the active destructive wishes that
hide out as passivity. She does not consider, as I would like her to have
done, why and how one becomes so frightened of active ownership of
hostile aggression that it must be so carefully hidden. As a result, Kristeva's psychoanalytic discussion of abjection tends to become reduc-
tionist.

Her discussion of Jewish and Christian religious ritual as sacred con-
trapuntal maneuvers for dealing with the abominable is well done. So
is her contrast between Jewish and Christian external and internal
modes for excluding and assimilating horror. Fascination with horror,
a central premise of her book, is taken as self-evident rather than
explored in detail. Fascination need not be only the other side of the
coin of repudiation. Fascination with drives, acts, and objects has a
more complex psychodynamic explanation, one that includes, for
example, sado-masochistic dependent wishes to submit to the power of
a fascinating object (for example, see Siegman 1964; Coen 1992).

Kristeva explains well how Céline's narrative is disrupted so as to
emphasize style. This occurs through use of spoken words (slang), the
words coming alive with emotion, as well as by the twists and turns,
starts and stops, of the narration, language, and semantics. Her semantic analysis of Céline's texts (expanding earlier work by the French lin-
guist Leo Spitzer) emphasizes the need for communication between
subject (writer) and object (writer as well as reader) as more significant
than the content of the statements. Intense awareness and anxiety
about the other's (the reader's) presence is well demonstrated in
Céline's narrative style. Kristeva connects this with the developmental
sequence of the child's pleasure in enunciation and awareness of the
person addressed that eventually leads to the establishment of imper-

sonal syntax. In Céline, there is not regression to such infantile levels but a conscious calling attention to them so as to heighten the emotional interplay between narrator and reader. Other techniques in the writing are shown to invite the reader's participation and fantasy and to intensify the speaker's affectivity.

I agree with Kristeva's emphasis that for Céline, "the speaking subject displays his desire and calls upon the reader to embrace it, beyond words, through the archaic configuration of melody—the original mark of syntax and subjective position" (p. 200). Aesthetic beauty through language—that is, style—is the only thing that is meaningful for Céline. Everything else is chaotic, evanescent, risky, frustrating, disappointing. I would add, which Kristeva does not, that Céline's narrators play out with their readers this passionately desired yet dreaded (as dangerous, frustrating, disappointing) relationship in which the literary creator of such beauty is to be admired forever.

In contrast to Kristeva's excellent discussion of Céline's style, is her unconvincing (psycho)analysis of thematic content in Céline's texts; for example, her discussions of mothers or of anti-Semitism. What is most important in this book is the connection between semantic and psychological analysis of literary style, a relatively neglected issue in applied psychoanalysis.

Literary Criticism Is Not Psychobiography

Here I want to consider further the problems caused by undue attention to the search for the author's unconscious organizing fantasy in a piece of psychoanalytic literary criticism. In Reed's practical criticism, careful attention to close literary analysis remains paramount and is successful, despite the search for the author's unconscious organizing fantasy. In the two examples that follow, heavy-handed imposition of psychodynamic interpretation impedes, rather than advances, literary criticism. The reader should be aware that these two authors, in contrast to those considered so far in this chapter, are practicing psychoanalysts but not literary critics. Simon (1992 unpublished), as chair of a subcommittee of the editorial board of the *Journal of the American Psychoanalytic Association* of which I have been a member, has recommended that work in applied psychoanalysis should integrate the methodological sophistication of this borderline between psychoanalysis and the field to which it is addressed. Thus, a psychoanalytic literary critic needs to be skilled in the methodology of literary criticism, of psychoanalysis, and of their integration as psychoanalytic literary criticism. In practice, this virtually seems to require that one be both a literary critic and a psychoanalyst.

Berman (1985) argued in "The Kidnapping of W. S. Gilbert" that the author's personal myth of a kidnapping at age two was of central importance in Gilbert's writing. Berman presents his readers with many samples from Gilbert's work of the theme of stolen and switched babies, sadistic impulses toward children, and jealousy and hatred toward a rival. The theme of switching places with another, whether sibling or father, can then be argued easily from the literary samples. Themes of separation and reunion and wishes for active mastery of childhood trauma are well argued within this model. So too is it plausible that forgetting in the works relates to wishes to defend against painful memories. Berman raises the issue, relatively neglected in applied psychoanalysis, of the functions of aesthetic form and uses this to advance his main thesis.

By the end of the paper, his readers can certainly agree with Berman that Gilbert's "creative efforts function as an obsessional defense" (p. 147) against painful memories and affects. At the start of the paper, however, Berman reminds his readers of the "healthy adaptations and sublimations" (p. 134) involved in creativity. Berman's perspective then is that Gilbert's art, although he shows his readers some exceptions, was a generally successful defense against conflict, involving healthy adaptation and leading to actual success. Nevertheless, pathography is central to this paper.

Berman (p. 9) refers to Gilbert's "assertion that the favorite theme in his literary works was also a real event in his childhood." The reader has not been shown that Gilbert's favorite theme was indeed kidnapping, only that kidnapping is a prominent theme in Gilbert's works. He has also quoted Gilbert's original biographer, Edith Browne as reporting the story of the kidnapping, which she says she heard from Gilbert. There certainly may be more evidence that establishes the importance of this story or memory for Gilbert, but Berman's readers have not been given this evidence. On the contrary, we have been told that some biographers assume that Gilbert was playing. Most crucially, we do not know what role this story or memory actually played in Gilbert's life, other than that he told it once to a biographer. Berman's suspicion that Gilbert's two youngest sisters were twins is certainly interesting in relation to images in the works of twins, divided people, splitting in two and coming together. Berman asserts twice (pp. 144–45) that we now know the artist's nuclear fantasy, which we can then refind in his literary work or in the episode when Gilbert at age 15 wanted to apprentice himself to the actor Charles Kean. We have no way of knowing the importance to Gilbert of the play, *The Corsican Brothers*, in which Kean was performing, with its twin motif, compared to other motivations. Once we have taken for granted we know Gilbert's nuclear fantasy, then, of course, we assume that his behavior is motivated by this. This is tautological and much too speculative.

This pathographic approach tends to reduce readers' pleasure in the author's writing and to reduce possibilities and meanings rather than to enhance them. The latter should be our goal in applied psychoanalysis. Thus Berman's attention to form, in relation to paradoxes, reversals, reciprocals, and opposites rather than being considered within the text itself for its literary and psychological functions is *assumed* to relate to wishes to switch places with the baby sister, as well as with the father (cf. Berman 1976). Ellis's (1970) introduction to *The Bab Ballads* stresses their pantomime quality, brutal jokes, startling surprises and transformations, and their ordered, controlled tempo and rhythm: "their spirited dactyls and anapests hurrying one along, their tempting but tongue-twisting alliterations and consonances, and their pompously reverberating syllabics" (pp. 21–22). Ellis contrasts the stiff, wooden quality with the occasional soaring or bounding. Self-importance, pomposity contrasts with greed, hunger, sadism, and childishness in theme, sound, movement, and so forth.

This is a fascinating area for further study; nonsense verse especially emphasizes playfulness, the need to be recited aloud, changes, twists and turns, and so on. Contrasts within the themes and style between reserve, order, and mocked goodness are especially well rendered in the poems "The Rival Curates" (Gilbert 1862–1884; reprint 1970, pp. 120–121), "Pasha Bailey Ben" (pp. 169–71), and "The Variable Baby" (pp. 266–67). Berman (p. 142) aligns these greedy and sadistic trends "toward children" with his major thesis. I am not sure that the poems justify his doing so. That is, the contrasts seem to be more between exaggerated adult reserve, respectability, and seeming virtue and all the greedy, envious, angry childish passions. Berman's reading of "The Baby's Vengeance" (Gilbert 1862–1884; reprint 1970, pp. 225–28) similarly narrows the theme too much in the direction of the rival, omitting a broader perspective of feeling slighted, so that one feels entitled to reparations, revenge, and greedy hunger.

From the perspective of examining the creative writer's nuclear fantasies, Berman thinks he knows which of the writing expresses the author's fantasies "almost too clearly" or which is the author's "own attitude toward his fantasies." I think this is unwarranted. It has been traditional in applied psychoanalysis to assume that when writing becomes raw and seemingly primitive the author's defenses have failed and we have been exposed to his neurotic fantasies. The other side of the argument is that good writing represents a successful defense against the author's nuclear conflicts. I think both assumptions have little to recommend them. A dream within a poem is treated here as a dream or a dream within a dream. This may be the reader's experience but we do not know that we have captured the author's experience. From a line in a text (p. 146), Berman states that Gilbert "could never forget his own 'tedious infancy and all its dangers.'" We would have to debate who is represented in the poem, what the relations are of themes, characters, and narrator to the author. Here again, Berman seeks closure of his material, arguing that the "precious baby" images relate (only) to wishes for active mastery of passive helpless childhood experiences. His interpretations pose other logical problems. Berman (p. 146) says what Gilbert thought of childhood: that "miserable . . . tedious . . . dangerous" time of life; how do we know whose view this is? Or, Gilbert's works "echoed the *wish* [emphasis added] that the infant remain a blank" (p. 146). There are many other possibilities for the ballad *My Dream* (pp. 280–81), besides this wish attributed to the author. Nonsense verse is understood exclusively as a defense against sadistic wishes. Indeed Berman asserts that this was Gilbert's "intention" (p. 140). This omits ideas about playing with language, babbling, regressive longings, freedom from adult restraints and painful reality, magic, and so on.

For example, Murray Schwartz (1982) has pointed out the interesting juxtaposition in *Othello* (act 3, scenes 3 and 4) of the clown scene, which involves punning, playing, and nonsense in contrast to Othello's rigid foreclosure of possibilities, literalness, inability to question or to play, and ultimately his inability to desire and possess Desdemona. Such excursions by Schwartz into Shakespeare's style are used to clarify psychoanalytic readings that can be argued from the text. But they begin with careful literary readings, in this case Schwartz's discovery of the juxtaposition of two sharply contrasting scenes and his posing the question of how the clown scene and the clown's nonsense function just at that point in the play.

In Berman's (1976) earlier paper on Gilbert, the literary theme of the "divided person" and Gilbert's own narcissistic vulnerability are well presented. However, the reader is not offered sufficient reason to reduce either of these themes to the single issue of castration anxiety. In both the analysis of literary themes and of biography it is better that we not reduce the issues beyond the available evidence at hand to single explanatory concepts. Kohut (1960) argues this well in contrasting Greenacre's *Swift and Carroll* with the Sterbas's biographical study of Beethoven's relationship with his nephew. Kohut argues for restraint and humility when psychoanalysts approach applied psychoanalysis, equal at least to what we require of ourselves within the consulting room.

We must acknowledge that with a text or an author, who is not our patient in analysis, our understanding must be imperfect and tentative. I think that not distinguishing clearly between the goals of literary analysis and biographical reconstruction adds to the unwarranted attitude that we can capture both author and text with a single stroke. This conflates two different goals, doing disservice to each. Psychoanalytic literary criticism does better to confine itself to clarification of the text and its reading experience. Beginning with a careful literary analysis, we must then demonstrate that a psychoanalytic perspective does indeed add something further to clarifying and enhancing multiple meanings and perspectives for enriching our reading experience of the text. Often the value in psychoanalytic literary criticism is not the psychoanalytic perspective or language but simply that it is good criticism. That must be the starting point before anything else "psychoanalytic" is added. There is danger of seeking unifying themes within the entire corpus of an author's work. We can easily find them but at the expense of clarifying each text as a separate literary entity. That the same author has authored them does not justify running one into the other. Once the work has been produced, the real-life author is no longer "the author." Criticism must stand on its own, according to the usual criteria for good criticism, apart from the author's biography or his stated or implied intentions.

Fleisher's (1990, 1991) two papers on Hemingway also demonstrate a psychoanalyst's overconcern with pathography in studying fiction. What is of interest to me is his linking of creativity and perverse trends in Hemingway. In effect, his hypothesis is that when Hemingway could draw on his own perverse trends, he could write creatively and well. But when these perverse trends are absent from Hemingway's fiction, Fleisher proposes, excessive vulnerability leads to psychological constriction, avoidance of introspection, and defensive focus on machismo action. Fleisher argues that at his best, Hemingway could explore his fascination with men's wishes to surrender to destructive phallic women. He illustrates well Hemingway's ability to render moving fiction in which men become captivated, helpless, and passive in their relations with women who want to rob and destroy their masculinity, identity, and creativity. Even the steers in the bull ring seem too willing to be gored by the bulls; once a male is damaged, he seems to invite others, especially androgynous others, to finish him off. We are given many images of men who cling to unloving, destructive women; these men are unable to stand up for themselves, to become angry, to put the woman in her place and to leave her. Indeed, I agree with Fleisher that Hemingway's posthumously published novel, *The Garden of Eden*, reads like perverse pornography.

There are two main points I want to raise. First, I want to comment on the theme of the phallic woman. Fleisher considers bisexuality, closeness, and anger as he attempts to explain the fantasy of the phallic woman in Hemingway's writing. I consider that *at times* his discussion of men's wishes to identify with the phallic woman as twin seems too benign, without sufficient acknowledgment of the rage and destructiveness in self and other involved in these fantasies. In his earlier paper, Fleisher (1990) elaborated the trauma of Hemingway's childhood and its relation to the theme of the phallic woman. Hemingway's mother (Lynn 1987) cross-dressed him until age five and sought to treat him and his sister, who was a year and a half older, as twins. During summer vacation, in contrast, she dressed both children as boys.

I would emphasize the mother's actual destructiveness of her son's masculinity, identity, self-confidence, and self-esteem. That Hemingway's mother encouraged her children to be twins similarly seemed to rob each child of his or her unique body and identity, as if these could be usurped by the mother. This was not primarily a game in which brother and sister played at being able to transform each into the other. The mother determined the children's performances and gender roles by directing the stage play, as if she were a perverse demigod. That is, within the mother's bisexual play there seems to have been intense destructiveness toward what was unique and different in her son and daughter. She seemed to want not only to play at being both sexes but to demonstrate an omnipotent ability to take what she wanted for herself through her destructive manipulation of her children.

Hemingway's destructive female characters do not tolerate their envy of men's unique abilities but seek to destroy and usurp such talent and creativity. In *The Garden of Eden*, Catherine does not only want to play at being David's boy twin. She relishes dominating him, making him feminine, passive, submissive, as in wanting to penetrate him anally. She envies his creativity and attempts to destroy it in the novel by taking him away from his writing, by devaluing and humiliating his pleasure in his abilities and accomplishments, and by actually burning his writing. Instead of feeling rage and destructiveness, David and other dominated men in Hemingway's writing, obliterate their feelings in alcohol or sexual excitement. This is the link with perversion, where excitement is used to patch over what is wrong within oneself and between oneself and the other person (see Coen 1992). Hemingway captures very well the intoxication with excitement that conceals humiliation, hurt, and rage. David seems uncertain whether he enjoys Catherine's feminizing him. He seems ambivalent about wishes to surrender to her domination, to have her take him over. However, it is not clear that he *wants* to be turned into a woman. He seems to patch this doubt over by attempting to persuade himself that he actually *enjoys* and is excited by Catherine's feminine transformation of him. Catherine repeatedly protests that this desire for feminization is not only her own, that David also wants to be feminized.

In this perverse tension, one defensively insists that he desires what the other will do to him, whether he actually wishes it or not. During childhood, such perverse tension restores the child's helplessness and passivity with a destructive parent except that the parent's destructive intrusion is now partly erotized and desired. As a result the child's, and later the patient's, rage can be calmed, at least so long as he or she remains addicted to such perverse play. Only within the illusion that both partners enjoy the domination, humiliation, and destructive robbery of one of them, is the child/patient's rage eased. Since the child/patient's rage continues and continues to endanger the vitally needed relationship with the other (parent/lover/analyst), such exciting perverse transformations become addictive and must be endlessly repeated. Of course, the balance of rage and destructiveness in self and in other will vary with the couple considered. But we begin with perverse defense against acknowledgment of rage at the other's (the parent's) destructiveness. Then we would proceed, *in a psychoanalysis*, to full ownership of one's own destructiveness without projection and justification of it because of past trauma.

However, in the study of fiction it is less clear how we are to connect these perverse trends with the author. We would expect creative writers to draw on themselves deeply and richly, and that trauma, conflict, need, desire, defense, and everything else will enter their writing. That is very different from our being able to determine from reading a text that authors have in fact attempted to master some specific unconscious fantasy and conflict through their writing. Even when we find psychic conflict within the characters and plot—in Hemingway's case bisexuality, dominance/submission, the "phallic woman,"—we do better to understand this within the text than attempt to guess where the authors themselves stand in relation to these trends. Unless, of course, our fantasies about the author actually enhance our readings of the text. The risk is that single-minded adherence to a particular conflictual theme attributed to authors will narrow our pleasure and grasp of their writing.

The second issue I want to raise is whether we can demonstrate that Hemingway's artistic decline actually related to a need to avoid facing his bisexual conflicts, as Fleisher proposes. That Hemingway could write about bisexuality, including phallic women and their destructiveness in short stories and in some longer fiction during the time of his apparent decline, seems to argue against this contention. Fleisher suggests that *The Garden of Eden* is repetitively stereotyped like perversion so that it is impaired as fiction. That may be, but that fact might suggest the author's (or the narrator's or the character's) greater need to hold onto his perverse images rather than a need to avoid them. That Hemingway could write successfully about bisexuality and the destructive phallic woman in his short stories during the 1930s does not suggest to me that he could manage to explore this conflict only for short periods of time.

The problem here concerns criteria for assessing the plausibility of interpretation. In many ways, this is the same dilemma as in clinical psychoanalysis. Although we may have biographical information and even a sense of the analysand's or the writer's predominant conflicts, psychoanalytic interpretation must fit the material examined in a coherent, cogent, and clarifying way. Otherwise, we have "applied psychoanalysis" in the sense of psychoanalytic ideas *pasted onto* patient or text. Readers who are not psychoanalysts may not appreciate sufficiently that skilled psychoanalysts, like thoughtful critics, do not just draw interpretations out of their theories and their knowledge of the patient. On the contrary, psychoanalysts are always seeking, through their interpretations and their silence, to heighten analysands' immediate affective experience of their conflicts.

Mahony once remarked to me with some impatience that psychoanalysts have no use for deconstruction in the consulting room. This literary critic, now more fully identified as a psychoanalyst, had shifted his stance pragmatically! The psychoanalyst needs to find an interpretation that will advance the analytic process; interpretations that will not do so are wrong, useless, and to be rejected. Literary critics, Mahony indicated, in contrast, have the luxury of insisting there is no correct interpretation. However, in my view, the literary critic, like the psychoanalyst, seeks affective immediacy—drama—that heightens the reader's tension and struggles between conflicting positions. Good readings, of patients and of texts, seek to grab the other person, so that by feeling something more deeply, she or he gains conviction. Ineffective interpretations will not grip the other so intensely.

Fleisher is persuasive that the themes of bisexuality, the phallic woman, and men's wishes for feminine surrender pervade Hemingway's fiction. He even convinces us that Hemingway infuses his fiction with a perverse thrust. I, as reader, feel an excitement reading *The Garden of Eden* over the unfolding perverse sexuality as well as over Catherine's destructiveness toward David. I disagree with Fleisher that Catherine simply announces her destructive aim at the beginning of the novel. Rather, in my reading, her aim is initially sexualized, as Catherine teases and excites David about what she will do to him. For example, Fleisher refers to the following passage (p. 5):

> "I'm the destructive type," [Catherine] said. "And I'm going to destroy you. They'll put a plaque up on the wall of the building outside the room. I'm going to wake up in the night and do something to you that you've never even heard of or imagined. I was going to last night but I was too sleepy."
>
> "You're too sleepy to be dangerous."
>
> "Don't lull yourself into any false security. Oh darling let's have it hurry up and be lunch time."

Will she harm David, or will she please and excite him as she introduces him to exotic, forbidden pleasures?

Compare this with Hemingway's diary entry about his fourth wife, Mary (Lynn 1987:533):

She has always wanted to be a boy and thinks as a boy without ever losing any femininity . . . She loves me to be her girls [sic], which I love to be . . . In return she makes me awards and at night we do every sort of thing which pleases her and which pleases me . . . Mary has never had one lesbian impulse but has always wanted to be a boy. Since I have never cared for any man and dislike any tactile contact with men except the normal Spanish abrazo . . . I loved feeling the embrace of Mary which came to me as something quite new and out-side all tribal law.

But how do we know that Hemingway's increasing difficulties as a writer had to do *primarily* with a defensive need to avoid facing and feeling his own bisexual desires? How do we really know what has inter-fered with Hemingway's creativity? We certainly can agree that Hem-ingway's later novels tend to shift from description of internal psycho-logical experience to an emphasis on external action. *The Garden of Eden* lacks the lighter, more imaginative, faster, and livelier pace of "The Short Happy Life of Francis Macomber" (1936). The themes of destructive envy and masochistic surrender are similar but the author seems able to play with and to take distance from these themes better in his earlier fiction. Can we explain this?

Fleisher describes how depressed feelings infiltrate Hemingway's fic-tion as they do his life. Would further biographical material help us understand Hemingway's deterioration as a writer and as a man? Has more intense depression led to impairment of his writing ability with greater pressure for relief through action and excitement? Does he become more self-destructive in his writing as he does in the rest of his life? Does he, as Fleisher suggests, wish to merge with the maternal phallic imago through suicide or has Hemingway despaired and come to believe that life is meaningless?

In other words, Fleisher is assuming that wishes to surrender to a destructive maternal imago were ever present in Hemingway's mind and in his fiction. Presumably, earlier he could fight against such regres-sive, self-destructive desires rather than give in to them. In "The Short Happy Life of Francis Macomber" (1936), Macomber struggles against his fear, and becomes able to kill dangerous animals and stand up to his envious and contemptuous wife. Even after Margot shoots Macomber, Wilson taunts her, putting her in her place. Men can indeed fight against destructive women! And Hemingway can create good fiction from fantasies of dying (see also "The Snows of Kilimanjaro" [1936]). David, in *The Garden of Eden*, comes across as helpless, passive, with great difficulty mobilizing his rage and asserting himself and his wishes to get rid of Catherine so as to go his own way.

In the earlier fiction, there is more space for shifts in intense feelings, wishes, and abilities. The writing is more passionate and optimistic, even in the descriptions of killing. The later writing is bleak, fixed, and pessimistic about its characters' abilities to feel and desire keenly and to change. The same applies to the narration; despite the erotic and destructive excitement, the writing seems static and lacks zest. Somebody is more depressed, resigned, and despairing. But even here we must proceed cautiously since we know that some writers are able to write well despite their depression, even able to use writing as an antidote to depression. Why couldn't Hemingway?

A Note on Responsible Psychoanalytic Psychobiography

Although psychobiography is not literary criticism, it can be rendered in a responsible psychoanalytically informed way. Stephen Weissman, in *His Brother's Keeper: A Psychobiography of Samuel Taylor Coleridge* (1989), writes an engaging, novelistic account of the life and creativity of Coleridge. Weissman tells his story very well—simply, elegantly, with a minimum of psychoanalytic jargon, using psychoanalytic formulations in a spare but effective manner. The reader easily becomes absorbed in Weissman's personal and convincing rendering. His psychological reading of the interrelations among Coleridge's life, conflicts, and creative work is fascinating. This is a moving but sad tale. I recommend it as an example of fine biography illuminated through psychoanalytic psychology. The criticisms I offer involve matters of taste, bias, and perspective. In no way should they be understood as minimizing Weissman's accomplishment.

Weissman is more concerned with telling his story well than with elaborating a psychoanalytic theory of artistic creativity. Thus the hypotheses he offers can be accepted or rejected, in whole or in part, without detracting from his overall work. In the introduction, Weissman briefly outlines his psychology of artistic creativity as involving issues of loss, separation, sensitivity, and depression, which are managed by the transformation of creative imagery into permanent works. Creativity is exhilarating, intoxicating, and addictive—certainly a useful theory to apply to Coleridge (and his opiate addiction). Weissman, however, connects this creative ecstasy only to wishes for immortality, in line with his idea of vital defense against loss and depression. This is too narrow a formulation. Creative excitement can be explained in many other ways, making creativity much more complex, both as conflictual and nonconflictual activity. But Weissman is not primarily interested in theories, psychoanalytic or literary; theory is not his passion. He excels as a clinical psychoanalyst organizing a set of narratives of the life of his subject. By not forcing his constructions upon us, like a good psychoanalyst (and writer) he succeeds in getting us to explore them. Unlike the two psychoanalytic writers discussed in the preceding section, Weissman uses himself as a psychoanalyst to enrich his narration rather than to impede or constrict it.

Weissman organizes his story particularly around fratricide, guilt, reparation and undoing, and the need for a supportive filial creative relationship. He does not refer to other psychoanalysts who have described this need for an intense, supportive relationship with another living person required by certain artists during a period of creativity (see chapter 1 in this book). This latter model seems to me a better way to organize Coleridge's need for a creative brother and his addiction to Wordsworth. Weissman prefers to tell this as a tale of Cain and Abel; his evidence is convincing.

When he refers (p. 6) to the aggression the artist must tolerate and express in order to create successfully, I agree and wish he had drawn this out further. He notes that Coleridge must have felt betrayed and rejected when his mother sent him away to London at age nine, six months after his father's death. There certainly are indications of persistent hunger for parenting, nurturance, and narcissistic supplies, including wishes for twinship, surrender, or merger with Wordsworth. That is, brother rivalry is only one explanation for Coleridge's depression, narcissistic neediness, selfishness and relative inability to maintain concern for his family, severe mood fluctuations, masochism, and addiction. Weissman suggests Coleridge may have had a manic-depressive disorder. Even in the wish to enact a foursome, there seems to have been the wish to recreate a family within which he could continue to feel that he was a central focus. Weissman's many examples of Coleridge's oratorical exhibitionism convince me of the poet's narcissistic hunger for recognition and acclaim. Certainly, as Weissman sug-

gests, Coleridge was angry at women but, more importantly, he needed their support and indulgence, as well as from men. At times (e.g., p.
71), Weissman suggests the brother hunger replaces the need for a parent (father).

His explanations of Coleridge's attempts to master conflict through
creative writing are well done. However, I would open his constructions further. For example, *The Rime of the Ancient Mariner* need not
be focused exclusively on survivor guilt related to fratricide but could
include various anxieties and guilts over destructiveness, loss, separateness, and success. Coleridge's envy, homosexual love and rivalry, and
difficulty with separateness from Wordsworth are well described.
Weissman tells us that initially this sharing relationship helped each
writer to create but that later Coleridge would do much better on his
own away from Wordsworth. Difficulties with separateness, with main-
taining self-esteem, with managing destructiveness without turning it
upon himself masochistically all could have been elaborated further. In
a footnote (p. 287) about Coleridge's *Christabel*, Weissman refers to
the symbiotic bond between vampire and victim both within this work
and in the relationship between Coleridge and Wordsworth (Coleridge
was primarily in the role of victim). But that would be a different story
than the one Weissman wants to tell.

Weissman notes briefly (pp. 304–5) Coleridge's idea of "willing sus-
pension of disbelief" in the dreamer and in the audience. He is also able
to derive a theory of wish fulfillment in dreams from Coleridge's writings, although the poet alternately relied on a theological explanation.
Similarly, Coleridge distinguished between wish (fancy) and imagination (complex creative fantasy). I would have liked more critical discussion of these ideas.

An Unexpected Resource for Studying Author-Reader Interaction: Translation—Notes on Ornston's *Translating Freud*

Although problems of reading Freud in translation are considered in
chapter 7 of this book, I want to note briefly here two themes that
emerge from recent writing on translation. First, most students of
translation now emphasize the translator's act of interpretation during
the act of translating. That is, close study of the choices made by the
translator in rendering a text into the target language shows that the

translator has his or her own agenda (one often not even fully known to the translator) for influencing the reader. The more fully the translator can acknowledge such motivation, the less he or she will be unconsciously driven by wishes to persuade the reader that the translator now offers the key to unveiling the true reading of the author's text.

The translator, like all readers of all texts, must struggle with multiple, often indeterminate, meanings, which he or she chooses to render in specific ways. When the translator is aware of the complexity and bias involved in such choices in translation, he or she can show the reader other possible renderings, involving the reader in the complexity of understanding the meanings of the text. When the translator is unable to acknowledge his or her own motivations concerning both author and reader, he or she may instead seek to compel the reader to follow him or her without involving the reader in a more dynamic conjoint creation of multiple meanings.

Second, all of the varied approaches to translation in Darius Ornston's *Translating Freud* seek to draw the reader into the creative *process* of translating and reading as shared experience between author, translator, and reader. Given that contemporary literary criticism has emphasized such creative reading process, it is not surprising that the contemporary study of translation also demonstrates this focus on the processes of reading and rereading. Further, psychoanalytic study of translation has been strongly influenced by three psychoanalytic readers (Mahony, Ornston, and Junker) who emphasize this interactive reading process between author, text, and reader. In Ornston's book these three psychoanalytic readers show how they have transformed the field of Freud translation by their literary critical emphasis on the complexities of author-reader interaction. This book is well worth reading for its literary critical study of readers (translators) struggling to read texts and to influence their own readers. I would suggest that attempts to decide Freud's meanings are of secondary importance here.

But note that the French contributors (Laplanche, Cotet, and Bourgignon) disagree with this approach, believing instead that a well-organized team of translators can succeed in conveying the text's varied meanings rather than offering just one set of readings of the text. They propose that a well-coordinated team of translators can collaboratively indicate various possibilities for understanding ambiguous, elusive, or contradictory ideas, images, and phrases. However, in their aim of not distracting from the text, they propose largely to *eliminate* consideration of the paths by which they arrived at their current choices in translating text that cannot be easily pinned down. I think that not sharing such deliberation with the reader tends to obstruct the reader's identification with the translator's own reading processes and keeps the reader from fully grasping the text and its complexities.

These French translators, unlike the other contributors to Ornston's volume, want to decide for the reader what will and what will not be problematic in understanding the text. I think the contention is illusory that collaboration by a group of translators can and should circumvent *some* of the reader's struggles with the ambiguities and complexities of a text.

Laplanche, Cotet, and Bourgignon seek in translating to render (p. 143) "the text, the whole text, and nothing but the text." They describe the process of creating meanings by using the target language in a manner similar to the ways in which the author draws upon his own language. These translators aim for a (p. 143) "Freudian French" that matches the German reader's experience of being grasped by Freud's German (Freudian) writing. They emphasize the translators' love of the work and its language, which the translators seek to bring to life with all the fullness and immediacy of the original text. Laplanche, Cotet, and Bourgignon suggest that the translator should work (p. 145) "in the same way that Montaigne loved Paris—'tenderly, with all its warts and stains.' " Although Laplanche, Cotet, and Bourgignon readily reveal their pleasure in translating Freud, Ornston (p. xv), Junker (p.49), and I believe that translation—like reading—is an act of interpretation. Hence, for us translation cannot produce a clear or even translucent rendering of the original text. Junker, emphasizing reading process, suggests that translation is always incomplete, that every reading will tend to lead us in new directions.

Mahony writes here (p. 46) that the "object relations" of Strachey's *Standard Edition* and the *Gesammelte Werke* are different (compare Mahony's idea with chapter 1 of this book). The *Gesammelte Werke*, Mahony argues, captures the reader more personally, more affectively, so that the reading experience differs from that of reading Strachey's more toned-down translation. Every contributor to Ornston's volume notes the political pressures on Strachey from Ernest Jones and the International Psycho-Analytic Society—which here becomes an exaggerated enemy of thoughtful scholarship—to standardize Freudian theory as a unified corpus in order to enhance organized psychoanalysis. Mahony's own Freudian reading of Freud's *unconscious* efforts to convince his readers via his texts leads Mahony to claim (p. 47) that the translator's own unconscious must capture him as he works so that he will be both faithful and traitorous to his source text.

Junker emphasizes that Freud compels his reader to participate actively in creating meanings as he or she reads Freud's text. According to Junker, Freud in German (unlike Strachey's rather more fixed renderings) engages the reader in "the ongoing and endless process of searching the repressed" (p. 55) as one reads about this search for the repressed. Junker is the first author I have read who questions the view commonly held in the United States and Great Britain that Freud's (1937) essay "Analysis Terminable and Interminable" is deeply pessimistic. Junker argues that Strachey's assessment of Freud's pessimism about the therapeutic efficacy of psychoanalysis (S. E. 23:211–215) has strongly influenced Anglo-American readers. French, Spanish, and Portuguese translations seem less pessimistic. Junker sees Freud as engaging his readers in this essay to consider with Freud the endless tasks of psychoanalysis. That analysis is interminable does not have to mean that Freud's readers should be discouraged by the necessary task of ongoing struggle with internal conflict. On the contrary, the reader needs to be encouraged to continue to struggle with the text and its problems just as he or she must be encouraged to go on struggling with his or her own internal problems. This is the essence of Freud's contribution, one that need not be gloomy but is affirmative and enhancing of the endless vitality of process—always partly conflictual—in reading as elsewhere in living.

Chapter 7

HOW TO READ FREUD: A CRITIQUE OF CONTEMPORARY FREUD SCHOLARSHIP

Contemporary Freud scholarship emphasizes new approaches to reading Freud's work, in which content is subordinated to process, style, and what transpires between author and reader. Readers' problems in reading Freud's texts now become the central focus. The move is away from what Freud said and meant, to how Freud said what he did, and what readers are to do with this. This current shift of emphasis should not be surprising.

First, psychoanalysts and others have been studying the content of Freud's work for so long that some may tend to feel that this approach has exhausted the material. What would be innovative and creative, the argument runs, would be questioning the basic assumptions with which we begin to read Freud. Raising questions, problematizing the reading of Freud's texts, now supersedes finding answers from Freud. Second, this is currently a popular mode in literary criticism (as elsewhere): raising questions rather than finding answers; studying the process of reading a text; what happens to readers as they read. Literary critics then may use the psychoanalytic process as further justification for reading texts as an interactional process between author, text, and reader. Third, we have become much more self-consciously aware of our ambivalently idealized relationship to Freud.

Current Freud scholarship considers how our feelings toward our psychoanalytic progenitor influence our readings of him. The conscious enterprise of seeking a more balanced perspective of Freud, less contaminated by idealizations and competitive denigration, is certainly to be welcomed. Whether we can achieve that is another story, a psychoanalytic story about our own needs and feelings. Freud scholarship has become a hot topic in psychoanalysis and in the popular press. The task of this chapter is to assess how helpful current attempts to reread Freud have been. It is my opinion that raising questions about what we are after in our returns to Freud *is* very useful. Most of current Freud scholarship does this. The most successful work seems to be most aware of its own reasons and needs to problematize Freud. The least successful seems able to question Freud's texts but not itself and its own enterprise.

For example, Masson's editing of *The Complete Letters of Sigmund Freud to Wilhelm Fliess: 1887–1904*, as well as his writing in *The Assault on Truth; Freud's Suppression of the Seduction Hypothesis*, tends to be marred by his need to call attention to himself and to enact his own seduction (of/by) and victimization by the psychoanalytic establishment. Even with his editing of the Freud-Fliess letters, much of which is very well done, he intrudes far too much, distracting our reading with his own ideas and his polemic about the seduction hypothesis. The long-awaited full version of the Freud-Fliess letters, produced under the sponsorship of the Freud Archives and Harvard University Press, should have had more of Masson edited out so that the reader could, less interruptedly, enjoy Freud and Fliess. More about this later. In "French Freud" (see discussion on Felman [1987] and Weber [1982] later in this chapter), as well as in Bruno Bettelheim's writing, competitive aims to decenter the psychoanalytic establishment tend to interfere. Felman's fine approach to literary critical reading, arguing persuasively against premature closure and dogmatism, is best read (as indeed I have attempted to persuade Felman) as the metaphor of Lacan as Freud's only successful (re)reader. Weber's fascinating Derridean reading of Freud, decenters Lacan, psychoanalytic theory and the psychoanalytic establishment, and everything else. This is heady stuff, perhaps too heady. That is, an exclusive emphasis on the role of unconscious conflict refuses to leave anything alone, as possibly, even temporarily, outside of conflict. This is not just a debate between the French and the

Americans about ego psychology, metapsychology, and the unconscious; it is also a critical position from which it is impossible to maintain perspective, in which unconscious conflict *must* always subvert one's position. In less extreme form, such radical questioning of Freud's texts by Weber and Felman is fascinating and useful.

Holt's Reading: Content and Conflict

A more balanced (for American psychoanalysts) approach to critical reading, allowing for more possibility for ego mastery of, or potential freedom from, unconscious conflict is taken by Holt and Mahony. Holt, unlike the other authors considered in this chapter, does not apply a literary critical (or processive) reading to Freud. Holt is a distinguished ego psychologist, not a literary critic. Indeed, he even points out (1983) that literary critical approaches do not, and should, consider their own methodology. They should demonstrate the uniqueness of what has been described by the use of "control" passages. Holt's (1974) "On Reading Freud" is the best introduction I know to reading Freud. Holt's approach is thematic, drawing on his interpretation of Freud's cognitive style and encouraging a sympathetic approach to learning from Freud, rather than idealization or fault-finding. Holt emphasizes Freud's "analytic" bent in contrast to systematic synthesizing and the construction of complete theories. He points to Freud's ability to tolerate contradiction and inconsistency and his avoidance of both precise definitions and deductive reasoning. Holt outlines a conflict in Freud between mechanistic and humanistic images of humanity, which persists throughout Freud's work. These two sides should be viewed as simultaneously present. Thus Bettelheim's view of Freud as only a humanist is tendentious and overly simplistic.

Contrasting Freud's self-critical doubting with Freud's self-consciousness, Holt notes Freud's tendency to move from initial hesitant presentation of hypotheses to later regarding them as "indispensable" and then finally as "established." Freud treated his assumptions as proven facts, despite pointing out the hypothetical or mythical quality of his conceptions. Holt relates this to Freud's struggle against his self-doubts in his new psychoanalytic field. Readers of Freud should bear in mind that Freud tended not to revise his work systematically or to discard old concepts. Thus contradictions, inconsistencies, and ambiguities are to be removed in Freud's work only at the expense of altering seriously Freud's own conceptions. Freud may at times read dogmatically with hyperbolic exaggeration.

Holt nicely shows Freud's style of undoing such statements with succeeding ones, which describe from contrasting or contradictory or qualifying perspectives. All these help the reader to picture Freud's ideas. Freud tended toward sweeping generalizations in contrast to cautious empirical generalizations from limited data. Holt is convincing that "proof" or "confirmation," for Freud, referred to probability of truth rather than to rigorous proof. Freud attempted to persuade the reader to believe that his ideas were true. How persuasive Freud's rhetoric is, how believable he is to the reader, becomes the measure of truth. One consequence of the mechanistic reductionism ("nothing but" [Holt 1978]) in Freud's work is the implication that only the underlying unconscious conflict matters, that nothing else is real ("French Freud"). Holt cautions that this perspective needs to be balanced with possibilities for conscious choice. My readers should keep this in mind when reading the rest of this chapter.

Strachey's Translation and Its Problems

A crucial problem in Freud scholarship is Strachey's translation in the Standard Edition. Weber (1979/1982), Ornston (1982, 1985a & b), Bettelheim (1982), and Mahony (1982, 1984a, 1984b, 1989) all point out biases and distortions in Strachey's English translation, which have significantly influenced readers. How much English-reading psychoanalysts have been led astray will have to be determined. Each commentator agrees on certain issues: Strachey was concerned with rendering an overall meaning at the expense of Freud's syntax, placement of words, and their repetition (Roustang 1977). Freud's present-tense fictional immediacy is often rendered in the past tense (for examples see Mahony 1977, 1982, 1984). Bettelheim, Ornston, and Mahony contend that Strachey's translation is overly formal and stiff in contrast to Freud's more flexible and forceful colloquial Viennese style. Strachey tends to make Freud's writing neater, simpler, less affectively charged, less open-ended, and less complex. Connotative meanings, in contrast to denotative meanings, are often lost in translation (Weber 1982). Strachey tends to conceal Freud's polemical aims (Mahony 1984a:116) and to translate under the influence of an idealizing transference to Freud. More vividly engaging terms are cleaned up into staid Victorian prose. Greek and Latin are used for familiar German terms that have intensely personal meaning.

Ornston contends that Strachey, unlike Freud, sought systematic definitions in artificial or technical terms, regarding Freud's work as complete. This tended to change Freud's hypothetical, subjunctive images into fixed statements. Ornston is convincing when he states that Freud wrote with a vividness of feeling that conveys intensely what the patient and analyst each felt, as well as what the reader is to feel. Strachey's translation tends to fortify analyst and reader against such feelings, to separate artificially the patient from the analyst and the reader. Brandt (1966) notes that Strachey changed Freud's descriptions of process, written in dynamic, active images into structures constituted by static, passive words. Ornston (1985) criticizes Strachey's belief that he could omit his biases in translating Freud, an assumption that must lead a translator (or critic) astray! He objects to Strachey's neglect of Freud's view, that the unconscious can only be described in approximations but never directly known. "*Beschreibende Psychologie*" (describing psychology) (Freud 1900:531, 582, 593) is a fine way to characterize Freud's strategy of describing a concept in multiple, vivid ways so that the reader can visualize and grasp it.

Ornston argues that Strachey "structuralized" Freud's images (e.g., turning "the repressing" into "the repressing agency," "the motive for repression" into "the motive force for repression"). Id, ego, and superego cut the reader off from the personal immediacy of "the it, the I, and the over I." The I, for example, would include the self, one's own person, and oneself as active agent. Ornston acknowledges that we need a systematic comparison between Freud's and Strachey's uses of the word, "structure." Ornston, in contrast to Holt, argues that Freud's scientific images are to be read only as metaphors rather than taken concretely, definitively, as forces and structures. Is Ornston correct that Freud is wry and ironic in sketching "*ein Schema eines Apparats*," or does Freud want to have it both ways, that is, as an imaginative, metaphoric guide as well as an image of "the thing in itself"? Ornston's argument is convincing only if we believe that Freud is ironic wherever he refers to images of mental apparatus. Irony may be less demonstrable in a text than as one way of interpreting a text (Fish 1983). My impression so far (in agreement with Holt) is that Freud both intended metaphoric description and, despite his frequent disclaimers, also—and simultaneously—an actual capturing of physicalistic events. I agree with Ornston that Strachey tends only toward the latter, toning down the quality of metaphoric description in Freud's prose. Ornston's examples of Strachey changing Freud's words into more concretely neurophysiological terms are persuasive. This certainly would lead English readers toward a more definitive, formal, complete structure of the mind. I am convinced by Ornston and Bettelheim that Strachey toned down Freud's more intensely suggestive sensual and hostile images into more neutral words. Ornston places Strachey's translation within an influential English tradition.

Bettelheim on Strachey's Translation

Moving from Ornston's lucid, thoughtful, scholarly, tempered appraisal of Strachey's translation to Bettelheim's (1982) tendentious attack is disappointing. Bettelheim makes points similar to Ornston's but assumes, far more than he should, that he knows what Freud had in mind—and he proceeds to tell us. His competitiveness with American medical psychoanalysis also distorts his presentation, overly skewing Freud and Bettelheim as humanists, in contrast to the rest of us as detached, defended, and mechanical. Bettelheim is certainly correct that students of Freud need to be familiar with the literary myths upon which Freud draws. Indeed, shouldn't all psychoanalytic students read Sophocles's *Oedipus Rex* in order to understand Freud's view of the Oedipus complex? (Felman tells us we also need to read *Oedipus at Colonnus* in order to have the whole story.) But how does Bettelheim know that Jocasta killed herself only because she contributed to the plot to kill Oedipus and not also because of her feelings about her incest? References to Goethe's *Faust*, on which Bettelheim draws to amplify Freud's meaning, would be better without Bettelheim's certainty that he knows the connections Freud made. Again, in his discussion of Freud's "A disturbance of memory on the Acropolis," Bettelheim shows us that Strachey's translation—the memory "troubled" Freud (*S. E.* 22:248)—misses the quality of the memory "visiting" him ("*so oft heimsucht*"). But he also tells us he knows the importance to Freud of this memory. That is, Bettelheim becomes a privileged reader, because he, like Freud, grew up in Vienna: "*heimsucht*" must refer to the Catholic religious holiday, *Maria Heimsuchung*. Bettelheim fails to indicate criteria for using his own subjective associations to the text, a central problem in reader-response criticism.

The trend, that the German original invites such personal affective resonance from the reader, is worth emphasizing and encouraging, as Bettelheim does—but more cautiously. Bettelheim is in agreement with Ornston and Mahony that Freud's German aims to stir the reader's unconscious emotions; process and allusions, as well as denotative meanings, vital in the original, are often lost in Strachey's translation. However, he makes too much of his own idiosyncratic rendering of "*Seele*" as soul rather than as psyche. This gives a cast of religion and spirituality to Freud, which does not fit. I concur with both Ornston and Bettelheim that in Strachey's translation "mind" overemphasizes the cognitive and conscious. Ornston correctly notes Bettelheim's faulty opposition of "*seelisch*" and "*geistig*"; the latter not only refers to the mental but also includes the "spiritual." The mistranslation by Bettelheim of "*geistig*" furthers his argument that Freud was in the camp of the "*seelisch*" rather than the "*geistig*."

Like Ornston, Bettelheim is convincing when he claims that Freud intended his readers to resonate with their own lifelong personal meanings to *das Ich, das Es*, and *das Über-Ich*. Note especially his points: that in German, the child (*das Kind*) is referred to by the neuter pronoun, "*es*," linking infantile impulses with "the it"; that in languages other than English, the translation of the three terms parallels the German. Bettelheim suggests that the title, *The Interpretation of Dreams*, is too definitively focused on interpretation; something like the "deeper meaning of dreams" would keep *Die Traumdeutung* more open. He makes the interesting connection between *Traumdeutung* and *Sterndeutung* (astrology), suggesting ancient efforts to make sense out of something incomprehensible, superstitious, and fantastic—an apt analogy for dreams. Bettelheim provides some background for the motto prefacing *The Interpretation of Dreams*, "If I cannot move heaven, I will stir up the underworld." He clarifies that in the *Aeneid*, Juno says this in desperation when she has been unable to obtain the gods' help; she turns then to the underworld. This can suggest that if the conscious mind does not respond to the unconscious, the latter will disturb the former. Bettelheim does not comment on the context within the Freud-Fliess letters in which this quotation appears. Freud takes the underworld for himself, while the higher regions and light are Fliess's (?ironically).

Bettelheim gives a number of good examples of Strachey's emotional understatement in translating Freud (pp. 80–81). When he discusses "The Psychology of Everyday Life," he correctly points out that the German title and subtitle both have qualifiers, indicating that the work is *about* the topic rather than a definitive statement. "Cathexis" as translation of "*Besetzung*" omits the military reference to forceful occupation; scoptophilia cannot convey the sensual pleasure in looking; defense does not render the "parrying" or "warding off" quality of "*Abwehr*."

One literary critic (Kendrick 1983) objects that in other disciplines, scholars would never work from translation but only from the original. Psychoanalytic scholars, this argument runs, should be educated at our psychoanalytic training institutes to cut their psychoanalytic teeth on Freud in German. Psychoanalytic trainees in the United States only read Freud in English translation. Mahony (1979) tells us that the Standard Edition is not a variorum text. A model for textual scholarship is Hawelka's (1974) French-German edition of the *Journal of the Rat Man*, which includes Freud's abbreviations, deletions, misspelling, marginalia, underlinings, and so on. A wise colleague, R. Michels, advised me, on reading a draft of the first solo psychoanalytic paper I wrote (1981) to consult Freud's German in order to learn more about the term and concept *sexualization*, which I was discussing. I did not. I did not take seriously enough the kind of bias and distortion in translation that I am discussing here. It certainly did not occur to me then that perhaps Freud did not regard the term I was investigating as a technical term. Strachey indeed sounded so definitive, so certain, as I also wanted to be as a beginning psychoanalytic writer. My colleague raised my doubts and I felt pleased to overcome (bypass) them.

Masson's Freud Work and Its Polemics

Masson's edition of Freud's letters to Fliess (1985) provides the fascinating opportunity to share with Freud the most momentous and creative period of his life. Here are Freud's creation of psychoanalysis; his struggles to understand and interpret so much of what now seems basic to us; his own inner turmoil and his attempts through self-analysis to master this; his passionate attachment to Fliess and his struggle against it toward greater self-confident autonomy; and glimpses of his everyday life—the setting in which he did all this.

Given the sensationalism in the popular press concerning new information about Freud, it should immediately be noted that these letters are not at all sensational. In fact, there are few surprises here. Schur (1966, 1972) and Mahony (1979) have already told us about Freud's organic heart trouble during the 1890s before Freud turned forty; the Emma Eckstein episode and Freud's conflict with his hostile criticism of Fliess; and the ending of the friendship. Masson (1984) certainly attempts to make the present letters seem incendiary, emphasizing Freud's failure of integrity in relation to Emma Eckstein and his abandonment of the theory of seduction and traumatization (see below). Much is made clearer from the additional portions of letters and the new letters provided. Certain things are newly revealed. Overall, this edition reads more intimately, more passionately, with Freud emerging in a more deeply personal way. In *Origins* (1887–1902), Freud's creative work and his relationship with Fliess are more prominent; his family life, his daily activities barely emerge. This is still largely true. Even in the new edition of these letters, the literary relationship seems so much more intense and important than the rest of the writer's or the reader's life. However, Freud does emerge as emotionally involved with Martha, Minna, his children, Breuer, Oscar Rie, and so forth. We learn for the first time about: Martha's colitis; Minna's tuberculosis; sufficient detail about Freud's cardiac symptoms to leave no doubt that Schur was correct that this was organic (not only the description of his symptoms but the fact that digitalis corrected his arrhythmia (Masson 1985:69–70; letter of April 25, 1894) and that he had rheumatic muscle nodes (Masson 1985:70–71; letter of May 6, 1894); and criticisms of friends (even the interesting mundane responses, such as the fact that Freud detested Melanie Rie's chicken and cauliflower). The editors of *Origins* claimed that they held back personal detail that would not materially affect a reading of these letters. It is understandable that concern for Anna Freud, Marianne Kris, and others personally connected to these letters and people influenced the suppression of intimate detail. Masson was correct to persuade Anna Freud that the time had come for the world to be able to read what else could be gleaned about Freud from these letters. They do no disservice to Freud's family.

The Emma Eckstein episode is now much clearer; Schur (1972) is certainly correct, and Masson (1984) is partly correct. Schur (1972) was persuasive that in the Irma dream, dreamt July 23–24, 1895 (Freud 1900; S. E. 4:107–121)—which, although referred to, is not presented in these letters—Freud was dealing (unconsciously) with hostile, critical feelings toward Fliess. These were immediately related to the latter's surgical mistreatment of Emma Eckstein and to Fliess's grandiosity. About this dream, in the dreambook, Freud acknowledges wishes to ridicule others so as to exculpate himself. The critical affects are, however, kept away from Fliess, who is here regarded positively. The thrust in Freud's presentation, of the Irma dream in the dreambook and in his references to it in these letters, is on his excited discovery of systematic free association to the manifest dream elements. Freud had found that this was the pathway to dream interpretation, through access to the latent dream thoughts and the dream work. It is clear in these new letters that Freud struggled with ambivalent feelings toward Fliess over Eckstein's hemorrhages; these resulted from Fliess having left a large wad of surgical gauze in her nasal cavity. Freud seems highly critical, accusatory of Fliess, while attempting to reassure Fliess that he is not to be blamed. Turning Eckstein's bleeding into hysterical wishes is an extreme form of denial of reality; it clearly protects Freud from accusing Fliess of incompetence and medical mismanagement. Masson (1984) does not present good evidence for his contention that this was the first extensive nasal operation performed by Fliess; nor for the claim that Freud showed a failure of integrity in denying his own responsibility for having turned Eckstein over to Fliess. Freud had turned himself over to Fliess—that was the problem. Freud's need to preserve his relationship with an idealized Fliess interfered with his critical, rational assessment of what had happened.

Ida Fliess's jealousy of the intimate relationship between Freud and Fliess is now more prominent (Masson 1985:187–190, letter of May 30, 1896; 1985:191–92, letter of June 4, 1896; Masson 1985:195–196, letter of August 12, 1896; Masson 1985:446–48, letter of August 7, 1901). The intensity of Freud's involvement with Fliess appears earlier than we had known: Freud calls Fliess (Masson 1985:134) "*Daimonie*" (demon) on July 24, 1895 ; by April 16, 1896 (Masson 1985:180–181), he asks Fliess to "Scold me!"; and uses even more explicitly seductive imagery (Masson 1985:193–194, letter of June 30, 1896): "I bring nothing but two open ears and one temporal lobe lubricated for reception." There is evidence that Freud felt ambivalent early in the relationship with Fliess (Masson 1985:49–50, letter of May 30, 1893): the first reference that Freud, although feeling capable, is not about to dissolve the partnership; irony in exaggerated and teasing praise of Fliess, before Freud's self-analysis; the letters about Eckstein's hemorrhages; more material (Masson 1985:173–176, letter of March 1, 1896) about Freud's angry disappointment with Breuer, which Freud connects with what may happen between himself and Fliess; early covert indications (Masson 1985:199–200, letter of October 9, 1896) that Freud regards Fliess (critically) as paranoid and grandiose.

Anxiety *about* sexuality is discussed (Masson 1985:49–50, letter of May 30, 1893) in two cases of virgins with a "presentient dread of sexuality."

Reading this new edition of the Freud-Fliess letters, one is certainly aware of Masson's presence. Some of his editing is very helpful indeed. He corrects and comments on certain prior mistranslations—e.g., Draft N, p. 251, where his correction emphasizes the new prominence of wishes for punishment in symptom formation, beyond the earlier idea of self-hindrance because of mistrust of one's desires. He provides some useful reference for quotations—their source, and when else Freud and/or Fliess used them (e.g., Masson 1985:205–206, fn. 2). Providing the German original for passages whose translation may be unclear or contested is valuable; so too are excerpts from contemporary reviews of Freud's work that add the flavor of the times, and some other background material (e.g., the discussion of a review by Eugen Bleuler). On the other hand, using chapter headings to organize the letters intrudes the editor's own bias. Masson tells us that Lottie Newman prepared the first draft of the translation, which Marianne Loring and he revised several times. A few lines further, he refers to the translation as "mine" (Masson 1985:xiii). Many footnotes distract the reader from the letters, especially those footnotes that involve Masson's own polemics, particularly about the seduction theory. There are far too many notes referring to the seduction theory, which interferes with the reader's own assessment (e.g., Masson 1985:205–206; Masson 1985:236–238; and Masson 1985:242, fn. 1).

I consider Masson to be wholly unconvincing in his attempt to demonstrate that Freud felt in conflict about his abandonment of the seduction theory. That is very different from acknowledging continuing doubts about this change. The relationship between external reality and internal reality has not been easy for psychoanalysts to explain. These can be overly polarized and have been. Masson is not correct, as many have noted, in stating that a contemporary intrapsychic perspective does not integrate external reality, trauma, seduction, and everything else that has happened in the patient's life.

Several years after the publication of Masson's *The Assault on Truth: Freud's Suppression of the Seduction Theory* (1984), it is sad to read but not at all dangerous. Masson, as Projects Director of the Freud Archives, was in a wonderful position to use his scholarly talents to edit and study fascinating, unpublished material. The story of his ouster reads like his own polemic of seduction and traumatization—in this case by the psychoanalytic establishment. Mutual seduction, idealization, and adoption lead to provocation, attack, dismissal, and victimization. Where Masson is able to keep himself to the task of serious scholarship, his work is useful. But he just cannot do that. His intellectual history of the medical literature on sexual seduction, incest, and physical abuse of children provides a useful context within which to understand Freud's emphasis on the psychological consequences of such trauma. He is even partly correct that the history of psychoanalysis can be read in terms of competition between different theories of etiology: trauma (seduction), wish-conflict, and constitutional endowment. Nor are we surprised that Freud had doubts about the correctness of his changing positions, which at times could lead to rigidity and dogmatism in Freud or in his adherents. A thoughtful, balanced appraisal of this would be helpful. Masson does not provide this but instead provides a provocative polemic. Masson (p. 92) reminds us of Freud's early discussions of aspects of sexuality (e.g., masturbation or ceremonials) that are adapted to protect against painful feelings from sexual trauma. But this is too either/or for a contemporary audience. Sexual trauma (seduction, rape, incest) and fantasy are not simply polar opposites, as Masson argues. Efforts to master and integrate such sexual trauma affect and involve the entire personality, in multiple, complex ways, as contemporary psychoanalytic authors have described. Masson bypasses this psychoanalytic perspective on mastery and integration.

Mahony on Freud: Writing and Reading As Process

Surprisingly, little has been written (especially in English) about Freud as a writer. Mahony's *Freud as a Writer* (1982) is thus particularly welcome, especially for those unable to read Schönau, Muschg, Schotte, and Roustang (not yet translated intro English). Mahony is both a professor of literature and a practicing psychoanalyst. It is a welcome trend that the number of those who combine both professions is increasing significantly. Fortunately, he eschews the writing style of "French Freud" (see discussion on Felman and Weber in this chapter), using clear explanatory (secondary process) language for his exposition. Mahony's is the best introduction to a literary critical reading of Freud's writing. He immediately identifies the argument between French Freud and Anglo-American psychoanalysis: whether anything (the ego) can be outside conflict. Although Mahony's position seems to be on the North American side, his argument in fact weaves the two sides together. Freud's writing is intended to be clear to the reader in secondary process terms, so that it may easily be understood. It still has traces of primary process instinctual elements within it; this leads to an enactment of the content during the reading process. The reader is neither read by the text nor the text read by the reader. The reader of Freud's texts reads and experiences, comprehends and feels, grasps the text and is grasped by the unconscious primary process living-out of the text. Mahony's emphasis is on process, on what happens, as we read Freud. In the German, unlike in the English translation, this induces the reader actually to experience what Freud is describing.

Mahony uses Derrida's analysis of "Beyond the Pleasure Principle" in order to demonstrate that Freud's writing has a mimetic structure while it is also a performance. Derrida noted that in "Beyond the Pleasure Principle" Freud enacts the *fort/da* game in his writing as repetition and detour. Four times Freud tries to explain repetition, only to interrupt his argument and claim it to be inconclusive. Mahony contrasts Freud's writing with Lacan's style. In Lacan, there is a self-conscious, deliberate attempt to overwhelm the reader with unconscious instinctual traces. The reader cannot simply proceed but must become caught in an instinctual "happening." With Freud, this occurs in a much more modulated way. What readers experience partially outside of their awareness, through resonating visual or auditory images, amplifies their conscious understanding. With Freud, communication is primary. With Lacan, communication and understanding having been rendered impossible (unreadable text), readers must draw on their own unconscious, making this primary.

Freud engages the reader by invitations, dialogue, and attempts to persuade, convince, and so on. Mahony suggests that Freud desired closeness with his audience, which he sought through this intimate conversational style. In Mahony's opinion, this served to reduce Freud's insecurity in revealing himself (his unconscious, which emerged through his secondary process elaboration in writing). Mahony and I suggest similar dynamics between author, text, and audience. Mahony shows how Freud's use of dialogue, the editorial "we" and self-revelatory use of "I," all engage reader and author. Freud treats his audience as if they were themselves analysands. This allows him to deal with their own resistances to understanding and experiencing what he tells them; it also encourages transferences to him. The text of "The

Introductory Lectures," Mahony suggests, is "a weaving of pedagogy and guided working through" (p. 95). Freud is aware that the text's affective tone strengthens the influence of its arguments (Freud 1914, 14:41). This seems to lead him to use words that will be persuasive: correct, right, justified, rightly, untrue, gone astray, and so on. Truth and dignity in the text aim to appeal to ego and superego. Mahony disagrees with Niederland (1971), that in his later work Freud used direct discourse with the reader less frequently.

What is the appropriate way to describe the psyche? Mahony selects Freud's comments; since the psyche cannot be directly represented, it must be described in analogies, in multiple images, none of which can actually grasp it. "Our understanding reaches as far as our anthropomorphism," Freud wrote (Scientific meeting of February 27, 1907, *Minutes of the Vienna Psychoanalytic Society* 1:136). Mahony emphasizes Freud's animation of mechanistic language and that Freud favors descriptive analogies and anthropomorphic approximations as the appropriate language for psychoanalysis.

Mahony, the literary critic, invites Anglo-American medical psychoanalysts to move away from content analysis toward a more literary immersion in the reading process when reading Freud. In moving away from dogmatic attempts to pin down what Freud really said, we are welcomed to the complexities of reading and experiencing what Freud wrote. The emphasis shifts from thoughts to a mind thinking, imagining, discovering (i. e., to process). Lessing was especially skilled in writing as the experiencing of thinking. There is evidence that Freud used Lessing as a consciously chosen literary model. The German language, Schotte and Mahony argue, is especially well suited for processive writing because of its activity and dynamism. For example, Mahony (p. 165) notes that Freud had a special preference for the prefixes *her-* and *hervor-* (forth; out) and that these prefixes capture the sense of dynamic process of the German language. Thus Freud often used *hervorziehen* (to bring forward, bring to life), *Hergang* (course), and *Herstellung* (setting up, restoration, cure). Or, to use another example, the German word for reality, *Wirklichkeit*, derives from *wirken* (to act), while in the Romance languages the word for reality derives from the Latin *res* (thing).

I am not sure how useful Mahony's repeated analogies are between reading Freud and the psychoanalytic experience (e.g., pp. 171, 173). On the other hand, Mahony describes well Freud's *fictional* dramatization of his cases, even his patient's dreams, by rendering them in the present tense (unlike the way in which most patients actually report their dreams). Freud orients the reader in time and space so as to keep the reader connected with him. As a result, the reader does not become lost in those portions of the writing that are more "instinctualized." I think that these are techniques more of fiction than of psychoanalysis, techniques that lead readers to find (in) themselves what is hinted at in the text or that enable authors and readers suddenly to take a new turn. However, Freud does, I believe, write both as a fine literary craftsman and as a thoughtful psychoanalyst attempting to influence his readers. Mahony and I agree on an interactional model between author (Freud), text, and audience. Mahony argues that psychoanalytic theory is processive. We can only attempt to describe the unconscious (or external reality) in figurative language; the unconscious remains unknowable in itself.

Mahony's subsequent book, *Cries of the Wolf Man*, is not primarily to be read as a psychoanalytic commentary on the Wolf Man's preoedipal psychopathology. Mahony reviews and amplifies what others have said about some of Freud's unlikely assertions, particularly the reconstruction of the primal scene, in all its imagined detail. Mahony is convincing that this is a polemical treatise, despite Freud's denials, aimed against Jung and Adler. As Mahony shows, Freud tries to give the Wolfman, and the reader, no choice with his reconstructions. After introducing the primal scene, Freud asks for the reader's provisional belief. He then asks the reader to assume that the primal scene has been educed in a technically correct way and that it is the indispensable solution. Freud then announces that we as his readers must choose whether everything is exactly as he has said or whether it is total nonsense. How are we to resist? To establish infantile sexuality through the primal scene would refute Adler and Jung. Freud sought the same goal by positing the phylogenetic inheritance of infantile sexuality.

Mahony wonders whether the primal scene is Freud's own. He suggests that Freud's difficulty with recognizing aggression toward his own father interfered with his interpretation of the Wolf man's negative transference. Freud was insistent. The Wolfman, yielding and compliant, seemed willing to do what Freud needed of him. Mahony gives examples, left out by Strachey's translation, that show the Wolf Man case to have been written up with polemical intent. Mahony also points to verbal traces suggesting (p. 116) "that the analysis, like a dream, was the fulfillment of a wish" (derived from *gewünschten Aufklärungen* as "wished-for explanations"). In Mahony's reading, the Wolf Man allowed himself to be penetrated from behind by Freud's fantasies.

Mahony argues that Freud's persuasive rhetoric is meant to overcome Freud's own doubts as well as his audiences, and notes that Freud, over and over, uses the words "conviction" and "convincing" in this text, unlike in any other. The German root, *zeugen*, means to witness and to procreate, as Freud acknowledges in his essay on the Rat Man. These, together, constitute the primal scene. Mahony argues that in this text, more than any other, Freud does not demonstrate, but attempts to persuade or convince through rhetoric. He considers this to be both polemical (against Adler and Jung) and a derivative enactment of primal scene fantasies (*überzeugen* as witnessing and copulation). Mahony regards the frequency of the word, *überzeugen*, as an oneiric trace, i.e., as *one* contribution to the writing. According to Mahony, there are lexical elements in the text relating to obsessional neurosis, which is being described as derived from the primal scene. "Convince," the word for the primal scene, is balanced by words representing obsessional neurosis (force, compel, belief, doubt, suspicion, and so on). The compulsive doubt in the text is negated by words such as "surely," "believe," "suspect." Mahony (pp. 113–14) assembles Freud's varied sentences relating to *überzeugen*; the reader is impressed with Freud's attempt to convince.

In *Freud and the Rat Man* (1986), Mahony is writing more as a confident practicing psychoanalyst, while retaining his literary critical approach. He now approaches Freud more as a professional colleague, whose work he is critiquing. Mahony is persuasive about Freud's distortions in exaggerating the psychoanalytic (therapeutic) accomplishment in this case. He is again convincing that Freud seeks to dominate and influence both patient and reader. At the same time, Freud's own defenses against his obsessional tendencies interfere with a coherent presentation of the patient's obsessional neurosis. Freud, like the Rat Man, must enact isolation and avoidance of contact, so that gaps and discontinuities must be preserved, precluding synthesis and integration.

Mahony is especially talented at demonstrating, by close affective reading, Freud's need for defense/distance from dangerous instinctual thrusts. For example, Mahony nicely shows (pp. 183–188) Freud's sudden shifts of tense, away from present-tense narration into the past, in the famous scene wherein Freud utters the words "into the anus." The Rat Man creates a gap, by withholding the words, enticing Freud to penetrate and fill this gap by his speech. Retranslating from the German, Mahony (p. 104) reveals Freud's active participation in the intrusive enactment: "What I [Freud] could do is to guess fully [*erraten*], from something hinted by him, *about what ought to happen*" (Mahony's italics). Mahony elaborates on the "omniscient," "correct" meaning of "*erraten*," which adds to the sense of Freud filling in the patient's gaps. Although other psychoanalysts have described a similar sadomasochistic homosexual transference/countertransference enactment between Freud and the Rat Man, none have been able to demonstrate this, and the defenses against it, within Freud's narration.

In *On Defining Freud's Discourse* (1989) Mahony's passion is louder about writing and reading. He shows us how (and encourages us to join him) he allows himself to resonate creatively as reader/rereader/interpreter of Freud as creative writer/mentor/psychoanalytic explorer. Writing and reading *both* become exciting, creative acts, when one allows oneself to discover where one is going, while immersed in writing or reading. Mahony encourages his readers to follow Freud's example ("Itzig, the Sunday rider") of writing as creative organization of as yet barely formulated inner experience. Writing becomes a creative act of self-discovery.

Various psychoanalysts (e.g., McDougall 1980) have described sitting down to write an article when they are troubled about a psychoanalytic case. I have certainly done this, most notably when I felt troubled that the work with certain patients was not progressing as well as they and I had expected (Coen 1989 and chapter 8 of this book). A patient who came to me after having read a paper of mine, left abruptly, angrily taunting me, "At least you'll probably get a paper out of this!" (He was wrong). In fact, Mahony takes his readers back earlier, to St. Augustine (Mahony 1989:vi): "I try to be among the number of those who write as they progress and who progress as they write." Mahony is inspired/energized by this model of creative writing/exploring, which he does so well. He invites the reader to join him, just as Freud invites his reader (here Mahony). However, Mahony allows his reader more creative space and imagination than does Freud, who is much more intent on influencing and dominating his reader/patient.

Mahony evokes a psychoanalytic emphasis on process, the writer's and the reader's. Because of its importance, I quote again the passage from the introduction to this book. Mahony writes (1989:94):

> My own approach presumes that Freud's texts, like crystals, have
> fault lines, and I wonder where they are and how wittingly as well as

unwittingly they are covered up. I muse about whether Freud's self-irony fully accounts for the gaps or contradictions in his report. Given the foiling nature of the unconscious, these questions are where I begin, not end, my enquiry. In addition, by splitting my ego into participant and observer role, I aim to respond antiphonally to the dual activity that characterized Freud's own compositional creativity."

Mahony tells his readers that he is working within a writing space and a reading space that are akin to the analytic space.

Mahony emulates with his reader, and with Freud-as-writer, Freud's interactive engagement with his reader and his work. This leads to a creative enactment in reading Mahony reading Freud. Writing and reading thus become creative, psychoanalytic experiences of working out and working through. Freud has contributed to what Mahony (p. 94) calls a "hermeneutics of suspicion" in reading; reading can never be complete and closed but must, on the contrary, aim to open and question.

Mahony is persuasive about Freud's conscious, preconscious, and unconscious efforts to deal with the readers' resistances so as to influence them. Mahony shows us a passionate Freud, writing under the sway of intense feeling that infiltrates his prose. He demonstrates persuasively, from the German, the erotized tone of Freud's writing about Katharina. Mahony arouses us too with images of the mountain setting in which Freud and Katharina meet, with references to climbing, falling, looking, penetrating, abstaining, and desiring. He convinces us that Freud's creativity involves expressing and managing his desire.

Mahony introduces us to Helmut Junker, who opens up the logical contradiction in the title of Freud's "Analysis terminable and interminable." The emphasis shifts to flow, movement, interweaving of this contradiction between "ending" and "nonending." Mahony (p. 85) shows us Freud's tendency to find "similarity-in-difference" within the psyche. Mahony will not simply accept Freud's well-known tendency to think in binary terms. Freud's writing becomes richer as Mahony twists and turns these polarities back on themselves and on each other. Whatever these seeming opposites may be, ending and non-ending, ego and id, eros and thanatos, and so on, they cannot be separated so easily. Freud's story of life and psychic conflict becomes a struggle among division, intermixing, synthesis, and integration, that can never be clearly and forever won. Mahony, the classicist, heightens Freud's tragic view of life. He returns Freud to the Scholastics (p.87): "*Distinguo ut uniam* (I distinguish in order to unite)."

Mahony and I agree about the importance of attempting to elaborate a psychology of writing and reading that is both literary and psychoanalytic. In Mahony's work, both author and reader struggle to work through conflicts in the acts of writing and reading, seeking creative expression and integration. In reading Freud, Mahony would have us be attentive to Freud's creative and conflictual needs, within his text and toward his readers. And he would have us attend to our own attempts to seek creative solutions to our conflicts as we read Freud, conflicts within ourselves and toward our progenitor, Freud. Writing and reading become "ending" and "non-ending." Our struggles and our creative efforts are never done. Eschewing such closure makes both writing and reading more exciting, more creative, worth turning to again and again. Mahony shows us this by his own creative rereadings of Freud (and himself), as he leads us to read, write, and create with and through him.

"French Freud": Felman

I want to examine "French Freud" through the lenses of two very thoughtful, innovative, and talented American academicians. Neither should be approached as an introduction to Lacan (Felman) nor to Derrida (Weber). Each author uses French criticism to make her or his own important points. Thus Felman's title, *Jacques Lacan and the Adventure of Insight* (1987), is deceptive. This is less a book about Lacan's influence than a use of Lacan as a metaphor for a questioning reader (of Freud). Felman writes about problems of reading and interpreting both texts and patients. Since Felman, Donelly Professor of French at Yale, has written some of the best "psychoanalytic" literary criticism (e.g., 1977), her cautions about reading and interpreting are worth the attention of both psychoanalysts and literary critics.

Felman's criticism is good because she helps us read better—more honestly, more complexly, by enjoying the difficulties and problems in reading, the ambiguities, contradictions, and uncertainties, rather than by trying to foreclose these by pressured interpretation. That is bad psychoanalytic practice in the consulting room just as it is in reading literature. Premature interpretation cuts us off from the complexities of manifold meanings, branching out in more directions than we can catch, the terrors of the unknown or unknowable, the uncertain or unstable. Psychoanalysts, who are so well aware of the need for open-ended listening with analysands, too often presume to have privileged access to *the* hidden meanings of literature. Thoughtful critics, such as Felman or Fish (1980), write "conservative" psychological criticism, where the psychological interpretations are very modest indeed. They provide us psychoanalysts with more reasonable and humble expectations for our reading and interpreting.

Literary critics may not realize that in the consulting room, the best psychoanalytic work is similar to their interpretive work. The skilled psychoanalyst attempts to move her or his patient forward with a minimum of intervention, without imposing too much on the patient. Idealization of the other, by psychoanalyst and by literary critic, tends to interfere with knowing that the best interpretation is the simplest and most elegant, the one that opens closed doors and allows the other (patient, reader) to proceed further on his or her own. For examples of this in the literature on psychoanalytic technique, see E. Kris (1956), A. Kris (1982), Gardner (1983), Schafer (1983), and Renik (1990).

Questioning, understanding, interpreting, and reading are actions to be understood by how they work, by their effects. Wisdom requires tolerance for ambiguity, uncertainty, and contradiction. "Of course," we reply, "we already know that!" Yet we do not, or we use a partial denial, so that we may grasp at meanings in order to reassure or stabilize ourselves.

Felman emphasizes that concern with difference and paradox opens the way to new readings of patients and texts. Focusing the reverberations between interpreter and interpreted, analyst and analysand, reader and text, conscious and unconscious, avoids mechanical repetition (as defense against the unknown/unknowable). The task of psychoanalyst, literary critic, or teacher is to raise questions rather than to provide answers.

Felman's readers may need to remind themselves that her book is not about Lacan but about the "myth of Lacan," as critically reflexive rereader of Freud. Felman aims to encourage identification with the position of analyst-reader, struggling with what is "other" within others, as well as within ourselves. The entire book is to be read as parable, with Lacan representing an advocate for Felman's way of reading. Lacan is not the hero who knows how to read but a problematic reader just as we all are. Felman decenters all stable reading positions, except the one she allows for "Lacan." Weber, as I shall demonstrate, will tumble Lacan, as well as everyone and everything else.

Lacan's view of the unconscious, as more the subject of psychoanalytic investigation than the object, as primarily "that which reads" rather than simply "that which must be read," is used to raise a set of questions about reading. What does it mean to be a reader and what does a reader do? These questions are central. In her section on practical criticism, Felman asks how poetry works and what leads to art's *effect*. She warns that (p.48) "there is no language in which interpretation can itself escape the effects of the unconscious; the interpreter is not more immune than the poet to unconscious delusions and errors." Situating the interpreter or analyst inside, rather than outside the text (in some privileged position), raises the question of (p. 49) "*how* to implicate psychoanalysis in literature" as "a question for interpretation."

Like Reed (1982), Felman suggests studying the contradictions and problems in the literary critical history of a given text as a way of approaching the *effects* of the text. Reed (1982) attempts this in a study on Diderot, drawing on the concept of parallelism in psychoanalytic supervision (between patient and analyst as between analyst and supervisor). Melanie Klein's text, as used by Lacan and Felman (as I reread this), is not to be understood as actually referring to clinical practice but to a metaphor of interpretation. It is intended to move the psychoanalyst's attention from the content of interpretation to interpretation as an act, a performance, with consequences and effects. The psychoanalytic narrative, as centrally involved with what is "other" to the self, is not just the province of Lacanians. Hermeneutists, object relations theorists, reader-response critics, Roy Schafer (despite Felman's opinion), and so forth, are in the same arena.

Each section of Felman's chapter "Beyond Oedipus" elegantly moves to one "beyond" itself, decentering each position. Following Lacan, she moves us beyond *Oedipus Rex*, where psychoanalytic writers stop, to *Oedipus at Colonnus*. Here there is an acceptance (at death) of what is "other" within oneself; death becomes birth, and desire and destiny become myth. The importance of "beyond" is that there is no end, no final resting place from which to understand. The important rereading of *Beyond the Pleasure Principle* is that beyond one myth there is always another myth, so that (p. 146) "the tale (Freud's, Oedipus's, Lacan's) is never ended".

Like the other authors I consider here, Felman also tells her readers that myth is central to psychoanalytic theory; it cannot be superseded. Psychoanalysis, like literary criticism, must continue to be self-reflexively self-critical or else become delusionally blinded. Psychoanalytic knowledge is similar to literary knowledge as (p. 92) "a knowledge which does not know what it knows, and is thus *not in possession of itself*." The model for this is the dream. Freud's work should be read as poetic texts, in the sense that Freud could not be master or sole authority of the meanings of his texts.

"French Freud": Weber

Weber's *The Legend of Freud* (1982) is a fascinating but difficult book that deserves to be read by American psychoanalysts and by literary critics interested in psychoanalysis. Already in 1979, Weber pointed out major problems with Strachey's translation; only Mahony (1977) had reported this in print. Weber is devastating to any psychoanalytic theory that claims to exempt itself from unconscious conflict, within the theory itself and within its proponents. However, readers need to keep in mind that Weber follows an extreme position: that nothing is conflict-free. All thinking and all theory are thus modeled on the dream. This extreme position is contradictory to American ego psychology. Weber idealizes the uncanny force of the unconscious, its power, its processiveness, its ongoingness, so that there cannot be relatively stable compromise formations. The latter would be delusional speculation on the part of the American psychoanalytic establishment, in the effort to secure itself against the dangers of unconscious forces. Nevertheless, Weber's argument is unsettling, as it is intended to be.

Weber gives fine examples of places where Strachey's translation misses the connotative meaning of Freud's words, overly emphasizing the denotative meaning (e.g., Weber:113, where he shows that Freud's image of "that play of mirrors (*Unter jener Vorspiegelung*) in the Joke Book is rendered by Strachey as "The pretense makes it possible that"). Or Weber (p. 89) shows that Strachey reverses Freud's meaning in the Joke Book that substantial thoughts are used as an envelope or guise by the unconscious. Strachey, more rationally, writes that important thoughts are served (preserved) in jokes. Weber claims that Freud in fact subverted this concept.

Weber tells us in his preface (p. xvii) that Freud's texts in German must be read like dreams, with the emphasis on *Entstellung*, disfigurement, dislocation, distortion. As a metaphorical model for reading Freud this is wonderful stuff, but Weber fully believes this, and that is quite another story. His project, reminiscent of Artaud or Céline, is to put the uncanny force back into Freud by unsettling his readers from any stable conflict-free position. We are to struggle with what our unconscious is doing with us. Weber uses Freud's own writing to argue that Freud's rejection of psychoanalytic heretics gives Freud a privileged position in judging what is and what is not psychoanalytic. Freud denies this to the heretics. Freud accuses others, who try to systematize theory speculatively, of narcissism, "the standpoint of the ego," missing the play of unconscious conflict. Freud wants to be rid of, to eliminate (*Abfallsbewegung*) most competing theories. Weber asks whether Freud's arguments against systematizing of theory, in his polemic against his competitors, do not also apply to Freud's own efforts. To a degree, one can grant Weber (and Freud) that all theorists have a narcissistic investment in their theories; the theories may help to protect against certain feared dangers (see Rothstein 1980; Coen 1987). Weber's task, however, is to use Freud against himself, to argue that any attempt to theorize about unconscious conflict must be subverted by the latter, which will always have the last laugh. That is, unconscious conflict cannot be pinned down once and for all within our theories. Unconscious conflict will, as it were, mock our naive attempts to control it within our theories by upending any fixed theoretical position.

Weber problematizes the relations between observation and interpretation in Freud. Freud writes in 1938 (*S. E.* 23:159): "We form our observations by means of the very same perceptual apparatus, precisely with the help of gaps in the psyche, by supplementing what has been left out with conclusions that lie close at hand, translating the omissions into conscious material." Weber questions how such "conclusions that lie close at hand [*durch naheliegende Schluss-folgerungen ergänzen*]" are reached, since "gaps" of the unconscious will be present in the analyst as well. He argues that *Entstellung* (distortion, dislocation) must be implicated in any Freudian description, which cannot merely be a representation of unconscious processes.

Although Freud attempts to posit description as the beginning of scientific activity, he quickly changes the beginning away from such description of experience to (Weber 1982:34) "certain abstract ideas which derive from 'various sources.'" Weber then attempts to argue that there are no such "beginning" positions in Freud's thinking. All theory is implicated in (by) the affects (e.g., anxiety) and unconscious forces it describes; there is no position before, beyond, outside of this.

The interpreter of the dream (Weber 1982:68), like the dreamer, or the dream theorist, is similarly implicated in a larger process of *verstellenden Entstellung* (dissimulating dislocation). Weber is at his (literary critical) best (pp. 68–75) in describing Freud's model dream, which requires *no interpretation* (from the Dream Book). This is a section worth many readings.

Weber is masterful in describing how Freud introduces this dream, whose source is unknown, as absolutely clear. Freud then, in passing, increasingly makes clear that the dream is not so clear, that there are problems of seeing and not seeing, of light and dark, that the dream cannot be simply unveiled (with the word play on the word "veil" and "veils"—*unverhüllt gegeben*). The dream interpreter is (Weber 1982:75) "a protagonist, and the results of his actions are determined by a relation of forces in which he is inscribed." From here, Weber moves (1982:75) to the "navel" of the dream (Strachey called it the "core"), "the place where it straddles the unknown (*dem Unerkannten aufsitzt*)." Weber translates Freud's *netzartige Verstrickung* as "netlike entanglement," emphasizing the "snares of a trap."

Weber argues against Lacan's view that the navel of the dream is something definite, like the abyss. That is, Weber argues that there is no center to the dream; the dream work does not have a starting point. Weber's meaning of the "*thallus*" is worth examining. Interpretation involves deception. That the navel of the dream straddles the unknown, Weber translates from the German into being duped or deluded, by the unknown. This is brilliantly done!

Using jokes and child's play, Weber argues against Lacan's attempt to distinguish the symbolic from the imaginary. Again, Weber tries to demonstrate how humans are duped by their intense narcissistic wishes for sameness. This is an interesting position, but, once again, it seems too either/or. The *fort/da* game becomes a performance in speech, a command to an illusory other summoned by the child when left alone. Not the actual mother but an illusory substitute is summoned, which contains revenge and ambivalent relatedness toward the actual, separate mother.

Weber's discussion of jokes in relation to the addressee, and in relation to id and superego, is well done. He nicely connects wit, knowledge, and *Schaulust* (pleasure in looking) in jokes and in their telling. Weber (p. 116) argues against any final or definite "proper place" within a psychoanalytic model. "A conflictual dynamics of displacement" (dislocation [*Entstellung*]) leads to unsettling any "proper place" (p. 146); rather, what becomes important is the relation between repetition involving alteration or dislocation and repetition involving identification or sameness. Thus, Freud's introduction of the death drive can be viewed as an attempt (narcissistic, illusory) to go "beyond," to reach origins, a final resting place. This being impossible, only more of the same kind of conflictual repetition, alteration, is discovered—it is unsettling!

Weber elegantly unsettles Freud's uses of the *Symposium* in *Beyond the Pleasure Principle*. He argues that Freud idealized psychoanalytic theory as a "beyond," where indeed things can be definitely known. Aristophanes, poet, storyteller of the absurd, in Weber's reading, disrupts any clear account of the origins of man, by the view that desire cannot be clearly fixed or defined. There is no definite, final story of origins, only more stories to be told. Weber writes (p. 158): "The navel is left wrinkled, knotted, interrupting the smooth surface of the body, which, as Freud knew, serves the ego as its model." Like the navel of the dream, the navel of the body or of the psyche cannot be (p. 159) "hermetically sealed." The same, for Weber, applies to psychoanalytic theory.

Contemporary Freud scholarship is a kind of revisionist enterprise. Traditional assumptions psychoanalysts have made about the content of what Freud said are now called into question by emphasis on context and process in Freud's writing. The style of Freud's thinking and writing (Holt and Mahony) are examined as guides for reading Freud's prose. The actual ideas Freud presented are to be understood within the conflicts and contradictions in Freud's mind and in his texts. How Freud attempted to persuade and influence his audience has been examined in detail. Psychoanalytic and literary critical methods converge in careful attention to the process and experience of being a reader of Freud. What Freud was doing in writing, in and out of his awareness, and what we, as readers, are doing in reading him, become foci for attention. The same applies to Strachey and to us, as readers of Strachey in English. Writing and reading become literary and psychological events, complex, multidetermined, not easily understood. Recent Freud scholarship begins to approach a psychology of writing and reading.

I have emphasized the reader's subjective experience in reading

Freud. There is disagreement about this, in terms of techniques of fiction versus techniques of psychoanalysis. Skilled writers involve their readers in themselves and their writing through the fictional techniques I have described. I assume that Freud, additionally, consciously attempted to place his readers in the position of analysands. He could then influence them transferentially and interpret resistance against the reader's connection of the writing with the reader's own unconscious instinctual trends. That is, Freud wrote as a fine literary craftsman and as a thoughtful psychoanalyst. Further, Freud's own unconscious traces and conflicts can be found in his writing. Literary criticism and psychoanalysis are integrated in attention to the reader's own affective responses, problems, doubts, and uncertainties in reading Freud's texts. Mahony tells his readers that this is how he in fact works.

Contemporary Freud scholarship attempts to move the audience away from idealized readings of Freud toward much greater emphasis on what Freud was doing with us, and on what we want to do with him. From this perspective, writing is neither wholly conflict-free nor wholly subverted by unconscious instinctual forces. A "both/and" perspective to writing integrates both conflict-free ego activities (or, perhaps, effective and stable compromise formations) and infiltration and enactment of instinctual derivatives in the writing. This should not be surprising. It offers a bridge between "French Freud" and traditional American ego-psychological Freud studies. Recent Freud studies call attention to the reader's own psyche while reading. This combines current literary critical methods with psychoanalytic ones. The goal of this contemporary scholarship, however, is not to psychoanalyze Freud. The emphasis is literary, textual, on what the writer is doing in his text with his reader. The best of this criticism seems well aware of what critics themselves are after in their rereadings of Freud. Where this is outside of awareness, the criticism (or translation) may become excessively marred by the writer's own conflicts. Hence: writer, know thyself!

Although I object to the either/or emphasis on the unconscious in "French Freud," Felman and Weber provide very important cautions against the illusion of freedom from one's own unconscious conflicts. Thus, the illusion of a "beyond," of a final resting place, or starting place, outside of conflict, from which smugly and safely, to view unconscious forces, will always tempt psychoanalytic critics. So too will we be tempted by dogmatism, certainty, answers, which safely foreclose doubt, uncertainty, and anxiety. We need to be reminded that Freud, Strachey, and every other psychoanalyst, has tried to bypass (mostly

unconsciously) their own doubts and uncertainties. Psychoanalysts
would expect that. Careful attention to the writer's and reader's own
motivations in writing and reading may help to keep us more open and
honest. Freud and Weber are wise to warn us that what seems not to
need interpretation, to be absolutely clear, may be otherwise.

Will any of this change our understanding of (Freudian) psychoanalysis? Will a new translation of Freud, or further study of Strachey's
influence, alter our psychoanalytic theory? The answer is that psychoanalysts have already made Freud our own. Now we are acknowledging
this more openly. That is a major advantage of processive readings of
Freud. Students of psychoanalysis, newcomers as well as experts, are
being welcomed to join in reading and interpreting Freud (enjoying
Freud), rather than exclusively trying "to get" Freud's ideas. We have
all been doing this. Now we are owning it.

What will Freud scholarship change? We now acknowledge the uses
we have been making of Freud (and Freud of us) all along. The role of
bias, need, conflict in our understanding, interpretation, and theories
becomes clearer. This is important for historical studies of psychoanalysis as well as for the psychology of belief. Freud would have welcomed this, especially from American psychoanalysts.

Chapter 8

CONCLUSION: TOWARD A PSYCHOLOGY OF WRITING AND READING

Method in Psychoanalytic Literary Criticism

Since so little psychoanalytic attention has been paid to the psychology of writing and reading, this chapter will outline a psychoanalytic psychology of writing and reading and indicate directions for further study. A psychoanalytic literary criticism should begin by examining the roles and needs of the writer and reader. My review of writings in psychoanalysis and literary criticism reveals (see chapter 1 in this book) that the author/reader relationship has not been examined psychologically in close detail: neither psychoanalysts nor literary critics have described comprehensively what happens to reader or writer during their literary encounter.

Psychoanalysts' formulations have tended to be abstract, general, and at some distance from the processes of writing and reading. Reader-response criticism has attended to details of the problems of reading, without, however, sufficient consideration of what happens psychologically to the reader as he or she reads, followed then by close examination of what the reader does with these experiences. That readers can now relate problems in their reading a text to the meanings they construct of that text directs the attention of critics and psychoanalysts to the process of reading. It does not, however, focus our attention on how individual readers or critics experience such problems during reading, or how they process these so as to differentiate idiosyncratic personal responses that are to be judged irrelevant to the reading task at hand from those responses that can be organized into relevant meanings for the text studied. Exceptions to this have largely included exercises for literature students in which students have been encouraged by author-teachers to draw upon their own subjective experiences during reading to construct meanings.

Skilled literary critics certainly do focus closely on the details of reading a text, including the problems, uncertainties, inconsistencies, traps, and so forth encountered. For example, Fish's (1980) very careful readings reveal close attention to the reader's problems during reading a text. But Fish gives his readers little sense of what happens to him during such struggles and what he then does with such experiences as he tries to interpret texts. This book has offered some examples of my own attempts to process my subjective reading experiences in reading certain texts (chapters 2–5) as well as somewhat similar accounts by Mahony (chapters 6 and 7). This is not to say that in order for psychoanalytic literary criticism to succeed it must draw upon the author's subjective reading experiences. I would assume, however, that most skilled critics draw upon their own emotional responses during reading, using them as one pathway toward interpretation, without explicitly formulating and acknowledging this procedure.

To my mind, what is most intriguing about linking psychoanalysis with literary criticism is precisely this union of the methods by which psychoanalysts and critics work. Less by theory than by the practices of interpretation can each discipline enrich the other and yield a distinctive psychoanalytic literary criticism. Again, my model is the combined psychoanalyst literary critic who succeeds at practicing both disciplines. Although few will be able to manage full formal training in both fields, the psychoanalytic literary critic should be able to draw upon the methods and practices of each discipline. That is, he or she should be able to read texts carefully and closely *and* have enough access to her or his own internal psychic resonances with the text to be able to utilize *some* of these to understand the text. Psychoanalytic literary critics, just like practicing psychoanalysts, need to be able to organize their inner responses hierarchically on a continuum of relevance to the text in contrast to relevance primarily to their own internal conflicts. In practice, the distinctive methods of criticism and of psychoanalysis should have been sufficiently integrated so that the psychoanalytic literary critic is able to work smoothly at an interface between both disciplines (Simon 1992 unpublished).

This model for the practice of psychoanalytic literary criticism differs from a model that uses aspects of psychoanalytic theory or the theory of the psychoanalytic process (Skura 1981) for interpreting texts. Although such theory can help illuminate problems of reading literature, the risk is of mechanically applying aspects of psychoanalytic theory to textual interpretation. Such misuse of theory for inappropriate interpretation is bad practice with texts as it is with patients. Literary critics may be disappointed if what they seek from psychoanalysis is primarily a theory of the human mind with which they can understand characters, narrators, and authors more fully. I would argue that it is the *method* of the practicing psychoanalyst that can enrich the work of the literary critic. The way to learn psychoanalytic method is through psychoanalytic training, full or partial. I refer to those colleagues, already skilled critics, who have sought training at a psychoanalytic institute. Some have become practicing psychoanalysts while continuing a distinguished academic career. Others have had partial psychoanalytic training with the aim of using this to enhance their investigative work in another area. To learn the method of the practicing psychoanalyst requires personal psychoanalysis and some experience with conducting psychoanalysis under supervision; theoretical learning alone is insufficient for freeing people to be able to draw upon their own psychic responses in order to understand and interpret (analyze) another, person or text. Some have compromised with partial psychoanalytic training that includes personal psychoanalysis and selected courses at a psychoanalytic institute, including some courses in psychoanalytic process and technique, in which actual cases are presented in detail. They have not, however, conducted analysis under supervision, which itself usually requires some preliminary clinical experience provided by the training institute. Not only literature professors have obtained such psychoanalytic experience but also professors of history, philosophy, aesthetics and art history, anthropology, sociology, and so on.

There is a parallel to the psychoanalytic situation here. The most persuasive psychoanalytic case writings are those in which the author presents considerable detail of the psychoanalytic process; details of what the patient said and did, what the analyst said and did, and also what the analyst imagined, thought, felt, and how the analyst reached his or her strategies with that patient. Since psychoanalytic treatment is indeed an intensely felt experience for both participants, outside observers need details of what has actually transpired within and between analysand and analyst. The reader is then able, to a degree, to resonate with both patient and analyst. Without such detail of the psychoanalytic process and the transactions between the analytic couple, the reader remains a total outsider, necessarily skeptical of the analyst author's unsubstantiated, and usually self-serving, assertions. Some will still argue that each analytic couple has already so shaped their interaction consciously and unconsciously that what is revealed to others may be very different from the actual pathways they have taken. Further, psychoanalytic authors almost always choose to reveal their treatment successes or at least to present their work as if it had been successful. When analysts have indeed disclosed their treatment problems, others have questioned those writers' motivation in revealing their "failings." The program committee of the American Psychoanalytic Association has recently (1991–1993) sponsored a series of panels at its meetings on analytic problems, difficulties, stalemates, and failures with the explicit aim of encouraging analysts to discuss such dilemmas publicly.

Aspects of the Psychology of Writing and Reading (with Dependent Authors)

Consideration of the psychology of writing and reading in this chapter must necessarily remain focused on the dependent authors discussed in this book. Hence, this chapter should be regarded as an outline of one model of the author/reader relationship, which may or may not apply to other authors and readers. It is presented as a summary of themes described in my exercises in practical criticism (see chapters 2–5), which provide the data for these hypotheses. I believe that there is *some* universal applicability to the themes here considered. Further, this model of the author/reader relationship is proferred to stimulate others to investigate other models of the author/reader relationship with other authors. The present model is one approach to a psychology of writing and reading, which will need to be amplified with detailed descriptions of what transpires between other authors and other readers.

Writing and reading will be regarded in this chapter as behaviors that, to varying degrees, can be adapted to manage conflict. At varying times, in different authors and different readers, writing and reading may be relatively free of conflict *or* heavily involved in efforts to manage conflict. I repeat for emphasis—writing and reading need not be dominated by conflict. Of course, what is in conflict will range over the entire spectrum of human struggle.

Given the authors I have chosen to study, I focus on the uses of fantasy in writing and reading especially for managing feared need and destructiveness with others. From this perspective, creative work and creative mastery are considered in relation to needs to manage destructiveness and dependency. Although this approach fits the authors I have studied, it neglects other conflicts. Of course, the narrowed focus of this chapter cannot encompass all the aspects of human conflict that can be played out in creativity. The reader should keep in mind that my approach must necessarily omit all the rest of what author and reader want from their encounter that is outside such conflict: the literary pleasures (e.g., Barthes 1973) and even other psychological needs. For example, although (feared) loss is a major issue in dependency, it is not my primary focus here; but see Aberbach's (1989) moving essay on creativity in holocaust survivors (also, Hamilton 1969; Pollock 1978).

I shall contrast differing meanings of creativity, especially how creative work avoids *or* assists creative psychological integration of dangerous conflict—a central theme in the authors I have studied. I consider creativity in writing and reading in relation to the capacity to integrate envy and destructiveness and to draw on this in creative work. I also discuss the inhibition of creativity in relation to the dangers of separateness and fantasied destructiveness. The reader of the authors considered here is imagined as contending with conflicts that are *somewhat* similar in content, although, I hope, far milder, than the author/narrator/characters face. That is, this chapter conceives of an emotional force field between and among author, narrator, characters, text, and reader that resonates with somewhat similar needs and struggles in each. To be a reader of the authors considered here seems to require emotional access to some of the same psychic strife as author/narrator/characters must contend. Of course, this fiction of a relatively symmetrical psychic force field between author, text, and reader is intended only for the authors considered here. This is a fictive model constructed to investigate dynamic interactions among these particular authors, texts, and their readers.

Who Is the Author and How Do We Find Him?

I ask my readers not to be offended at my putting the early Freud (of the letters to Fliess, 1887–1902) in the company of Genet, Céline, and Sade. I chose to study *these* authors because each is unusually involved with his reader/audience. Their writings provide ready access to this interaction. The author/reader interaction in these writings especially centers on issues of dependency and destructiveness. I shall highlight certain similarities and substantial differences in their *psychological* goals and accomplishments in writing. I have argued earlier about Genet, Céline, Sade, and Freud, that the intensity of certain authors' efforts to elicit affirmation and acceptance from their audience is actively in the foreground of their writing rather than embedded in the background as an unconscious wish. There is a psychoanalytic analogy that, for some patients, the basic early maternal relationship with the analyst cannot be taken for granted as the background for the whole psycho-analytic venture but must be brought out front right from the start. I have emphasized these authors' attempts to engage and force their audience into an intensely responsive relationship, representative of loving parent and child, whose task is to provide the authors with affir-mation, admiration and acceptance, despite their badness, which is now to be safely contained within the relationship. I have regarded this as an essential, partly conscious but largely unconscious, purpose of the writ-ing. Other, less needy authors are not so preoccupied with a desire for connection and acceptance by their audience. They are less driven to attempt its enactment by eliciting intense responsiveness from reader, narrator, or characters; such desires tend to remain less consciously in the background of their writing project without thrusting themselves so much into the foreground. Of course, for writing to work, the read-er must become engaged. Ordinarily, this occurs without our becom-ing aware of it, without such obvious self-conscious preoccupation in reader and author about their relationship.

Each author I studied was depressed at the time of his writing and each sought to be healed through writing. Each attempted this through mastery of painful feelings by writing about and through them. Each sought a creative experience that would interrupt his depression, open-ing the path to confident assurance that he could manage himself bet-ter. These authors sought greater control over their feelings and their worlds (in relation to which they felt helpless) by creating new imagi-nary worlds of their own. The reader too is to be controlled and manipulated, so that he takes on the writer's feelings of uncertainty and help-lessness, and thereby reassures the writer of his influence and power. I have emphasized *psychologically* in these authors an intense dependent need for contact and reassurance, especially about guilt and anxiety related to rage and destructiveness. These are certainly central issues in pathological dependency (Coen 1992) and it is not surprising that dependent authors would enact such themes in their writing. I have been impressed by the (temporary) usefulness of creative writing for transforming what is most awful within oneself into creative, poetic, exciting, or universal images and themes, thereby (temporarily) reas-suring the author of his worth. Thus one's badness is made not to count. Dependent people have multiple ways of *avoiding* what they fear they cannot tolerate and integrate within themselves. Dependent writ-ers are no different. Writing becomes a kind of literary magic for seek-ing to transform badness into beauty and truth.

This contrasts with efforts to face and integrate what is most awful and intolerable within. To do so requires tolerance of the anxiety and guilt associated with such dangerous feelings and wishes. This is, of course, a major goal of a psychoanalysis. The writers I have studied have instead sought a magical reassurance (a *writing cure*) that their badness does not preclude their being accepted and loved. This has been a vital function of the reader/audience. To a degree, Freud attempted to go beyond this. He did seek to use his relationship with his reader for reassurance against self-doubt, grandiosity and ambi-tion, destructiveness, and competitiveness. In so doing, as in a psy-choanalysis, he became aware (to a degree) of his resentment, ideal-ization, and competitiveness with his reader/supporter (Fliess). To a certain extent, he tried to face his anger at his reader and to have the reader tolerate his doing so. However, the writer (Freud) did not seem able to face his anger fully and directly and his reader (Fliess) could not bear to be the object of this hatred, as a psychoanalyst would have had to be. Consequently, this had to become an incomplete analysis. We see here an attempt at a *writing cure* that is not just based on magic and avoidance but on a genuine attempt to face and integrate what is dangerous within. Thus, Freud's psychological project (and accom-plishment) differs from the other writers I consider even though it is incomplete.

I would expect that all writing, as a creative effort, *may* involve con-flict (to varying degrees, in different authors, at different times) between attempts to stabilize (reassure) oneself in the face of inner dangers and efforts to confront and integrate these dangers (i.e., to change, move forward to a more mature level of psychic integration). For example, Genet, Céline, and Sade each repeatedly describes threatened craziness in his writing and seems to reassure himself that he has faced this down and written through it. Henry James in "The Jolly Corner" and Guy de Maupassant in "The Horla" each attempts a similar confrontation with dangerous disintegration. Maupassant's attempt is especially impressive because of his awareness that he was deteriorating from general paresis. That Maupassant can write such a fine short story about increasing (organic) madness must reassure him that his talent (mind) is still intact. Crews (1990) suggests that Flannery O'Connor managed to confine to her writing much of the helplessness, claustrophobia, and rage she felt in her losing struggle with systemic lupus erythematosus. The deterioration of a creative writer's brain and mind is a terrible threat, which can be *undone* (denied) only by further creative writing. This was the case with a creative writer I saw in consultation who had become panicky and somewhat depressed that his writing was now partially impeded by such illness. He felt under enormous pressure, as if his psychic survival required it, to demonstrate that he could still write creatively. The other (progressive) side of this is the very painful attempt through such writing to confront and bear such illness, loss, and death.

It takes considerable courage and strength to confront and integrate what is most troublesome within, so as to progress to a new, healthier, more autonomous position. This is true for patients in psychoanalysis just as it is true for creative writers. What most people seek is temporary reassurance in order to stabilize themselves and to preserve their present adaptation. That should not be surprising, for patients or for writers. Nor is it surprising that troubled writers would turn to their talent and craft, within the written text as well as within the imaginary and real relationship with an audience, to accomplish this. It should be remembered, even as we seek psychological meanings, that creative writers write primarily because they enjoy it and are good at it; it is their craft (cf. Crews 1990). Of course, creative writers will draw on what is within them, conflicted and unconflicted.

My focus here is on attempts to manage such conflict in creating, either by avoidance and magical reassurance, or by genuine attempts to master and integrate it. I am impressed by the ability of seriously depressed, troubled people to create during such periods, or even, like Sade and Genet, to begin to write creatively at such a time, and to feel better/nurtured by such creative effort. Aberbach (1989) suggests that creative writing may give purpose, meaning, and commitment to the life of the despairing (in this case, holocaust survivors with pathological mourning and survivor guilt). Gedo (1972, 1983) describes geniuses as driven to creative effort, in part, because they know this will enhance their self-esteem and counter negative self-images. Thus I disagree with the commonly held view (e.g., Stein 1988) that an author needs distance from his conflicts in order to write creatively. Unlike Kohut (1976), I emphasize the capacity of creative work to reassure, revitalize, and sustain, rather than placing emphasis on its emotional drain.

Troubled creative writers expect, despite their doubts, that writing will help them to feel better. They consciously expect that writing about whatever troubles them will result in their being able to handle it better because of the insights they reach. They also expect that their talent for creative writing will *per se* help them to feel better about themselves, transcending whatever has disturbed them. Affirming their identity as talented creative writers reassures them against negative feelings.

Psychoanalytic writers talk readily about their need to write about what troubles them, be that problems with their analysands or problems within themselves. Numerous colleagues (McDougall 1980; Stein 1988) have reported this, especially informally. Sometimes writing about a patient or about oneself does indeed clarify what the author had not been able to let himself grasp. Sometimes the writer can gain more distance from himself and get beyond his own defenses, by sitting down to write about what is wrong, as a kind of self-analysis. Writing about a patient can similarly become a kind of minisupervision, in which psychoanalyst-authors can more openly criticize what has been in their way with their analysands. And sometimes writing allows one to generate significant, original ideas.

However, as in all writing, such goals may be illusory. They easily provide the chimera of change and mastery *because* of the creative effort. This promise of insight and mastery through writing can indeed be compelling, leading authors to attempt to write through what troubles them. Without question, this can lead to new *ideas*, which they and their colleagues will value. Most of the time writing seems to offer illusions and reassurances, which temporarily comfort and sustain the author. This even includes the reassurance that by writing about what has been wrong, the author has now faced and integrated it, rather than denied it further through such illusions. Often the writing provides an illusory sense of mastery as creative writing, transcending one's temporary feelings of helplessness and inadequacy. Perhaps we can sustain ourselves more easily by holding onto what we have written. Of course, sometimes such writing does allow for newly creative integration of something we had been unable to tolerate. Writers must continue forever to struggle with what is unacceptable, within and without. In our quest for illusions and shortcuts, we may seek to bypass the unacceptable. Thus I am differentiating writing that leads to insight and change from writing that strengthens defensive illusions. Of course, it is more likely in writing, as in any behavior, that defensive positions will be enhanced rather than new integration achieved of what had been previously been intolerable.

For example, inspired by McDougall's (1980) report of writing about difficult cases, I sat down one Saturday to write about a group of patients whose progress I had found unsatisfactory. This became a successful paper (Coen 1989b), clarifying problems of avoiding responsibility for internal conflict. However, I did not really resolve something that had interfered, in my patients or in myself. What did become clearer through my writing this paper was my own partial denial of the reality of the serious difficulty these patients had with facing and integrating their conflicts. I affirmed through my writing what I had known and in part did not want to accept: that one of the three patients I would not be able to help further, and that what I could accomplish with the others would be limited. Although I did not reach something new in myself or in my patients, I did need to validate through my writing the therapeutic limitations of these treatments. This is a more positive way of saying that I needed to interrupt my own partial denial of what I could not accomplish with them. However, I certainly did feel better through this act of writing.

For any creative writer, the act and process of writing can feel joyful, liberating, and creative. As Freud described in the metaphor of Itzig the Sunday horseman (Freud 1954:258), it is exciting to abandon oneself to the imagination, not knowing what is about to happen, where one will go. Freud wrote to Fliess: "It [a chapter of the dreambook] was all written by the unconscious, on the well-known principle of Itzig, the Sunday horseman. 'Itzig, where are you going?' 'Don't ask me, ask the horse!' At the beginning of a paragraph I never knew where I should end up." Here, it becomes less important actually to capture a new insight or achieve a better integration. What matters most, like the

Sunday rider, is the excitement, the twists and turns of the imagination in writing. It is exhilarating for writers to let themselves go, wherever their imagination will take them (cf. Mahony 1989; Shengold 1990). In writing, one's controls *virtually* disappear as writers can imagine whatever they desire. To keep such writing readable for others, all restraints cannot be abandoned. The writer's own idiosyncratic primary process (and gestalt-free) imaginings must be presented with sufficient conscious, secondary process synthesis so that they can be grasped by others (e.g., see Coen 1988; Mahony 1982; Gadamer 1975; Gedo 1983).

Fantasy and Its Narration

Unlike Freud, Genet, Céline, and Sade seem to prefer a literary world to relations with other separate, autonomous people. Relations with literary figments, characters, or readers, seem safer than with living people, who are not a symbiotic part of oneself. Even the infamous Sade desires symbiosis, despite his denials! Without the control and domination of the author, reliance on living people who are able to make their own moves seems too unreliable and dangerous. Each author (including the early Freud) seems to feel that his destructiveness cannot be managed within, that he needs a literary outlet for it, a space within which he can attack and torture others—characters and imaginary readers. Turning inward to fantasy and its narration provides a safer haven for intense need, rage, and destructiveness, which the writer fears he cannot manage in relation to living people. Freud has much less trouble with relying on others, although intense dependent need (Freud/Fliess) is largely managed through a distant letter-writing relationship.

Sade is much more destructive in writing than in living. The world of the imagination becomes a substitute for reliance on other, separate people and on oneself, since neither self nor others can be trusted. This literary imaginary world is safer and more satisfying than external reality. Sade, Genet, and Céline try to convince their readers of this, inviting them to dematerialize and to meet as figments in this literary playland. The literary world becomes a new universe, created by the angry, child-god who refuses to tolerate his place as one among others. In his writing, he enacts his fantasy of being the only one who counts. Everyone else, characters and readers, exists to serve his needs in this *literary* world; they cannot leave, frustrate, disappoint, hurt, or interfere with him. On the contrary, others are to admire and confirm the grandeur of his imagination. To a degree, these authors (not Freud), being despairing about real life, seek refuge in a fantasy world of their own creation. Freud's letter writing to Fliess helps to counter his feelings of being neglected by his Viennese colleagues.

Turning inward to fantasy as a retreat from reliance on others and as an avoidance of one's own destructiveness in human relations is countered by writing these fantasies down and sharing them with others (in imagination and in reality). Here creative writing may offer an adaptive and restitutive (literary) reconnection with others. Writing becomes a mode for bridging one's solipsistic, near-delusional world and the world of everyday reality. The reader, not the author, becomes the outsider, who struggles to find his way in the author's world, whose reality is now affirmed as we live out this folie à deux. Of course, creative writers differ in their need to use writing as a link to others.

For each of these authors, feeling alone, isolated, and depressed, writing becomes a wished-for connection with admiring, accepting others. This can, of course, include others lost or absent (cf. Aberbach 1989). For Sade in solitary confinement, writing becomes a means of preserving sanity and human connectedness. Writing as communication with others becomes as significant as the attempt to create literary aesthetic objects. The imagined audience is always near at hand, warming and nurturing the writer. The parallels drawn by Holland (1975), about the wished-for connection with the other as comforting parent in reading, apply as well to writing. As Holland (1975) suggests about the development of reading, narrating stories evokes memories of listening to stories, of shared intimate experiences between child and parent, which feel comforting and protective. The writer's entering the world of the imagination in the fantasied presence of a distant reader reevokes childhood experiences and wishes of sharing thoughts, hopes, imaginings, stories with an accepting parent. Regressive longings are evoked to return to such intimate sharing with another/parent. During childhood one learns to do this in one's own mind, but even then, to a degree, there is the imagined presence of an accepting/listening other/parent. As writers turn inward to their own minds and write this down, to a degree, they are going backward temporally and spatially, turning from reality to fantasy, in the imagined presence of another. They may then feel freer and safer to open up and explore aspects of their psyches that are ordinarily closed off. In a sense, this becomes similar to psychoanalytic regression, in that action (other than narration) is foreclosed and the writer feels encouraged to enter more deeply into his or her own world of fantasy, protected by the distant presence of his or her imagined other/reader.

What writers imagine and narrate is not to be regarded as primarily their own fantasy. Instead, to a degree, we as readers accept the convention that writers' imaginings are to be treated as fictional, that we are not to ask, although we certainly want to, what these have to do with the writers themselves. This further helps writers to open up their minds creatively and to transform what is inside them into something fantastic/fictional, which exists outside and apart from them. Their writing is always simultaneously "me and not-me," a very personal part of them, as well as crafted as a separate object, as other than themselves, for others.

In writing and reading, there is the potential for turning reality into fantasy and fantasy into reality. To make feelings, wishes, experiences less real, makes them less painful, less true. The other side of this is the possibility of temporarily tempering something too painful to bear, so that it can be tolerated and assimilated gradually. This is the more mature, integrative task of fantasy, and the forward-moving possibility of writing and reading. This is ordinarily one adaptive function of all defense, the temporary avoidance of mental content, so that it can be metabolized piecemeal (see Coen 1989b). An example is denial, conceived of as an emotional shield, which may be moved aside *gradually*, allowing for processing and integration of what had previously been too painful to bear (cf. Dorpat 1985, 1987, in psychoanalysis; Aberbach 1989, in literature).

Creative writing is not only the province of lonely, dependent, or schizoid people. To a degree, everyone has needs to retreat from relations with others, to seek imaginary companions to accept and love them, to flee their rage and destructiveness, to soothe intolerable pain, to turn reality into fantasy for so many reasons. Although these mechanisms may stand out more sharply in the writers I have discussed, they are universal themes. Turning inward to fantasy, using fantasy creatively to manage what is painful and threatening, reassuring oneself through the imagined presence and acceptance of others—these are all human stratagems.

On Creativity in Writing and Reading

I have been drawing on two very different meanings of creativity. Ordinarily one would think of the ability to create something original, meaningful, significant, beautiful. One would think of new synthesis and integration, of something substantially different from what has come before. In the writers I consider here this applies especially to novel representation of the mean, ugly, dangerous underside of life. Creative representation of the dark side of life is a major theme and task of this writing. A second, less readily apparent meaning of creativity refers to the ability to change what is wrong by confronting and integrating it. To bring forth darkness fully into the light of day is an act of creation, in the Biblical sense of "to form out of nothing" (*Oxford Dictionary of English Etymology* 1979). Here creativity transcends temporary magical transformation by allowing for the possibility of adaptive mastery of what had previously been too terrifying and painful to bear. Creative representation of the dark side invites our attention of it, opening the potential for genuinely facing this in ourselves. Turning horror and destructiveness into poetry draws us toward it, encouraging us with the model that it can be managed and used as the stuff of wisdom, strength, and creativity. Analysand, reader, and writer, all need to become convinced that they are strong enough to tolerate what seems so terrifying within. All can sustain themselves with images of poetic transformation of badness into beauty. Here creativity refers to the ability to imagine—as a wondrous accomplishment—the task of responsibly managing one's rage and destructiveness. One pictures oneself as an epic hero confronting the forces of evil (within), surviving and containing them.

The writers considered here have advanced this task by clarifying that the enemy is within and not, primarily, without. Hence, turning inward to fantasy can also be an adaptive acknowledgment that what needs to be confronted exists *within* oneself. Fantasy offers the potential to represent what is wrong in such a way (creatively) that it can be tolerated, faced, and remedied. Creative writers offer themselves and their readers such potential creative fantasy representations and solutions to universal human dilemmas. That does not mean that creative writers succeed in reaching more mature levels of integration as a result of their writing. On the contrary, like most ordinary uncreative people, they are more likely to avoid what is wrong than really to work their way through it. Of the writers here considered only Freud, and only in part, was able to use his writing to effect psychic change. However, each of the other writers was able to manage himself *somewhat* better through his writing, especially by affirming his creative powers to transform badness into beauty.

And what do we, as readers, get out of our reading? Pretty much the same thing, except that we can attribute to the author whatever in this we cannot tolerate in ourselves. As readers we can similarly seek comfort and connection with the author as other, for whatever needs of another we may have. We too in reading are in a potentially safer, if less directly gratifying, world. We too can seek to heal our loneliness, isolation, unhappiness, and despair by joining the author in her or his imaginary literary world, jointly leaving behind the unsatisfying world of external reality. We too can (temporarily) reassure ourselves that our badness does not count, as we collude with the author in her or his poetic transformations of badness into poetry. And for us, it is easier, because the badness ultimately belongs to the author, not to us. Even as the reader identifies with the author's badness or destructiveness, what matters most is what the reader eventually does with this. My argument is that what happens most commonly is that the reader, just like the author, stabilizes and reassures herself or himself through the illusion that she or he has managed or disposed of what is unacceptable within, rather than masters this by actually facing and integrating it. Writing and reading, like all behavior, tend most easily to preserve current defensive positions rather than to lead to newly creative mastery and integration of the dark side. To think otherwise is overly to idealize writing as magical creative transformation, an attitude so central to the authors I have discussed here.

More should not be expected of the reader than of the author. By and large, neither reading nor writing will lead, *per se*, to emotional growth. This is different from the writer, and the reader, developing greater confidence in their skills, talents, and creativity as writers and readers. That is to be expected. There is, of course, the possibility that the reader will be able to use the author's imaginative representations creatively in order to face and change what is wrong within himself or herself. The author's fantasy depictions and transformations of the dark side may aid the reader in a successful struggle to integrate and manage his or her own evil forces, by temporarily making these seem less odious and deadly, more the basic stuff of human tragedy, with which every hero or heroine must contend.

The Inhibited Writer and Reader

Inhibitions in writing and reading may, of course, involve any conflicts, just as with any other behaviors. However, since I focus in this book on dependent authors, who especially struggle to manage their unacceptable rage and destructiveness, I would like now to consider some of the ways these themes may complicate writing and reading. To think and express something original must involve the confidence that one has separate talents and gifts on which one can draw, for which one does not need others (cf. Kohut 1976; Eissler 1971). Dependent writers and readers may hesitate to acknowledge their abilities; if they can manage on their own, this tempers their claims on others. Even to sit alone, and to read or write, requires tolerance for separateness and the anxiety it engenders. To feel and become creative and successful may require relinquishing a neurotic posture of helplessness and disability aimed at preserving a dependent parent-child relationship within which one disowns one's (creative) rage and destructiveness.

It should be reiterated here that Freud (see chapter 4 in this book) needed originally to attribute to Fliess a portion of his creativity and grandiosity before he could claim these fully for himself. He needed a sharing relationship with Fliess within which he felt sustained and protected before he could feel safe to challenge accepted wisdom. Freud's competitiveness could be somewhat tempered and denied by imagining that he wished *only* to move in tandem with Fliess rather than to leave him behind in the dust. That one dares to think something original speaks to criticizing, robbing, outdoing, destroying those who have come before: other writers and readers, and one's own progenitors. Writers and readers must be comfortable with such impulses in themselves as part, rather than the predominant goal, of the writing or reading project (cf. chapter 7 in this book). Otherwise, anxiety, guilt, and the fear of gross destructiveness may lead to constriction of one's imagination. Or, writers may unconsciously attempt to manage the feared destructiveness of their successful writing by varied compromise formations of getting themselves and their unfinished work arrested, so as to contain themselves. Because of the fantasy terror of the destructiveness of successful, completed writing, the writer may resort to various dependent, masochistic restraints. The danger here is of writers really taking off *on their own* into their grandiosity and destructiveness. On the other hand, the relatively uninhibited writer may achieve a focal resolution of such conflict, when felt at a distance from others, as in writing. Or, relatively uninhibited authors may actually be able to enjoy dipping into their grandiose and destructive fantasies as they create.

That a Genet, despite his massive childhood deprivation, is able to begin to write in prison contradicts the psychoanalyst's assumptions about developmental contributants to confidence in creative ability. How indeed did Genet gain the confidence that he could write creative work that others would admire? Even if his narrator seems to crave the reader's admiration, the marvel is that he can *expect* to get it. In contrast, Sade's narrator seems to expect little admiration from his reader, so that he must force the reader to respond with outrage, disgust, and revulsion.

Inability to integrate one's exceptional gifts may serve as background for the grandiose, destructive dangers attributed to creativity; instead, one feels inferior, different, or defective (Bychowski 1951; Greenacre 1958; Gedo 1972, 1983). The more such abilities need to be disavowed rather than used, exhibited, and enjoyed, the more likely one will be to develop grandiose, omnipotent illusions, which will need to be sequestered. The more endangered one feels in acknowledging one's abilities, the more difficult it will be for one to integrate these. For one example, when creative children perceive their superiority in intellect and ability to vulnerable, insecure parents, they may become terrified of linking their anger and destructiveness to the power of their minds. The more powerful they feel in relation to parents who cannot manage them, the more terrified they become of their quasi-delusional destructive omnipotence (cf. Novick and Novick 1987, 1991); then they feel they must be stopped, punished, contained. As a result, they maintain contradictory self-images as angry, creative, capable, and as weak and disabled. The more anger and ability need to be kept apart, the more difficult it is to integrate the knowledge that they have a powerful mind. Such childrens' age-appropriate envy and competitiveness with the parents tend to be defensively focused, more than is usual, on the other's superiority. Envy, idealization, and surrender attenuate the dangerous, destructive power of their minds. To integrate robbing the parents of their gifts, adding these to their own, would lead to a terrifying, grandiose, destructive sense of superiority. Of course, there may be many other background scenarios that would explain why certain creative writers and readers fear acknowledging fully their creative powers with their attendant destructive potential.

Successful writing, in these terms, becomes an unconscious acknowledgment that the authors have indeed committed their fantasied crimes. Chasseguet-Smirgel (1984) emphasizes sadistic, castrative meanings in the creative act but limits this to appropriation of the paternal phallus. More generally, being creative and successful may mean that the writers have indeed robbed (destroyed) the parents of their most wondrous attributes, that they have really taken this away from them, adding them to their own gifts. To feel creative, in this sense, may mean that one has good stuff inside, and that it is both one's own and has been robbed from the parents. Childlike envy, rage, and competitiveness toward the creativity and strength of the parents, the mother's breasts and womb, the father's phallus, their brains and good insides, may lead to anxiety and guilt when one feels creative and successful. To feel more consistently capable and creative, as writer or reader, one must tolerate and pull together one's wishes to rob, devour, destroy, murder the other as parent/predecessor. Otherwise, persistent guilt and anxiety need to be managed by denial and undoing. One then feels depressed, empty, doubtful, anxious following successful creative work, as if to negate that one has it in one to be creative (as opposed to Kohut, 1976). Or, one remains uncertain whether one is indeed the parent of one's work or has fraudulently usurped it. Similarly, persistent doubting that one can repeat creative activity negates such talent. Analysands may tend to maintain contradictory views of their creativity: that it is their own *and* that it is pilfered. Ongoing denial precludes integration of the intended destructive robbery, so that it is made not to count. This contrasts with responsibility for one's fantasied crimes, together with integration of what one has robbed from the parents, so that it can become internalized and amalgamated with one's own innate talents and creativity. Otherwise, creative writers may continue to seek what they need from others, who remain idealized and envied, rather than to feel that what they need to draw on is now fully within themselves.

In order to feel talented and capable, writer or reader must relinquish dependent, envious reliance on idealized others who, knowing better, will provide (magical) protection and safety. These are childhood illusions of the magical perfection and power of the parent, who knows and has everything (e.g., the magical phallus or breast), and can prevent fantasied disaster. If one believes this, then of course one wants to rely on or to grab this from the idealized and envied other. So long as the other one has better stuff, or is better, writer or reader need to remain behind as pupil, receiving or appropriating what belongs to the other. Then one will (guiltily) feel fraudulent and inauthentic, ready to be caught and judged for one's dependency and rivalry. This dependent envy and idealization of the other contains and undoes the fantasied robbery of the other's (parent's) wondrous attributes, by exhibiting one's defectiveness. One can go through cycles of fantasied robbing of the other, followed by guilty surrender to the other of all one has taken. This is equivalent to an undoing. By such repetition, creative writers may continue to hide their dangerous, powerful minds and the full acknowledgment of their own talent and ability. To create successfully on one's own, this destructiveness must be borne in oneself, without regressive reliance on the need for fantasied containment and punishment by others. If one can tolerate one's destructiveness, then one can bring together one's own ability, talent, and creativity as something separate and special, which one can cherish within oneself.

For example, Mr. A. during his analysis had come to value his creative writing, imagination, and ability as his own gifts. Heretofore, he had felt that he needed a mentor or the analyst to fill him up with sufficient encouragement and admiration so that he could begin a new project. He had approached new work with great anxiety and feelings of insecurity and inadequacy. Now, he felt exhilarated by his creative powers and the recognition accorded him. Indeed, Mr. A. found it very difficult to relinquish his endless craving for admiration when he completed a project and to be on his own again for awhile. In his mind, he would cling to images of himself in the limelight, wanting more enthusiastic applause. He now believed in his own creative power and ability. Yet each time he completed one project and needed to begin another, he felt anxious and uncertain that he could proceed on his own. Fears of loss and separateness continued as did his terror of fully and consistently acknowledging and integrating his competitive rage and destructiveness. Thus, after each success he would need to retreat into helpless self-doubting, presenting himself to the analyst as passive and ineffective. Although he could tolerate his envy and rivalry with the analyst for awhile, he would need to undo these strivings and surrender once more. The violence of his rage and wishes to rob and destroy the analyst as father and mother remained too terrifying for him to assimilate. So he would oscillate between feeling angry, strong, and powerful and feeling helpless, passive, and terrified of being on his own. He could now enjoy being a generous adult and father, yet he clung to feeling he needed to remain the dependent boy who received warm caring. He postponed a final bloody battle with the analyst as father and mother whom he would defeat, destroy, and rob. Or, more accurately put, he could feel like usurping the analyst's place, murdering and castrating him, taking what he envied in the analyst. He would then feel enraged, exhilarated, and triumphant. However, he could not persist with such intense feelings long enough to consolidate them. Rather, he would undo and deny them, retreating to the safer position of the passive boy who wants his father's encouragement and admiration.

To accept one's creativity fully, one must first integrate one's own destructiveness. Creativity and destructiveness go together; they are not opposites, they cannot be separated. The latter is a defensive illusion, writers and readers (and everyone else) resort to in the magical attempt to get rid of one side of the conflict. I think that part of the idealization of creativity, in literature and in psychoanalysis (e.g., Eissler 1964, 1971; Kohut 1976) involves this illusion that creativity transcends and replaces destructiveness. Creativity tends to be valued as something only good; it is terribly disappointing when creative people turn out to be bad (say Céline) or mediocre (say, John Berryman). On the other hand, it is reassuring that bad people (say Sade or Céline) have it in them to be creative. As readers, we then feel reassured that our own badness does not preclude our ultimate redemption. A more realistic attitude toward our own, and others', badness and goodness, would lead to a more accurate assessment of creativity, one less hindered by the magical idealization of transmuting shit into gold.

REFERENCES

Aberbach, D. 1989. Creativity and the survivor: The struggle for mastery. *Internat. Rev. Psycho-Anal.* 16: 273–86.

Arlow, J. A. 1981. Unpublished. Contribution to the Panel on Interpretation, American Psychoanalytic Association, May 1981, San Juan, Puerto Rico.

Bach, S. and L. Schwartz. 1972. A dream of the Marquis de Sade: Psychoanalytic reflections on narcissistic trauma, decompensation, and the reconstitution of a delusional self. *J. Amer. Psychoanal. Assn.* 20: 451–75.

Barthes, R. 1973. *The Pleasure of the Text.* Trans. R. Miller. New York: Hill and Wang, 1975.

—— 1979. From work to text. In J. V. Harari, ed., *Textual Strategies: Perspectives in Post-Structuralist Criticism,* pp. 73–81. Ithaca: Cornell University Press.

Baudry, F. 1979a. Discussion of "The perverse author and his audience: A psychoanalytic essay based on Jean Genet's early work" by S. J. Coen. Unpublished. Presented to the American Psychoanalytic Association, December 1979, New York City.

—— 1979b. On the problem of inference in applied psychoanalysis: Flaubert's *Madame Bovary. Psychoanal. Study of Society* 8: 331–58.

Berman, L. E. A. 1976. Gilbert's first night anxiety. *Psychoanal. Quart.* 45: 110–27.

—— 1985. The kidnapping of W. S. Gilbert. *J. Amer. Psychoanal. Assn.* 33: 133–48.

Bernfeld, S. 1952. Letter to the Editors. *Bull. Menninger Clin.* 17: 70–72.

Bettelheim, B. 1982. *Freud and Man's Soul.* New York: Knopf, Vintage ed.; New York: Random House, 1984.

Bleich, D. 1967. The determination of literary value. *Literature and Psychology* 27: 19–30.

—— 1975. The subjective character of critical interpretation. *College English* 36: 739–55.

—— 1976. The subjective paradigm in science, psychology, and criticism. *New Literary History* 7: 313–34.

—— 1977. The logic of interpretation. *Genre* 10: 363–94.

—— 1978. *Subjective Criticism.* Baltimore: Johns Hopkins University Press.

Bollas, C. 1984–85. Loving hate. *Ann. Psychoanal.* 12/13: 221–37.

Booth, W. 1979. *Critical Understanding: The Powers and Limits of Pluralism.* Chicago: University of Chicago Press.

Brandt, W. 1966. Process or structure? *Psychoanal. Rev.* 53: 374–78.

Brenner, C. 1982. *The Mind in Conflict.* New York: International University Press.

Brody, S. 1980. Transitional objects: Idealization of a phenomenon. *Psychoanal. Quart.* 49: 561–605.

Buxbaum, E. 1951. Freud's dream interpretation in the light of his letters to Fliess. *Bull. Menninger Clin.* 15: 197–212.

—— 1952. Letter to the Editors. *Bull. Menninger Clin.* 16: 73.

Bychowski, G. 1951. Metapsychology of artistic creation. *Psychoanal. Quart.* 20: 592–602.

Céline, L.-F. 1924. *La vie et l'oeuvre de Philippe-Ignace Semmelweis, 1818–1865.* Thesis for the Faculté de Médecine de Paris, no. 161.

—— 1932. *Journey to the End of the Night.* Trans. J. H. P. Marks. New York: New Directions, 1960.

—— 1936. *Death on the Installment Plan.* Trans. R. Mannheim. New York: New Directions, 1971.

—— 1957. *Castle to Castle.* Trans. R. Mannheim. Middlesex, New York, Victoria, Ontario, Auckland: Penguin, 1976.

—— 1960. *North.* Trans. R. Mannheim. New York: Delacorte, 1971.

Certeau, M. de 1983. History: Science and Fiction. Originally published in R. Bellah et al., eds., *Social Science as Moral Inquiry.* New York: Columbia University Press, 1983, pp. 125–52. In M. de Certeau, *Heterologies: Discourse on the Other.* Foreword W. Godzich. Trans. B. Massumi. Minneapolis: University of Minnesota Press, 1986, pp. 199–221.

Chasseguet-Smirgel, J. 1978. Reflexions on the connexions between perversion and sadism. *Int. J. Psychoanal.* 59: 27–35.

—— 1983. Perversion and the universal law. *Int. Rev. Psychoanal.* 10: 293–301.

—— 1984. Thoughts on the concept of reparation and the hierarchy of creative acts. *Internat. Rev. Psycho-Anal.* 11: 399–406.

Coen, S.J. 1980. Unpublished. Toward a psychology of the relationship between author, text, and audience. Presented to the American Psychoanalytic Association, New York City, December 1980.

—— 1981a. Notes on the concepts of selfobject and preoedipal object. *J. Amer. Psychoanal. Assn.* 29: 395–411.

—— 1981b. Sexualization as a predominant mode of defense. *J. Amer. Psychoanal. Assn.* 29: 893–920.

—— 1982a. Louis-Ferdinand Céline's *Castle to Castle*: The author/reader relationship in its narrative style. *Amer. Imago* 39: 343–68.

—— 1982b. Essays on the relationship of author and reader: Transference implications for psychoanalytic literary criticism. Introduction. *Psychoanal. Contemp. Thought* 5: 3–15.

—— 1984. The author and his audience: Jean Genet's early work. *Psychoanal. Study Society* 10: 301–20.

—— 1985. Perversion as a solution to intrapsychic conflict. *J. Amer. Psychoanal. Assn.* 33 (Supplement): 17–57.

—— 1987a. Pathological jealousy. *Int. J. Psychoanal.* 68: 99–108.

—— 1987b. The analyst's uses and misuses of clinical theory: Interpretation. *Yearbook Psychoanal. Psychother.* 2:200–24.

—— 1988. How to read Freud: a critique of recent Freud scholarship. *J. Amer. Psychoanal. Assn.* 36: 483–515.

—— 1989a. Why is Sade angry? Notes on the management of destructiveness and need. Abstract in *Proceedings of The New York Freudian Society* 5 (1989–90): 52. Presented to American Psychoanalytic Association, San Francisco, Ca., and New York Freudian Society, New York City, 1988.

—— 1989b. Intolerance of responsibility for internal conflict. *J. Amer. Psychoanal. Assn.* 37: 943–64.

Cooper, A. M. 1982. Some persistent issues in psychoanalytic literary criticism. *Psychoanalysis and Contemporary Thought* 5: 45–53.

Crews, F. 1990. The power of Flannery O'Connor. *New York Review of Books* 37 (7): 49–55.

Culler, J. 1975. *Structuralist Poetics: Structuralism, Linguistics and the Study of Literature.* Ithaca: Cornell University Press.

Deleuze, G. 1971. *Sacher-Masoch: An Interpretation, Together with the Entire Text of "Venus in Furs."* London: Faber and Faber.

Dorpat, T. L. 1976. Structural conflict and object relations conflict. *J. Amer. Psychoanal. Assn.* 24: 855–74.

—— 1985. *Denial and Defense in the Therapeutic Situation.* New York and London: Jason Aronson.

—— 1987. A new look at denial and defense. *Annual Psychoanal.* 15: 23–47.

Eissler, K. R. 1964. Mankind at its best. *J. Amer. Psychoanal. Assn.* 12: 187–222.

—— 1971. *Talent and Genius: The Fictitious Case of Tausk Contra Freud.* New York: Quadrange.

English 692 (from Colloquium for Psychoanalytic Criticism, State University of New York at Buffalo) 1978. Poem opening: An invitation to transactive criticism. *College English* 40: 2–16.

Erikson, E. 1954. The dream specimen of psychoanalysis. *J. Amer. Psychoanal. Assn.* 2: 5–55.

—— 1955. Freud's "The Origin of Psychoanalysis." *Int. J. Psychoanal.* 36: 1–15.

Esman, A. 1982. Psychoanalysis and literary criticism—a limited partnership. *Psychoanal. Contemp. Thought.* 5: 17–25.

Feder, S. 1980. Discussion of "Towards a psychology of the relationship between author, text, and audience" by S. J. Coen. Presented at the Annual Meeting of the American Psychoanalytic Association, New York City, December.

Felman, S. 1977. Turning the screw of interpretation. *Yale French Studies* 55/56: 94–207.

—— 1987. *Jacques Lacan and the Adventure of Insight: Psychoanalysis in Contemporary Culture.* Cambridge: Harvard University Press.

Fish, S. 1970. Literature in the reader: Affective stylistics. In *Is There a Text in This Class? The Authority of Interpretive Communities.* Cambridge: Harvard University Press, 1980, pp. 21–67.

—— 1980. *Is There a Text in This Class? The Authority of Interpretive Communities.* Cambridge: Harvard University Press, 1980.

—— 1983. Short people got no reason to live: Reading irony. *Daedalus* 112: 175–91.

Fleisher, M. L. 1990. Twin fantasies, bisexuality, and creativity in the works of Ernest Hemingway. *Internat. Rev. Psycho-Anal.* 17: 287–98.

—— 1991. Hemingway's failure and the phallic woman. Unpublished. Presented to the New York Psychoanalytic Society, New York City, January 1992.

Foucault, M. 1971. Nietzche, genealogy, history. Originally published in *Hommage à Jean Hyppolite.* Trans. D. F. Bouchard and S. Simon. Paris: Presses Universitaires de France, 1971, pp. 145–72. In *Language, Counter-Memory, Practice: Selected Essays and Interviews* by M. Foucault, ed. D. F. Bouchard. Ithaca: Cornell University Press, 1977, pp. 139–64.

Freud, S. 1887–1902. *The Origins of Psychoanalysis* ed. M. Bonaparte, A. Freud, and E. Kris. New York: Basic Books, 1954.

—— 1900. The interpretation of dreams. *S. E.* 4 and 5.

—— 1907. Delusions and dreams in Jensen's "Gradiva." *S. E.* 9: 3–95.

—— 1910. Five lectures on psychoanalysis. *S. E.* 11.

—— 1914. The Moses of Michelangelo. *S. E.* 13: 211–36.

—— 1937. Constructions in analysis. *S.E.* 23: 255–69.

—— 1938. An outline of psychoanalysis. *S. E.* 23.

—— 1985. *The Complete Letters of Sigmund Freud to Wilhelm Fliess, 1887–1904.* Trans. and ed. J. M. Masson. Cambridge: Harvard University Press.

Gabbard, G. O. 1991. Technical approaches to transference hate in the analysis of borderline patients. *Internat. J. Psycho-Anal.* 72: 625–37.

Gadamer, H. G. 1975. *Truth and Method.* New York: The Seabury Press.

Gardner, M. R. 1983. *Self-Inquiry.* Boston and Toronto: Little Brown.

Gedo, J. E. 1972. On the psychology of genius. *Internat. J. Psycho-Anal.* 53: 199–203.

—— 1983. *Portraits of the Artist: Psychoanalysis of Creativity and its Vicissitudes.* New York and London: The Guilford Press.

Genet, J. 1943. *Our Lady of the Flowers.* Trans. B. Frechtman. New York: Grove Press, 1963.

—— 1947. *The Maids.* In B. Frechtman, trans., *The Maids and Deathwatch: Two Plays by Jean Genet.* New York: Grove Press, 1961.

—— 1948. *The Thief's Journal.* Trans. B. Frechtman. New York: Grove Press, 1964.

—— 1951. *Miracle of the Rose.* Trans. B. Frechtman. New York: Grove Press, 1966.

—— 1963. As quoted in P. Thody, *Jean Genet: A Study of His Novels and Plays.* New York: Stein and Day, 1968, p. 175. Original source is Genet's preface to the 1963 French edition of *The Maids* (Les bonnes).

Gilbert, W. S. 1862–1864. *The Bab Ballads.* Reprint 1970. Ed. J. Ellis. Cambridge: The Belknap Press of Harvard University Press.

Gorney, J. E. 1980. The field of illusion in literature and the psychoanalytic situation. *Psychoanalysis and Contemp. Thought* 2: 527–50.

Green, A. 1975. The analyst, symbolization, and absence in the analytic setting (on changes in analytic practice and analytic experience). *Internat. J. Psycho-Anal.* 56: 1–22.

—— 1978. The double and the absent. In A. Roland, ed., *Psychoanalysis, Creativity, and Literature: A French-American Inquiry* pp. 271–92. New York: Columbia University Press.

Greenacre, P. 1957. The childhood of the artist: Libidinal phase development and giftedness. In *Emotional Growth* Vol. 2, pp. 479–504. New York: International Universities Press, 1971.

Grossman, W. I. 1982. The self as fantasy: Fantasy as theory. *J. Amer. Psychoanal. Assn.* 30: 919–38.

Hamilton, J. W. (1969) Object loss, dreaming, and creativity: The poetry of John Keats. *Psychoanal. Study Child* 24: 488–531.

—— (1980). Personal communication. See also (1979). Transitional phenomena and the early writings of Eugene O'Neill. *Int. Rev. Psychoanal.* 6: 49–60.

Hawelka, E., ed. 1974. *L'Homme aux rats: Journal d'une analyze.* Paris: Presses Universitaires de France.

Heisenberg, W. 1958. *The Physicist's Conception of Nature.* London: Greenwood.

Holland, N. 1968. *The Dynamics of Literary Response.* New York: Norton.

—— 1970. Discussion of "Criticism and the experience of interiority" by G. Poulet. In R. Macksey and E. Donato, eds., *The Structuralist Controversy: The Languages of Criticism and the Sciences of Man,* pp. 86–87. Baltimore and London: Johns Hopkins University Press.

—— 1973. *Poems in Persons: An Introduction to the Psychoanalysis of Literature.* New York: Norton.

—— 1975a. *Five Readers Reading.* New Haven and London: Yale University Press.

—— 1975b. Unity, identity, text, self. *PMLA* 90: 813–22.

—— 1976. The new paradigm: Subjective or transactive? *New Literary History* 7: 335–46.

—— 1978. Literary interpretation and three phases of psychoanalysis. In *Psychoanalysis, Creativity, and Literature: A French-American Inquiry,* pp. 233–47. New York: Columbia University Press.

Holt, R. R. 1974. On reading Freud: Introduction to C. Rothgeb, ed., *Abstracts of the Standard Edition of Freud,* pp. 3–71. New York: Aronson.

—— 1978. Ideological and thematic conflicts in the structure of Freud's thought. In S. Smith ed., *The Human Mind Revisited: Essays in Honor of Karl A. Menninger,* pp.51–98. New York: International Universities Press.

—— 1983. A new type of analysis for Freud. (Book review of P. Mahony, *Freud as a Writer*). *Contemp. Psychol.* 28:397–98.

Isakower, O. 1963. Minutes of faculty meeting of the New York Psychoanalytic Institute, October 14 and November 20.

Iser, W. 1978. *The Act of Reading: A Theory of Aesthetic Response.* Baltimore and London: Johns Hopkins University Press.

Jakobson, R. 1960. Linguistics and poetics. In T. A. Sebeok, ed., *Style in Language,* pp. 350–77. Cambridge: Massachusets Institute of Technology Press, 1966.

Jones, E. 1953. *The Life and Work of Sigmund Freud,* Vol. 1. New York: Basic Books.

—— 1955. *The Life and Work of Sigmund Freud,* Vol. 2. New York: Basic Books, pp. 366–67.

Kavka, J. 1975. Oscar Wilde's narcissism. *The Annual of Psychoanalysis* 3: 397–408.

Kendrick, W. 1983. Thallic symbols and other Freudian slippages. *Village Voice Literary Suppl.* 14 (February 1983): 16–18.

Khan, M. M. R. 1965. The function of intimacy and acting out in perversions. In R. Slovenko, ed., *Sexual Behavior and the Law*, pp. 397–412. Springfield, Ill.: Thomas.

Kligerman, C. 1980. Art and the self of the artist. In A. Goldberg, ed., *Advances in Self Psychology*, pp. 383–96. New York: International Universities Press.

Kohut, H. 1960. Beyond the bounds of the basic rule: Some recent contributions to applied psychoanalysis. *J. Amer. Psychoanal. Assn.* 8: 56–586.

—— 1971. *The Analysis of the Self.* New York: International Universities Press.

—— 1976. Creativeness, charisma, group psychology: Reflections on the self-analysis of Freud. In P. H. Ornstein, ed., *The Search for the Self: Selected Writings of Heinz Kohut*, Vol. 2, pp.793–843. New York: International Universities Press.

Kris, A. 1982. *Free Association: Method and Process.* New Haven: Yale University Press.

Kris, E. 1951. Ego psychology and interpretation in psychoanalytic therapy. In *Selected papers of Ernst Kris*, pp. 237–51. New Haven and London: Yale University Press, 1975.

—— 1952. Approaches to art. In *Psychoanalytic Explorations in Art*, pp. 13–63. New York: International Universities Press.

—— 1956. On some vicissitudes of insight in psychoanalysis. *Internat. Jour. Psycho-Anal.* 37: 445–55.

Kris, E. and A. Kaplan 1948. Aesthetic ambiguity. In *Psychoanalytic Explorations in Art*, pp. 243–64. New York: International Universities Press.

Kristeva, J. 1982. *Powers of Horror: An Essay on Abjection.* Trans. Leon S. Roudiez. New York: Columbia University Press.

Lacan, J. 1966. *Ecrits.* Paris: Editions du Seuil.

—— 1977. The function and field of speech and language in psychoanalysis. In *Ecrits*, pp. 30–113. New York: Norton.

Leavy, S. A. 1980. *The Psychoanalytic Dialogue.* New Haven and London: Yale University Press.

Lély, G. 1961. *The Marquis de Sade: A Biography.* Trans. Alec Brown. New York: Grove Press.

—— 1966. *The Marquis de Sade: Selected Letters.* Sel. by G. Lély. Trans. W.J. Strachan. Ed. M.Crosland. New York: October House.

Lipton, S. 1977. The advantages of Freud's technique as shown in his analysis of the Rat Man. *Internat. J. Psycho-Anal.* 58: 255–78.

Lynn, K. S. 1987. *Hemingway.* New York: Fawcett Columbine.

McCarthy, P. 1975. *Céline: A Biography.* Middlesex, New York, Victoria, Ontario, Auckland: Penguin. (Quotation [a] on p. 277 of McCarthy's book from letter, Céline to Paraz, June 19, 1957, *L'Herne* 3: 15. Quotation [b] on p. 277 of McCarthy's book from Pierre Audinet, "Dernieres rencontres avec Céline," *Nouvelles Litteraires* [June 7, 1961]: 4).

McDougall, J. 1980. *Plea for a Measure of Abnormality.* New York: International Universities Press.

Mack, J. 1980. Psychoanalysis and biography: Aspects of a developing affinity. *J. Amer. Psychoanal. Assn.* 28: 543–62.

Mahony, P. 1977. Friendship and its discontents. *Contemp. Psychoanal.* 15: 55–109.

—— 1982. *Freud as a Writer.* Madison, Ct.: International Universities Press.

—— 1984a. *Cries of the Wolf Man.* Madison, Ct.: International Universities Press.

—— 1984b. Further reflections on Freud and his writing. *J. Amer. Psychoanal. Assn.* 32: 847–64.

—— 1986. *Freud and the Rat Man.* New Haven and London: Yale University Press.

—— 1987. *Psychoanalysis and Discourse.* London and New York: Tavistock Publications.

—— 1989. *On Defining Freud's Discourse.* New Haven and London: Yale University Press.

Masson, J. M. 1984. *The Assault on Truth: Freud's Suppression of the Seduction Theory.* New York: Farrar, Straus and Giroux.

Matthews, J. H. 1978. *The Inner Dream: Céline as Novelist.* Syracuse: Syracuse University Press (Quotations on pp. 223, 227 of Matthews's book are from Céline 1955, *Entretiens avec le Professeur Y.*).

Myers, W. A. 1979. Imaginary companions in childhood and adult creativity. *Psychoanal. Quart.* 48: 292–307.

Niederland, W. 1971. Freud's literary style: Some observations. *Amer. Imago* 28: 17–23.

—— 1976. Psychoanalytic approaches to artistic creativity. *Psychoanal. Quart.* 45: 185–212.

Novick, J. and Novick, K. K. 1991. Some comments on masochism and the delusion of omnipotence from a developmental perspective. *J. Amer. Psychoanal. Assn.* 39: 307–31.

Novick, K.K. and J. Novick 1987. The essence of masochism. *Psychoanal. Study of Child* 42: 353–84.

Noy, P. 1979. Form creation in art: An ego-psychological approach to creativity. *Psychoanal. Quart.* 48: 229–56.

Ornston, D. G. 1982. Strachey's influence. *Int. J. Psychoanal.* 63: 409–26.

—— 1985a. Freud's conception is different from Strachey's. *J. Amer. Psychoanal. Assn.* 33: 379–412.

—— 1985b. Book review of *Freud and Man's Soul* by B. Bettelheim. *J. Amer. Psychoanal. Assn.* 33 (Suppl.): 189–200.

—— 1987. Book review of *Cries of the Wolf Man* by P. Mahony. *J. Amer. Psychoanal. Assn.* 35: 259–63.

—— 1992. *Translating Freud*. London and New Haven: Yale University Press.

Panel 1972. Panel on "Creativity." (From the 27th International Psycho-Analytic Congress, Vienna, 1971). Rep. C. Kligerman, *Int. J. Psycho-Anal.* 54: 21–30.

Pao, P.-N. 1965. The role of hatred in the ego. *Psychoanal. Quart.* 34: 257–64.

Parkin, A. 1980. On masochistic enthralment. A contribution to the study of moral masochism. *Int. J. Psychoanal.* 61: 307–14.

Pollock, G. H. 1978. On siblings, childhood sibling loss, and creativity. *Annual Psychoanal.* 6: 443–81.

Poulet, G. 1970. Criticism and the experience of interiority. In R. Macksey and E. Donato, eds., *The Structuralist Controversy: The Languages of Criticism and the Sciences of Man*, pp. 56–72. Baltimore and London: Johns Hopkins University Press.

Reed, G. S. 1982. Toward a methodology for applying psychoanalysis to literature. *Psychoanal. Quart.* 51: 19–42.

—— 1985. Psychoanalysis, psychoanalysis appropriated, psychoanalysis applied. *Psychoanal. Quart.* 54: 234–69.

Renik, O. 1990. Analysis of a woman's homosexual strivings by a male analyst. *Psychoanal. Quart.* 59: 41–53.

Richards, I. A. 1929. *Practical Criticism: A Study of Literary Judgment.* London: Kegan Paul, Trench, Trubner.

Roland, A. 1978. Towards a reorientation of psychoanalytic literary criticism. In A. Roland, ed., *Psychoanalysis, Creativity, and Literature: A French-American Inquiry*, pp. 248–70. New York: Columbia University Press.

Rose, G. J. 1978. The creativity of everyday life. In S. A. Grolnick and L. Barkin, eds., in collab. with W. Muensterberger, *Between Reality and Fantasy: Transitional Objects and Phenomena*, pp.345–62. New York and London: Jason Aronson.

—— 1980. *The Power of Form: A Psychoanalytic Aproach to Aesthetic Form. Psychological Issues* Monogr. 49. New York: International Universities Press.

Rosen, V. 1967. Disorders of communication in psychoanalysis. *J. Amer. Psychoanal. Assn.* 15: 467–90.

Rosenblatt, L. 1938. *Literature as Exploration*, rev. ed. New York: Noble and Noble, 1968.

Rothenberg, A. 1978. The unconscious and creativity. In A. Roland, ed., *Psychoanalysis, Creativity, and Literature: A French-American Inquiry*, pp. 144–61. New York: Columbia University Press.

Rothstein, A. 1980. Psychoanalytic paradigms and their narcissistic investment. *Jour. Amer. Psychoanal. Assn.* 28: 385–96.

Roustang, F. 1977. Du chapitre VII. *Nouvelle Rev. Psychoanal.* 16: 65–95.

Sachs, H. 1942. The community of daydreams. In *The Creative Unconscious: Studies in the Psychoanalysis of Art*, pp. 11–54. Cambridge, Ma.: Sci-Art Publishers.

Sade, D. A. F. 1785. *The 120 Days of Sodom*. In A. Wainhouse and R. Seaver, comp. and trans., *The Marquis de Sade: The 120 Days of Sodom and other writings*. New York: Grove Press, 1966.

—— 1791. *Justine, or Good Conduct Well Chastised*. In R. Seaver and W. Wainhouse, comp. and trans., *The Marquis de Sade: The Complete Justine, Philosophy in the Bedroom and other writings*. New York: Grove Press, 1965.

Sartre, J. P. 1952. *Saint Genet: Actor and Martyr*. New York, Toronto and London: New American Library, 1963.

Schafer, R. 1976. *A New Language for Psychoanalysis*. New Haven and London: Yale University Press.

—— 1980. Action and narration in psychoanalysis. *New Literary History* 12: 61–85.

—— 1981. Discussion of "The psychoanalytic prototype of the supportive literary relationship: Freud and Fliess" by S. J. Coen. Presented to the Association for Psychoanalytic Medicine, New York City, October 1981.

—— 1983. *The Analytic Attitude*. New York: Basic Books.

Scholes, R. 1977. Towards a semiotics of literature. *Critical Inquiry* 4: 105–20.

—— 1979. *Fabulation and Metafiction*. Urbana, Chicago, London: University of Illinois Press.

Scholes, R. and R. Kellogg 1966. *The Nature of Narrative*. New York: Oxford University Press.

Schur, M. 1966. Some additional "day residues" of the "specimen dream of psychoanalysis." In R. M. Loewenstein, L. M. Newman, M. Schur, and A. J. Solnit, eds., *Psychoanalysis: A General Psychology*. New York: International Universities Press, pp. 45–85.

—— 1972. *Freud: Living and Dying*. New York: International Universities Press.

Schwartz, M. M. 1975. Where is literature? *College English* 36: 756–65.

—— 1978. Critic, define thyself. In G. Hartman, ed., *Psychoanalysis and the Question of the Text*, pp. 1–17. Baltimore and London: Johns Hopkins University Press.

—— 1980. Shakespeare through contemporary psychoanalysis. In M. M. Schwartz and C. Kahn, eds., *Representing Shakespeare: New Psychoanalytic Essays*, pp. 21–32. Baltimore and London: Johns Hopkins University Press.

—— 1982. The literary use of transference. *Psychoanal. & Contemp. Thought* 5: 35–44.

Schwartz M. M. and D. Willbern 1982. Literature and psychology. In J-.P. Berricelli and J. Gibaldi, eds., *Inter-relations of Literature*, pp. 205–24. New York: Modern Language Association.

Scott, J. W. 1988. *Gender and the Politics of History* New York and Oxford: Columbia University Press.

—— 1991. The evidence of experience. *Critical Inquiry* 17: 773–97.

—— 1992. Multiculturalism and the politics of identity. *October* 61 (Summer 1992): 12–19.

Sharpe, E. F. 1940. Psycho-physical problems revealed in language: An examination of metaphor. In M. Brierley, ed., *Collected Papers on Psycho-Analysis*. London: Hogarth Press, pp. 155–69.

Shengold, L. 1990. A conversation with Leonard Shengold, reported by E. Gann. *The American Psychoanalyst* 24: 14–16.

Siegman, A. 1964. Exhibitionism and fascination. *J. Amer. Psychoanal. Assn.* 12: 315–35.

Simon, B. 1992 unpublished. Criteria for accepting papers on applied psychoanalysis for the *Journal of the American Psychoanalytic Association*.

Skura, M. A. 1981. *The Literary Use of the Psychoanalytic Process*. New Haven: Yale University Press.

Slochower, H. 1946. *No Voice is Wholly Lost: Writers and Thinkers in War and Peace*. New York: Farrar, Straus and Giroux, 1975.

Socarides, C. 1974. The demonified mother: A study of voyeurism and sexual sadism. *Int. Rev. Psychoanal.* 1: 187–95.

Steele, R. S. 1979. Psychoanalysis and hermeneutics. *Internat. Rev. Psycho-Anal.* 6: 389–411.

Stein, M. H. 1988. Writing about psychoanalysis: I. Analysts who write and those who do not. *J. Amer. Psychoanal. Assn.* 36: 105–24.

Stone, L. 1954. The widening scope of indications for psychoanalysis. *J. Amer. Psychoanal. Assn.* 2: 567–94.

Strachey, J. 1953. Editor's footnote. *S.E.* 13, no. 1: 230.

Thirer, A. 1972. *Céline: The Novel as Delirium*. New Brunswick: Rutgers University Press.

Thomas, D. 1976. *The Marquis de Sade*. Boston: New York Graphic Society.

Thomas, M. 1979. *Louis-Ferdinand Céline*. New York: New Directions. (Quotations on pp. 84–89 of Thomas's book come from Céline, 1955: *Entretiens avec le professeur Y.*).

Waelder, R. 1965. *Psychoanalytic Avenues to Art*. New York: International Universities Press.

Wallerstein, R. S. 1981. The bipolar self: Discussion of alternative perspectives. *J. Amer. Psychoanal. Assn.* 29: 377–94.

Weber, S. 1982. *The Legend of Freud*. Minneapolis: University of Minnesota Press. (Originally published as *Freud Legende: Drei Studien Zum Psychoanalytischen Denken*. Olten, Switzerland: Walter Verlag AG.) Rev. and trans. by the author.

Weissman, P. 1971. The artist and his objects. *Internat. J. Psycho-Anal.* 52: 401–6.

Weissman, S. M. 1989. *His Brother's Keeper: A Psychobiography of Samuel Taylor Coleridge*. Madison, Ct.: International Universities Press.

Wimsatt, W. and M. Beardsley 1954. *The Verbal Icon.* Lexington: University of Kentucky Press.

Winnicott, D. W. 1953. Transitional objects and transitional phenomena. In *Playing and Reality*, pp. 1–25. New York: Basic Books, 1971

—— 1967. The location of cultural experience. In *Playing and Reality*, pp. 95–103. New York: Basic, 1971.

INDEX

31762904R00126

Made in the USA
Middletown, DE
13 May 2016